Boredom and Academic W

Introducing the notion of boredom into the academic context, *Boredom and Academic Work* proposes a fresh sociological perspective on boredom and academic work alike.

It invites a reader to reflect on the essence of boredom and the nature of academic work from the sociological perspective. It constitutes methodological and conceptual guidance for all those interested in their own emotions both at work and outside. It also provides an original, interactional and essential definition of boredom and a novel standpoint for observing academic work, both in its systemic and practical level, and shows how the academic system influences its subjects' well-being, motivation, emotions, and practices.

Covering various approaches from the qualitative methodology, linguistics, sociology of work, emotions, and higher education, and telling a story of research and teaching university staff, the book will be of interest to researchers in a broad range of areas and the general academic public as well.

Mariusz Finkielsztein, PhD, is an adjunct at the Institute of Sociology, Collegium Civitas, Poland. His main interests include sociology of emotions, work, higher education, and creative occupations. He is the sole organizer of the International Interdisciplinary Boredom Conference in Warsaw between 2015 and 2017 (3 editions) and a co-founder of International Society of Boredom Studies (2021). For more details on him, see https://mariuszfinkielsztein.com/.

Routledge Advances in Sociology

310 **Exploring Welfare Bricolage in Europe's Superdiverse Neighbourhoods**
Jenny Phillimore, Hannah Bradby, Tilman Brand, Beatriz Padilla and Simon Pemberton

311 **The Home in the Digital Age**
Antonio Argandoña, Joy Malala and Richard C. Peatfield

312 **Coronavirus Capitalism Goes to the Cinema**
Eugene Nulman

313 **Suicide Social Dramas**
Moral Breakdowns in the Israeli Public Sphere
Haim Hazan and Raquel Romberg

314 **Understanding China through Big Data**
Applications of Theory-oriented Quantitative Approaches
Yunsong Chen, Guangye He and Fei Yan

315 **Transnationalism and the Negotiation of Symbolic Boundaries in the European Commission**
Towards an Ever-Closer Union?
Daniel Drewski

316 **Anxiety in Middle-Class America**
Sociology of Emotional Insecurity in Late Modernity
Valérie de Courville Nicol

317 **Boredom and Academic Work**
Mariusz Finkielsztein

For more information about this series, please visit: https://www.routledge.com/Routledge-Advances-in-Sociology/book-series/SE0511

Boredom and Academic Work

Mariusz Finkielsztein

Routledge
Taylor & Francis Group
LONDON AND NEW YORK

First published 2022
by Routledge
2 Park Square, Milton Park, Abingdon, Oxon OX14 4RN

and by Routledge
605 Third Avenue, New York, NY 10158

Routledge is an imprint of the Taylor & Francis Group, an informa business

© 2022 Mariusz Finkielsztein

The right of Mariusz Finkielsztein to be identified as author of this work has been asserted by him in accordance with sections 77 and 78 of the Copyright, Designs and Patents Act 1988.

All rights reserved. No part of this book may be reprinted or reproduced or utilised in any form or by any electronic, mechanical, or other means, now known or hereafter invented, including photocopying and recording, or in any information storage or retrieval system, without permission in writing from the publishers.

Trademark notice: Product or corporate names may be trademarks or registered trademarks, and are used only for identification and explanation without intent to infringe.

British Library Cataloguing-in-Publication Data
A catalogue record for this book is available from the British Library

Library of Congress Cataloging-in-Publication Data
Names: Finkielsztein, Mariusz, author.
Title: Boredom and academic work / Mariusz Finkielsztein.
Description: Abingdon, Oxon ; New York, NY : Routledge, 2021. | Series: Routledge advances in sociology | Includes bibliographical references and Index.
Identifiers: LCCN 2021006259 (print) | LCCN 2021006260 (cbook) | ISBN 9781032018355 (hardback) | ISBN 9781032018386 (paperback) | ISBN 9781003180258 (ebook)
Subjects: LCSH: Boredom. | Boredom--Research. | Boredom--Study and teaching (Higher)
Classification: LCC BF575.B67 F556 2021 (print) | LCC BF575.B67 (ebook) | DDC 152.4--dc23
LC record available at https://lccn.loc.gov/2021006259
LC ebook record available at https://lccn.loc.gov/2021006260

ISBN: 978-1-032-01835-5 (hbk)
ISBN: 978-1-032-01838-6 (pbk)
ISBN: 978-1-003-18025-8 (ebk)

Typeset in Times NR MT Pro
by KnowledgeWorks Global Ltd.

To my wife
ma renarde, ma souris, ma plus sage sorcière

Contents

List of figures xi
List of tables xii
Acknowledgements xiii

Introduction 1
  A serious issue 1
  Underestimation 2
  Psychology domination and sociology negligence 4
  Book overview 5
  Methodology 6
    Methodological approach 6
    Research questions 7
    Sampling and data collection 7
    Interviews 9
    Participant observation 10
    Autoethnography 10

PART I
Defining boredom 13

1 **Methodological problems in dealing with boredom** 15
  Phenomenological problems 15
    Boredom and sleepiness and fatigue 15
    Elusiveness and invisibility of boredom 17
    Researcher as a distraction 19
  Reactions for boredom 19
    Underestimation of boredom as a research subject 19
    Denials of ever being bored 22

*The principle of busyness and interestingness
    of the world 25*
Shameful vice of boredom 26
Experience without qualities 28
Poor conceptualization of boredom 30
  *Definition of boredom: respondents
    (general population) 30*
  Definitions of boredom: dictionaries and literature 35
  *Transcultural/Translingual differences between
    boredoms 38*
  *Lack of consensus on definition: multidimensionality
    of boredom 42*

2 Theories of boredom   45
Divisions of boredom 45
Psychological perspective 49
  Arousal theories 49
  Cognitive theories 50
  Psychodynamic theories 53
  Existential psychology 54
  Philosophical perspective 56
Microsociological perspective 63
  Role distance 64
  Low emotional energy 65

3 Conceptualization of boredom   69
Non-essential elements in defining boredom 69
  Idleness 69
  Rest 70
  Laziness 70
  Apathy 70
  Repetition/monotony 71
  Lack of interest 71
  Dragging time 72
Essential elements in defining boredom 72
  Emotion/feeling 72
  Negativity/aversion 73
  Listlessness/restlessness 73
  Disengagement/attention withdrawal 74
  Meaninglessness 75

Frustration 76
Liminality/transitionality 76
Definition and its applicability 78
Chronic boredom 79

PART 2
Work-related boredom of academics   81

4   Academic boredom as a systemic issue   83
(Post)modern academia and (post)modern boredom 85
Secularization - academic work as a job 85
Rationalization 86
Bureaucracy - clerk academic 92
Dirty work 101
Workload 103
Qualitative underload 104
Quantitative underload 105
Quantitative overload 106
Lack of belonging 108
Precarity 109
Recruitment system 112
Non-Place 114
Hierarchy 116
Identity disturbance 118
Comparative failure 120
Boredom and career dynamics 121

5   Academic boredom in practice   125
Scientific conferences 126
Format and content of presentation 128
Overload of conference assembly line 136
Opportunism 138
Disturbances in integration 142
Staff meetings 148
Boringness of the meetings 150
Prevention and coping techniques 153
Teaching 157
Teaching overload 160
Underestimation of teaching 162

*Between teaching and researching - teaching
     disengagement 163*
  Boring didactic tasks 166
  Prevention and coping techniques 168
 Research-related work 170
  Tediousness 170
  Satiety/overload 172
  Field boredom 173
  Laboratory boredom 176
  Communicating science 179
  Prevention 183

Conclusions   **187**

Bibliography   194
Index   220

List of figures

1.1	The most frequently used words in definitions of boredom	43
2.1	Mean values of negative valence and arousal for latent boredom classes	48
C.1	Passion triangle	192

List of tables

0.1	Sample according to disciplines and degree	8
1.1	Occurrences of boredom in academics in non-job-related time	25
1.2	Respondents' connotation with the word 'boredom'	34
2.1	Dychotomical distinctions of boredom	46
4.1	Workload typology (collated by the author, source: Fisher, 1987, 1993)	103
5.1	Frequencies of respondents' boredom according to activities and disciplines	126
5.2	Frequencies of respondents' boredom according to activities and degree	126
C.1	Systemic contributors to work-related boredom of academics	191

Acknowledgements

Writing this book was a long and challenging process. Since 2011, when I began this journey, boredom studies have developed, I have found colleagues worldwide sharing my research interests, and I have met many people I am deeply grateful for support, words of encouragement, and valuable discussions or inspiration.

I would like to express my deepest gratitude to:

Izabela Wagner, my BA, MA, and PhD advisor between 2010 and 2019, my mentor, my friend for her open-mindedness, unconditional support, unbreakable belief in me and my 'quirk' subject, always providing me with encouragement in times of academic dispiritedness, sharing with me her knowledge, experience, and approach, directing me towards bigger pictures and greener pastures, giving me full creative freedom with my work being a vigilant gardener instead of conventionally boring, tedium advocates advisors that impose boredom on those under their care, and surviving all the nuisance that I caused for all these years of our collaboration.

Michael Gardiner and Wojciech Burszta, the reviewers of my PhD thesis of which this book is a lighter version, for their suggestions, notes, and words of encouragement and prof. Gardiner for all the time and effort he made to come from Canada to Poland and attend my PhD thesis defence.

Randy Malamud, an excellent scholar, and an admirably positive man, for his enthusiastic participation in the International Interdisciplinary Boredom Conference and vigorous advocacy for the idea of boredom as a research subject, taking all the way from Georgia to attend the Conference in Warsaw, writing a marvellous, beautifully written article on boredom and the Conference in *Times Higher Education*, and supporting me from a distance since our first and only meeting in the summer of 2016.

Guido Borelli for his genuine interest in boredom, active participation in the Conference, all the trust and belief he showed by inviting me to Venice for lecturing on boredom (November 2016) when I was still an unfledged academic – it has meant a lot to me, and for inspirational conversations about boredom and academic career.

Lee Anna Maynard, Erik Ringmar, and Wijnand van Tilburg for being enormously kind people and for agreeing to be keynote speakers at the Boredom Conferences I organized in Warsaw.

Maria Flakus, Iga Kazimierczyk, and Małgorzata Kubacka, boredom researchers and my Polish colleagues for active support of the idea of boredom studies, encouraging discussions on boredom, inspirational presentations at the Conferences (multiple times), incessant work directed toward establishing boredom a valid research subject and being an invisible 'support group.'

Jakub Motrenko, a chief editor of the journal *Stan Rzeczy*, for open-mindedness, kindness, and vast support in establishing boredom studies in Poland by giving a green light for the idea of an issue on boredom.

All academics that agreed to take part in my research and sacrificed their precious time to talk with me and share their experiences, observations, and reflections. All students of the course 'Time without qualities' who conducted interviews with academics. Marcin Zaród for valuable discussions on brights and sorrows (especially sorrows) of being a PhD student.

My parents for unceasing support and unconditional belief in me and all my projects.

All whom I cannot mention out of their excessive numbers and the fear of defamation who inspired this research in the first place. All those who openly expressed their disbelief in boredom as a research subject for motivation for further work.

Introduction

Although everything is meaningless and there is nothing new under the sun (Ecclesiastes, n.d., 1:2,9), this book constitutes one more attempt to create meaning and novelty in a subject of which probably everybody has at least some experience, and about which equal numbers of readers feel either omniscient regarding, or immune to. Boredom is almost universally disregarded, and many treat it as a shameful emotion (Toohey, 2011), and as such is subjected to a process of individual and group denial. As the popular statement says, 'an intelligent person never gets bored' and since, as Descartes noted, the reason is the most widespread thing in the world – insofar as everyone thinks they are well stocked in it – the majority of people maintain that they never get bored. Sometimes, after a moment of reflection, some concede to an occasional feeling of boredom with the qualification that it was due to other people, or to trivial activities they had been forced to do (especially at work or school). Generally, however, boredom can be compared to venereal disease – no one wants to have it and no one wants to be accused of being its cause.

A serious issue

It has already become a boring platitude, included in almost all papers on the subject, that boredom is a widespread and fairly prevalent phenomenon, 'one of the most unexpectedly common of all human emotions' (Toohey, 2011, p. 1). Moreover, many authors have considered it to be a serious matter, 'a major social problem' (Klapp, 1986, p. 26), 'a central twenty-first-century problem' (Avramenko, 2004, p. 108), 'an inherent part of the human being' (Velasco, 2017, p. 184), one of the greatest miseries of humankind (Nisbet, 1983; Fromm, 2011) and 'that part of hell which Dante forgot to describe in *La Divina Commedia*' (Casanova, cited it in Bergler, 1945, p. 38). Science fiction writer, Isaac Asimov (1964) even predicted that in 2014 the 'disease of boredom' having 'serious mental, emotional and sociological consequences' will constitute one of the most severe sufferings haunting humankind. Boredom is positioned with such serious phenomena as 'alienation,' 'anomie,' 'disenchantment,' and/or 'depression' (Irvine, 2001) and is even believed to be the quality that makes us human (Kołakowski, 1999).

Boredom is also claimed to be significant because, as according to Walter Benjamin, who summarized Émile Tardieu's (1913) book on the subject, 'all human activity is shown to be a vain attempt to escape from boredom, but in which, at the same time, everything that was, is, and will be appears as the inexhaustible nourishment of that feeling' (Benjamin, 2002, p. 102). Similar claims have been made by many well-known authors, inter alia by German philosophers Arthur Schopenhauer and Martin Heidegger; German-born American social psychologist, Erich Fromm; French poet Charles Baudelaire; French philosopher and novelist Albert Camus; or American writer, David Foster Wallace; who all indicated in one way or another that 'most of us spend nearly all our time and energy trying to distract ourselves from [the] feeling' (Wallace, 2011, p. 85). In this vein, Schopenhauer suggested that boredom was the foundation of all religions – '[m]an creates for himself in his own image demons, gods, and saints; then to these must be incessantly offered sacrifices, prayers, temple decorations, vows and their fulfilment, pilgrimages, salutations, adornment of images and so on' (1969, p. 323; cf. Helvétius, 1810). Mihalyi Csikszentmihalyi, American social psychologist, the creator of the theory of flow (optimal experience) explained that an understanding of boredom is of central importance to all 'interested in enhancing the quality of life' (2000a, p. 444) because it is one of the main disturbances to human's well-being.

In general, people are believed to be led by imperative towards activity, and by a fear of boredom, which, as Bertrand Russell, British philosopher and mathematician, claimed is 'one of the great motive powers throughout the historical epoch' (1932, p. 57) and which effect 'on a large scale in history is underestimated' (Inge, 1940, p. 386). Scrutinizing the relevant literature suggests that it seems to be a justified conclusion that many agree that boredom is an essential incentive for social change and (r)evolution, and, thus, for the historical process. As Tardieu (1913, p. 195, 283) indicated, 'the infinite evolution of societies, their progress and decay, express their eternal boredom' and 'boredom, which is the sting that precipitates the race of this world, will never be blunted'.[1] Boredom is credited with the rise and decline of civilizations, heresies, reformation, the rise of nationalism and radical political movements (e.g. the Nazis), and all kinds of revolutions and wars (Inge, 1940; Moravia, 1965; Kuhn, 1976; Maeland and Brunstad, 2009; Kustermans and Ringmar, 2011; Laugesen, 2012).

Underestimation

It seems to be a paradox that the social prevalence of boredom and its social significance, which I only briefly suggested, has not been adequately reflected in either scientific and popular reflection and that boredom 'as a factor in human behaviour has [still] received ... far less attention than it deserves' (Russell, 1932, p. 57). Boredom, 'like normality, is a taken-for-granted part of everyday life' (Misztal, 2016, p. 109; cf. Barbalet, 1999, p. 633), it 'is generally paid scant and superficial attention, passed over lightly as transitory and insignificant' (Healy, 1984, p. 9) as most people 'do not fully acknowledge or ... are not fully conscious of what a grave affliction boredom is' (Fromm, 1986, p. 14). This includes many scholars as well; for instance, Reinhard Kuhn (1976), who in his erudite analysis of the notion of ennui in Western literature tradition totally dismissed boredom as worthy of scientific attention. Boredom is still usually not considered a part of the basic curriculum of any discipline, as 'there are no courses [on boredom] offered at the universities, apart from the fact that one is often bored during one's studies' (Brodsky, 1995; Svendsen, 2005, p. 18) and the limited exceptions confirm that tendency rather than contradict it.

Many authors observed/noted little scientific interest in boredom (expressed in the number of relevant publications: see O'Hanlon, 1981; Fisher, 1987; Vodanovich and Watt, 1999; Vodanovich, 2003; Martin, Sadlo, and Stew, 2006; Pekrun et al., 2010; Nett, Goetz, and Hall, 2011). During my desk research, I, similarly to Josefa Ros Velasco (2017), observed that such 'complaints' seem to constitute an oft-repeated fixed phase, frequently cited in many papers with reference to works that are 10 or 20 years old. This statement, while perfectly correct in the 1980s or 1990s, is no longer valid. Although boredom still (a) has received far less attention than other affective states[2] (Tze et al., 2013; Goetz et al., 2014), (b) is rarely mentioned in disciplinary and/or subject handbooks (for instance, in handbooks of emotions), and (c) is underdeveloped in some (sub)disciplines, such as sociology, anthropology, academic philosophy, neuropsychology, work studies, or leadership, the scientific interest in the phenomenon seems to be increasing. No more than one paper on boredom was published on average per year in psychology, between 1926 and 1980 (Smith, 1981), whereas in 2015 alone, according to ScienceDirect, 326 articles on the subject were released (van Tilburg and Igou, 2017; a similar tendency was found for PsychINFO by Vodanovich and Watt, 2016). Velasco (2017) found (using Google Scholar) 2,878 academic studies on boredom in 29 languages, covering various disciplinary spectra. Despite the limitations of all these searching engines and their databases, it still strongly suggests that researchers worldwide have become more interested in boredom, and that we should talk about lacunas in the research into boredom, rather than a lack of studies altogether. There are plentiful publications raising the issue of boredom, but their thematic scope is limited – for instance, in psychology, there is an overrepresentation of papers on individual differences in proneness to boredom, and in philosophy Heidegger's approach towards boredom is commonly examined, while other subjects are considered significantly less often.

Psychology domination and sociology negligence

As Michael Gardiner and Jason Haladyn (2016) observed, boredom studies are dominated by quantitative, questionnaire-based psychological research. This conclusion was entirely confirmed in my own literature analysis – out of 572 scientific texts with the word 'boredom' in the title to which I have had access (journal articles, books, books chapters, MA/PhD theses written in English (507) and Polish (65)[3], as many as 273 (47.73%) are from the field of psychology. To the best of my knowledge, psychology, including psychology-based research in education studies, is the only discipline in which knowledge on boredom has been accumulated on a regular basis. New studies are launched and publications released each year, providing colleagues with new data, discussing previous results, and/or as a continuation of some strand of theoretical or methodological consideration. In many other disciplines, a reflection on boredom has a rather incidental character, lacks regularity and, for the most part, does not result in establishing any research traditions or institutionally based groups of researchers. Outside psychology, boredom researchers work rather in isolation frequently surrounded by colleagues who have little or no understanding for their field.

Somehow in contrast to the well-developed field of the psychology of boredom, sociology 'has largely ignored boredom, although producing a rather large amount of it' (Darden and Marks, 1999, p. 33). This conclusion was confirmed in my analysis of the literature on boredom. Out of 572 academic texts I gathered, only 35 (6.12%) can be classified as 'sociological,' and fewer than 20 were written by a sociologist.[4] Boredom still seems to be perceived as having little or no social effect, and as a result is not considered a serious issue worth an incisive investigation in sociology. Although more and more researchers are noting the social side of boredom, the tradition of thinking about it as an individual (psychology) and/or existential (philosophy) malaise is still very much alive. Many authors speculate that the perception of boredom as a strictly individual phenomenon is the prime cause of the lack of sociological study (Zijderveld, 1979; Darden and Marks, 1999; Anderson, 2004; Kenny, 2009; Misztal, 2016), and hence the lack of theoretical and/or methodological frameworks/traditions that may be useful in such an investigation. Even the sociology of emotions thus far seems to exclude boredom from its area of interest (boredom is not mentioned in the existing handbooks, e.g. Stets and Turner, 2006). Moreover, although everyday life is recently gaining more and more interest, and researching subjective states and minor, 'vulgar' issues of social life has become a part of the sociological mainstream (see, for instance, Routledge's series 'The New Sociology'), the vast majority of the sociology of 'everydayness' still ignores boredom altogether (although there are initial signs of change to this attitude; see Jacobsen, 2019). Even when sociologists raise the issue of boredom, they frequently use the term 'in a commonsense manner,' and take 'its disvalued nature for granted' (Darden and Marks, 1999, p. 14) or underestimate it, like Peter Conrad who concluded that 'in the pantheon of human problems it is a relatively minor irritation' (Conrad, 1997, p. 474). Sociology thus 'has not contributed much to our understanding of the concept and lived experience of boredom' (Kenny, 2009, p. 262). The primary aim of this book is to change this situation.

Book overview

The main goals of the book are to (1) provide a detailed overview of existing conceptualizations of boredom in various academic disciplines, (2) propose a sociological definition of boredom, and (3) describe and analyse work-related boredom through the example of academic work. The book is divided into two parts, the first dealing with the conceptualization of boredom (Chapters 1–3), and the second with work-related boredom of academics (Chapters 4 and 5).

The first chapter reflects on methodological problems in researching boredom: (a) difficulties in observing boredom in vivo (phenomenological problem), (b) frequent denials of ever being bored, and (c) the poor common conceptualization of the feeling, which handicaps deeper reflection upon it, as boredom is often perceived as a synonym for idleness, rest, or laziness (depending on moral interpretations). This section summarizes the main problems in the operationalization of boredom for the purposes of research, and reveals the need for much definitional reflection – it may also be perceived as a 'manual' for possible obstacles to researching boredom, especially using qualitative methods.

Chapter 2 is a detailed description of existing approaches to the conceptualization of boredom, and covers much of the existing literature on the subject. Various disciplinary theories of boredom are offered, starting with the psychology of boredom (arousal, cognitive, psychodynamic, and existential theories), then the philosophy of boredom and microsociological perspective (interactional approach). This chapter aims to provide an interdisciplinary comparison of existing theories of boredom as well as interpretations of them.

Based on the concepts gathered in Chapter 2, the next chapter provides definitional reflection upon boredom, and results in an original proposition for the sociological, interactional definition of the state – boredom is defined as an emotion/feeling of engagement withdrawal from interactions with the social/physical environment due to a sense of meaninglessness. Considerations regarding the applicability of the definition are also included, and an original distinction between situational and chronic boredom is proposed.

The main, empirical part of the thesis (Chapters 4 and 5) consists of the description and analysis of academic work with respect to work-related contributors to the boredom of academics, and the preventive/coping techniques that they employ. The first empirical chapter concentrates on systemic factors that may potentially result in boredom – analyses organizational/institutional/normative effects on academic well-being in general, and the occurrence of boredom specifically. Chapter 5 provides a detailed description and analysis of various academic activities (scientific conferences, staff meetings, teaching, and research-related work) in terms of boredom, and is at least partial illustration of the systemic issues discussed in Chapter 4. All chapters supplement each other and provide justification for the main thesis that boredom is far from being a 'minor irritation,' an issue not worth further reflection, a laughing matter. I hope this work will contribute to changing the common perception of that underestimated emotion, at least among (some) academics.

Methodology

My incentive to research the subject many years ago was the boredom I felt as MA student during some of my classes. Out of boredom, I began to reflect on the nature and causes of the feeling, while sitting in boring classes and observing my colleagues suffering from the same affliction. The present study constitutes a continuation and expansion of my project devoted to the boredom experienced by students during university classes (Finkielsztein, 2013).

Methodological approach

The current study is based on qualitative methods of data gathering and analysis. The main methodological approach from which this research draws inspiration is grounded theory by Barney Glaser and Anselm Strauss (1967), which is based on the assumption that social reality is best understood by the actors that are involved in it. Therefore, the research process assumes building a theory not by verifying previously accepted hypotheses, but through systematic inductive concept building, based on empirical data collected during fieldwork. Data collection, hypotheses building, and their verification are therefore not clearly separated in time, but are procedures that repeatedly intertwine during the long process of theory generation. In accordance with this premise, the whole research project was conducted from 2011 in cycles, which consisted of field work (data gathering), data analysis (coding and category development), and a literature review (theory building). I have not employed any specific kind of grounded theory methodology and use it only as a general methodological approach and inspiration – not a strictly defined methodological set of procedures.

An important foundation of the current research is also the triangulation of methods and data (Salkind, 2010), i.e. combining multiple methods of investigation and materials from various types of sources. In this study, I employed various qualitative methods of data gathering – individual in-depth interviews, participant observations, and autoethnography – and combined data derived from my empirical study; the scientific literature, both empirical and theoretical; from various disciplines (psychology, sociology, anthropology, philosophy, cultural studies, education, and management/vocational studies); popular articles (newspapers, magazines, environmental journals, for example, on higher education); and fiction and essays. Boredom, although increasingly accepted in the scientific discourse, is still neglected by many – triangulation is meant to support the legitimacy of the subject.

The 'idiosyncrasy' of the empirical part of the book is the extensive quoting of the interviews. It is employed both as a premise of qualitative sociological methodology and a technique to dynamize the analysis and make it less boring, since original material is frequently the part of the work that is best remembered, and which makes the whole narration inherently more interesting. Quotes also bring the context to the analysis and epitomize a more reflective approach towards the sociological research – a researcher does not pretend, through a distanced, 'objective,' jargon-ridden style, to be omniscient, but shares expertise with the respondents, gives them voice and space, describes not only or even not primarily, the state of the facts, but more the participants' interpretations, perceptions of, or attitudes towards, the facts.

Research questions

The main questions that this research aimed to answer included: (1) do academics experience boredom and/or related emotional states in their work?; (2) in what kinds of activities/situations do they feel/declare/connote boredom the most prevalently?; (3) what are the main factors contributing to the sensation of boredom among academics?; (4) what effect do systemic/organizational/institutional factors have on occurrences of the feeling?; (5) what strategies, both deliberate and indeliberate, do academics employ to prevent/cope with work-related boredom?; and (6) how do academics define and understand the concept of boredom, both in the context of their vocational and everyday life?

Sampling and data collection

All participants were recruited from among the employees of the University of Warsaw. This university was chosen for several reasons: (1) it is the biggest university in Poland, with 21 departments, which allowed data collection covering a wide variety of academic disciplines and thereby deepens the analysis of the phenomenon at the university milieu; (2) I have been a student and PhD student at this university, which allowed me to reach a better understanding of the inner processes, for instance, through facilitating entrance to staff meetings and classes; and (3) my MA project was located at this institution and my initial aim (not realized eventually in this book) was to compare the perspectives of students and teachers on class-related boredom, and thus it was natural choice to use the same institutional environment. The choice of only one institution for analysis was dictated by: (a) the limited possibilities for a one-person research team, (b) an emphasis on the depth of analysis of the researched phenomenon, and (c) the size (a dozen or so faculties) and complexity of the institutional structure of the University of Warsaw.

Purposeful sampling was used to recruit participants to this study (Patton, 2001; Silverman, 2004; Seale et al., 2006). Respondents were chosen to represent (1) all fields of knowledge – humanities, social, and natural sciences according to the division of OECD (2007), and (2) all professional career stages (advanced PhD students, PhDs, habilitation holders, and full professors) in order to provide the widest coverage possible. Five faculties were selected from each of the three groups of sciences. A total of 15 (out of 21) faculties were included in the study – natural sciences (mathematics, geology, biology, chemistry, and physics), social sciences (education, sociology, geography, psychology, and journalism), humanities (history including archaeology, philosophy, linguistics including modern languages philology, book and information studies, ethnology, and cultural anthropology).

The respondents within the chosen institutions were selected randomly from the list of employees available on the University of Warsaw website with regards to maintaining equal representation of each career category within the institution. Prospective participants were recruited using e-mail invitations. A total of 251 study invitations were sent, and 72 university employees were interviewed. The exact sample distribution according to disciplines and career stages is presented in the following Table 0.1.

The interviews were conducted in two main waves, the first between November 2015 and January 2016, with the assistance of students from the Institute of Sociology enrolled in the course 'Time without qualities: University towards boredom' (interviews 1–19), and the second (the rest

Table 0.1 Sample according to disciplines and degree

	Humanities	Social Sciences	Natural Sciences	Total	%
MA	5	4	2	11	15.28
PhD	7	8	8	23	31.94
Hab.	6	7	7	20	27.78
Prof.	6	6	6	18	25.00
Total	24	25	23	72	
%	33.33	34.73	31.94		

of the interviews) between October 2017 and March 2018. The majority of interviews took place in the respondent's employer institutions (prevalently in unit rooms) and only a few were conducted outside the university (in cafes). The interviews were recorded with permission via mobile phone. The recorded data was then transcribed by the researcher. A total of 74 hours of recordings were gathered, which resulted in almost 900 standard pages of transcriptions. The shortest interviews lasted 25 minutes and the longest 150 minutes, the median was 55 minutes and mean 62 minutes.

In accordance with the standard ethical procedure, consent for participation was obtained from each respondent and participants were assured of the confidentiality and anonymity of their contribution to the study. To fulfil this promise, all interview quotations in the book are described by the record number of the interview (interviews were numbered in chronological order of conducting), category (teacher/students – sometimes I used the data from my MA project), gender (this was neither devised nor analysed as an independent factor yet the number of males and females in the study was equal: 36 participants represented each gender), career stage (MA, PhD, hab., prof.), and scientific area of the respondent's faculty (humanities, social sciences, natural sciences).

Interviews

Interviews were semi-structured and were opened by the question about the circumstances of starting working at the university and about the advantages and disadvantages of academic work. The first set of questions was derived from common contributors to the state as identified in the literature, without using the word 'boredom' directly. I asked whether the participants had ever experienced situations or performed tasks/duties associated with academic work that they would perceive as disliked, unchallenging, monotonous, not interesting, bereft of meaning, underutilizing their skills and competences or causing the sensation that time was stand still or dragging. I only asked directly about boredom itself after this set of questions. In some cases, this was only after 40, 50, or even 60 minutes of the interview. Some respondents use the word 'boredom' before I asked about it; for others, it came as a surprise. In a few interviews, I did not manage to reach the subject at all, for example due to a strongly negative reaction against the concept itself (see more in Chapter 1). Firstly, I asked general question of whether they had ever experienced boredom in connection with their academic work. Then, irrespective of the answer to previous question, I asked about occurrences of boredom during subsequent academic activities (scientific conferences, staff meetings, teaching, organizational-bureaucratic duties, and research-related activities). I also asked about the respondent's boredom coping strategies or the reasons they do not feel bored in particular activities. The last set of questions was devoted to the feeling of boredom outside the university context – I asked about respondent associations with boredom, their understanding of it, their definition of boredom and a bore, and their experiences of boredom in everyday, non-vocational life.

Participant observation

Another research method I used was covert participant observation, employed primarily to increase the relevance of the study (McCall, 1984; Patton, 2001). This method constitutes, in my opinion, the connective tissue of all qualitatively inspired social research, as it can be used for merging information from various sources. It enables research questions to be raised, empirical hypotheses to be formulated, the cross-checking of data derived from interviews, and making sense of various data as it encourages reflection about a research subject. About 450 hours of participant observation was conducted including: (1) 320 hours observing scientific conferences (as a participant in 36 conferences, including 11 international conferences held in Poland, Italy, Great Britain, the Netherlands, and Greece, and 25 national conferences), held between May 2013 and March 2019; (2) 30 hours of the observation of faculty councils (I was a representative of PhD students) held between January and December 2014; and (3) 100 hours of observation of other kinds of staff meeting (unit meetings, open seminars as a participant and on the institute's council in the capacity of minute-taker) held between October 2013 and June 2017. Almost 75 standard pages of field notes were produced.

Autoethnography

A facultative method of data gathering was autoethnography, an approach that seeks to describe and systematically analyse researcher's personal experience as a member of the studied group in order to obtain more accurate and reliable data (Anderson, 2006; Ellis, Adams, and Bochner, 2011). In this method, a researcher is both the subject and the object of the research that enables exploration of the nuances of the internal world of the respondents. This research did not apply autoethnography as a narrative method, but merely as an approach to the research process. This research, thus, hopes to be a continuation of the rich tradition of qualitative studies that vigorously encourage instead of dismiss biographical data (see the tradition of Chicago sociology under the guidance of Robert Park or Everett Hughes, see Chapoulie, 2001; Helmes-Hayes and Santoro, 2016). In this study, I used my experience as: (1) a PhD student and both internal and external grant holder, (2) a scientific conferences attendee and organizer (I have organized nine events: four international and five national conferences between April 2014 and August 2017, two events I co-organized and in seven I was a sole organizer); and (3) an academic teacher (I taught 250 teacher hours between academic year 2014/15 and 2018/19).

Notes

1 All quotes from non-English sources were translated by the Author.
2 Browsing PsychINFO (at psycnet.apa.org) for 'boredom' resulted in 2,788 records; depression – 301,167, anxiety – 235,587, interest – 130,798, anger – 31,976, burnout – 12,548, frustration – 11,041, joy – 8,223, and sadness – 8,018 (as of 18-04-2019).
3 The body analyzed included 397 articles (25 in Polish and 372 in English), 29 books (5 in Polish and 24 in English), 90 chapters in books (33 in Polish and 57 in English), and 31 master's and doctoral dissertations (2 in Polish and 29 in English).
4 The rest of the texts represent broadly understood cultural studies (literature, cinema, art) – 90 texts (16.73%), philosophy – 57 texts (9.97%), and education – 34 texts (5.94%). A small number of texts can be assigned to management studies (21), history (11), or anthropology (9).

Part I

Defining boredom

Chapter 1
Methodological problems in dealing with boredom

There may be distinguished three main genres of problems pertinent to researching boredom: (1) phenomenological problems (problems with detecting and observing boredom in vivo), (2) reactions to the research subject (various kinds of denials of ever experiencing boredom), and (3) the lack of a clear and unambiguous conceptualization of boredom (both in the relevant literature and in the common perception thereof) or a very simplistic understanding of the phenomenon. Some of those are connected to boredom exclusively, and others are examples of well-established, traditionally identified problems in qualitative studies, or examples of more general methodological problems with studying sensitive subjects such as emotions (especially negative ones), social taboos, etc. I argue that, in the case of boredom, the problems encountered in the research process can reveal nuances and speak eloquently about the nature of the phenomenon itself. I claim, therefore, that elaborating on the problems in question is a good introduction to the subject, regardless of whether they proved particularly vital to the present study.

Phenomenological problems

One of the basic problems in doing qualitative research on boredom is how to detect and measure boredom in vivo. The typical symptoms of boredom can be misleading, and the researcher is almost immediately faced with the crucial methodological consideration of how to obtain certainty that a given person is bored and not just sleepy, exhausted, listless, contemplative, or depressed. Indeed, since all these different states may have similar or even identical phenomenology (Prinz, 2005), it can be hard to correctly diagnose them and tell them apart (Loukidou, 2008, p. 12; Vogel-Walcutt et al., 2012, p. 100).

Boredom and sleepiness and fatigue

The literature enumerates several observable characteristics of boredom that may partially overlap those of sleepiness, fatigue, or depression.

The most visible ones are motor expressions. These include the collapsed and slouched upper body, a slumped posture, supporting one's head with one's hand, leaning one's head backwards, rubbing or clutching one's face, putting hands behind one's head or neck, engaging in few bodily movements, or performing sudden movements (Wallbott, 1998; Kroes, 2005). This is how one of the respondents described her fellow students looking bored in class:

> You can see people leaning forward on their elbows or slumping [on their chairs or over the desks]. Sometimes you can tell that they are bored by the way they are sitting. They are lying down somewhere on a piece of bench, and trying to snooze. When someone is bored, well you can see that he is rather lying on the chair than sitting, looking around the room for some interest in whatever.
> (Student, FGI_5, sociology, female, undergraduate)

Another ambiguous feature is a glazy look. One may be keeping his/her eyes widely open and yet staring fixedly, as if without sight. 'The gaze is directed beyond the immediate and lost in an undefined distance' (Toohey, 2011, p. 40), being not focused on anything in particular around. Eyes browsing the environment, blinking a lot (Kroes, 2005), or 'lids slightly drooped' (Bench and Lench, 2013, p. 465) are believed to be indicators of boredom as well.

However, all of the above-mentioned characteristics are actually likely to be inconclusive for the observer to decide unambiguously on the spot whether the observed person is bored. This stems from the fact that all those may be (and frequently are) indicative also of fatigue or sleepiness. Getting fatigued, sleepy, or – for that matter – bored are the most common reactions to situations where one is (partially) passively participating in a compulsory or highly recommended gathering. Since exactly such situations (university classes/lectures, university staff meetings, academic conferences) are at the core of the present study, it is imperative that the issue be highlighted.

Indeed, many academic teachers whom I interviewed in my research somehow associated boredom with fatigue, used these two terms interchangeably, and were generally unsure of the actual nature of their own experience in this respect (i.e. were uncertain whether they had been bored or fatigued in the situations in question). This problem was addressed by Eran Dorfman in his chapter *Boredom and Fatigue*: 'Did I lie? Was I really tired or simply bored? It's hard to say ...' (2016, p. 180).

Yet the question is far more complex in the case of the Polish language, where the nouns 'boredom' and 'fatigue' (most strikingly in the gerund forms *znudzenie* and *znużenie*) and the respective verbs 'to bore' and 'to fatigue' (*nudzić* and *nużyć*) are etymologically and semantically interconnected. In dictionaries, the two words are each other's closest synonyms (Tomczyk, 2008;

Szmidt, 2013) and specified as deriving from the word of the Russian or Ukrainian origin *nuża* meaning 'poverty' (connection with a shortage of something, a void), 'effort,' or 'hardship' (Brückner, 1989; Malmor, 2009). Another etymological clue is the Proto-Slavic verb *nudit*, which used to mean 'to coerce' and in its dialectical forms also 'to fatigue,' 'to torment,' or 'to bore' (Boryś, 2005). I found my awareness of the relevant linguistic intricacies really helpful in conducting the research. During my interviews with academic teachers, on many occasions I was under the impression that the interviewees were using the word 'fatigue' (*znużenie*) to talk about something that actually should be called 'boredom' (*znudzenie*).

Sleepiness is another state that, to the general way of thinking, is strongly associated with boredom. Some use it as a synonym of boredom, others as a symptom of it, but in the common perception of the phenomenon it means virtually the same thing. Interestingly, the connection between boredom, fatigue, and somnolence is apparent in the English word 'weary' (weariness, wearisome), meaning 'worn out; tired; fatigued' as well as 'discontented or bored' (Merriam-Webster, 2004). An interesting statement came up in the research carried out among college students by psychologist Linda Wechter-Ashkin (2010); one of the participants remarked: 'When I'm bored, it feels like I've overslept' (p. 93). In conclusion, the interrelation between boredom, fatigue, and sleepiness occurs to be strong and multifaceted, and for this reason it is hard to employ the concepts in a clear-cut way. This is bound to prompt serious phenomenological problems in doing research.

Elusiveness and invisibility of boredom

Yet another issue contributing to methodological difficulties in researching boredom is the fact that even if we were capable of determining precise and reliably observable measures of boredom, we would still need to consider that 'the same emotional signals may cause very different feelings in dissimilar people' (Meyer, 2012). In other words, the same physiological markers may eventuate in different feelings, depending on the situation, individual characteristics, etc. Additionally, these feelings may be attributed differently by different people. Thus, one person may feel something that he/she would call fatigue, but the researcher would define as boredom, whereas another person – in the same situation and showing similar symptoms – may feel differently and use the word 'boredom' to describe the state, and so forth.

This leads us to addressing two probably self-evident but crucial issues. Firstly, boredom is a highly subjective experience – what may beget boredom in one person may be a source of fascination to another. 'Boredom is not a characteristic of an object, event or person, but exists in the relationship between individuals and their interpretation of their experience' (Conrad, 1997, p. 468; cf. Raposa, 1999, p. 38). It is the interpretation that matters most in the end, because even if someone looks bored, we cannot obtain certainty that he/she actually feels bored and that 'boredom' is a proper label for what we are observing. Secondly, boredom is a state of 'nonverbal character' that 'cannot be recorded (at least not on tape), but only permits a description' (Breidenstein, 2007, p. 96), which means it is not self-explanatory in vivo. In other words, it is much more productive to collect descriptions and explanations of boredom in hindsight. This is why most studies in the field rely mainly on verbal expressions rather than on observations in vivo. However, in practice, few people are capable of gaining insight into their own emotions to the extent that they can neatly name them all, and verbally capture them in detail. Indeed, most participants of the present study had difficulties with describing/defining boredom. Some of them claimed not to have experienced boredom, hence not being able to talk about it. But the alleged lack of life experience of boredom was not the main reason why the respondents were struggling with the introspection in this respect. As a matter of fact, the challenge resulted mostly from the nature of boredom itself. Usually, one's own boredom is so self-evident and obvious that one finds it elusive.

Another facet of the phenomenological problem is measuring the outcomes of boredom instead of boredom itself. Boredom hardly ever appears in a 'pure' form, as people learn how to hide their boredom, to minimize its visible symptoms or to alleviate it as soon as it emerges. As several authors suggested, '[w]hat we as observers often see, then, is not the direct expression of boredom itself but the secondary manifestations of the frantic and desperate efforts of the chronically bored to find relief from their misery' (Bernstein, 1975, p. 515; cf. Maeland and Brunstad, 2009, p. 5). One, 'for the most part, can only observe the killing of time' (Breidenstein, 2007, p. 104), the products and epiphenomena of boredom (Kenny, 2009, p. 42). Using the metaphorical description of the nature of emotions, we can say that with boredom

> [it] is a bit like with the wind. We all know it is, but we do not see it. We only see hats falling from human heads and leaves rushed along the road. But flying hats and leaves are not the wind.
> (Strelau and Doliński, 2011, p. 513)

Thus, boredom is difficult to be caught red-handed, because people are socialized to effectively hide it or to sublimate it (by various mitigation techniques). In addition, it tends to get submerged by other states and emotions, such as frustration, irritation, etc. Therefore, boredom is a transitory period in between the preceding and subsequent engagement. Moreover, people frequently are capable of accessing their experience of boredom only through techniques employed to alleviate the state itself. In this context, boredom seems to be an ontological void and the researcher needs to probe it in an apt way. '[F]or the investigator of boredom, we can see only a para-reflection of the experience' (Kenny, 2009, p. 195).

Researcher as a distraction

The researcher himself/herself may also become a distraction to bored participants, a remedy for their boredom. This consideration constitutes a significant factor especially in ethnographical, prolonged research. In the vast majority of cases, it is beneficial for the research purposes, because it facilitates the participants' engagement in offering their feedback in exchange for the researcher's anti-boredom presence. The researcher provides the bored participants with a kind of entertainment, and, in return, he/she receives gratitude and patience which he/she needs to collect valuable data. This gateway is mentioned by several anthropologists (e.g. Rabinow, 1977; Barley, 1983, 1989). The below-quoted excerpt from the study of the homeless in Bucharest, Romania may serve as an adequate example of this whole category.

> I proved endlessly entertaining. It was not uncommon, in fact, for even my most distant acquaintances to greet me on the street with exclamations like, "Thank God you're here—I was so bored! Let's go get a coffee!" In a testament to the reflexive nature of ethnographic research, my presence proved to be one powerful antidote to the boredom that otherwise shaped life on the streets. I became mindful that small gestures, like providing a shot of Nescafé or photographing someone's portrait, were great distractions. These gifs beat back people's boredom, and, in exchange, I received gratitude and patience.
>
> (O'Neill, 2017, pp. xiii–xiv)

However, what proves beneficial in the majority of research cases may be an obstacle in studying boredom itself. The fact that the researcher is 'recruited in the fight against boredom' makes it difficult to study the participants' own boredom, because 'wherever the ethnographer appears, boredom is vanishing' (Breidenstein, 2007, p. 96). The subject of the study is being destroyed by the presence of the researcher. This is especially valid in the case of overt observation but may also have some influence on cover observation, which was employed in the present study.

Reactions for boredom

Underestimation of boredom as a research subject

The second category of methodological problems associated with researching boredom is reactions of other people (academic colleagues and participants) to boredom as a research subject. It is not uncommon for researchers investigating boredom or just interested in the topic to be considered a bit extravagant. In the academic context, the subject itself is regarded as intriguing but slightly whimsical, 'weird, crazy or unworthy of study'

(John Eastwood cited in Rhodes, 2015, p. 278). Some colleagues of mine and/or my supervisors used to deliver pithy one-liners upon seeing me in the university corridor: 'Aren't you bored with boredom yet?,' 'Are you bored yet?,' or 'You must be extremely bored to be researching boredom.' Despite the genuinely amusing nature of the friendly jokes, the inner message seems to be quite clear: boredom as a research subject appears quite ridiculous. Moreover, many people get openly perplexed when told that I am researching academic boredom. Most of them simply ask in disbelief: 'Really?!' As Randy Malamud recollected: 'When I told colleagues that I was travelling 5,000 miles to attend a conference on boredom, the first reaction was, inevitably, a sardonic chuckle' (Malamud, 2016).

In extreme cases, suggesting boredom as an object of a regular scientific endeavour is interpreted openly as an unkind joke. At the beginning of 2016, I was sending email invitations to a scientific conference on boredom that I was to organize. The information was sent from the official university email address to academic institutions throughout Europe, with a kind request to forward it to their employees and PhD students. One of the institutes from Germany responded as follows: 'Our institute received the invitation below (see also attachment). This probably is a gag of maybe some students of your institute with a specific sense of humour.'

Trivializing boredom as an area of academic discussion rests mainly on comparing boredom with study subjects, which are commonly viewed as strictly scientific, serious, or vital. Guido Borelli sheds light on the issue:

> Facing the seriousness of migration flows, of world economic crisis, of climate changes or the combined effects of these three plagues of contemporaneity, a sociologist stating that he deals with boredom would be considered snob, earning the reputation of at least a 'strange person,' devoted to studies of doubtful social usefulness. This [is] because boredom can be easily stigmatised as: 'a problem for those who have not more important problems.'
>
> (Borelli, 2021)

The prevailing opinion on the idea of studying boredom is that it looks like a leisure activity for bored academics with no serious issues to reflect on. It is 'a relatively minor irritation' (Conrad, 1997, p. 474), a 'mild psychic disturbance' that 'can hardly be the purview of a rigorous social science concerned with altogether weightier issues, and the reassurance of dealing with such solid, measurable facts as income disparities or the rate of violent crime' (Gardiner, 2012, p. 38). Perhaps, as Malamud suggested, researching boredom violates 'the taboo of that which shall not be named in our scholarly endeavours' (Malamud, 2016).

To furnish a real-life illustration of the point, I would like to mention the initial reaction of the PhD recruitment committee at the University of Warsaw to my PhD proposal. I had fulfilled all formal and scientific requirements, and the objective assessment of my candidature was perfectly sufficient to pass, but the members of the committee appeared to be unconvinced about the significance of my research subject. The question of boredom was deemed unworthy of a scientific attention and the proposal was rejected without further ado. Moreover, it is not unlikely that raising the topic of academic boredom could have offended them, if they were to interpret it as a tacit though serious and unfair accusation of themselves possibly being boring and/or bored in the context of university work. Interestingly, it might have been the case, indeed. The chairwoman opened the conversation with a sardonic quip: 'So you think that we are boring?' Her strong reaction made me realize that – to some academics – bringing up the topic of boredom at university might act like a red rag to a bull. To explain it more clearly, I realized that, in the academic milieu, the mere idea may constitute a taboo which, when touched upon, would shock, give offence, or cause an aggressive or ironic reaction of refusal.

The PhD committee did not change their opinion about my proposal, nor did I change my mind about the research subject. However, thanks to a favourable turn of events (a PhD candidate happened to drop out), I eventually did embark on my doctorate research. Gradually, the academics at my institute got used to the subject and began to perceive it as more and more legitimate. This part of the story (accustoming oneself to a novelty through prolonged exposure) spotlights my intuition that the rejection of the idea of researching academic boredom could also result from the novelty of the subject in sociology. Indeed, depending, e.g. on the national/institutional culture, academic establishments do vary in their attitudes towards introducing new, non-classical, potentially controversial subjects within the domains of scientific interest. For instance, in his review of my grant proposal concerning the subject of boredom, an expert of the Polish National Science Centre[1] expressed his scepticism towards the concept: 'If boredom was as important as the project's author claims, it would have become an object of interest of social thought and sociological research a long time ago.' The proposal was ultimately accepted, but the reviewer's reservations about the subject itself show how unfamiliar it still is in sociology.

Another reason for denying acknowledgement of boredom's relevance may be one's alleged lack of life experience of boredom. Indeed, some people claim never to have experienced it, and they believe that it must be therefore of no scientific importance altogether. The following expression clarifies this way of thinking: 'If I do not find the issue significant to myself, most certainly it is not significant at all.' This reaction is linked with the belief that boredom is the domain of bores, people of low intellectual capacities or of weak character.

Certainly, there may be quite many other reasons for trivializing boredom as a research subject in the university milieu. I have listed only the ones which I identified in the course of doing my research and which were corroborated in the findings of this study.

Having discussed the unfavourable/sceptical approaches to the subject of the present study, I would like to underline that there is also a group of academics who generally react in a positive way in this regard. They find the direction of my research interesting, promising, and/or needed – as they admit to struggling with academic boredom themselves (see John Eastwood, cited in Rhodes, 2015, p. 278), observing it in others at university or just perceiving boredom in general as a vital problem of the contemporary society.

Denials of ever being bored

Asking participants (directly or indirectly) about their boredom is the most commonly employed method of researching boredom in the social sciences. Thus, the researcher vitally relies on the participants' feedback. In the case of this study, collecting data by employing the above-mentioned method was not a straightforward task. In the academic milieu, boredom occurs to function as a taboo to many people. For this reason, the word 'boredom' had to be deleted from the invitation emails, because many recipients had refused to participate in the research altogether because of its subject. The most common reply was that one had nothing to say because of the lack of personal experience. Such an adamant denial to have ever been bored signalled a generally negative attitude towards the subject and turned out to be the most challenging reaction to my request/invitation to take part in the research. Quite many of those did eventually agree to participate in the study, but their initial resistance to talking about their own boredom resounded in the interviews. Here come apt examples:

> RESEARCHER: Do you ever get bored?
> RESPONDENT: Pardon me?
> RESEARCHER: Do you ever get bored?
> RESPONDENT: No, sir, I never get bored. This is probably impossible.
> (Teacher, interview_47, female, prof., social sciences)

> I don't understand your questions, to be honest. Huh? Boredom at the faculty councils? The faculty councils are to deal with specific matters that are extremely important to the functioning of the department, personal matters also. I don't understand these questions about boredom at all. You know, this is some total abstraction, because I don't understand how you can ask if I'm bored at the faculty councils. No, sir, I'm not bored, because there are a lot of things which have to be dealt with and which are necessary to settle, and that's it. So what boredom can we talk about here? It has to be done quickly and efficiently, that's it.
> (Teacher, interview_47, female, prof., social sciences)

> In general, my reaction to your question about boredom is astonishment that you can ask about it.
> (Teacher, interview_66, male, PhD, humanities)

In the first quote, the respondent was so surprised by the question (as if she could not believe that I had actually posed it) that I needed to repeat it. From the perspective of the whole interview, it is clear that the theme of boredom triggered a negative reaction and poisoned the atmosphere of our conversation, because the respondent seemed to feel offended just by me uttering the taboo word itself. The subject of boredom turned out to be so sensitive that it would provoke in a few interviewees of mine a strong defence mechanism, a kind of unconscious psychological reaction which aims at reducing anxiety arising from unacceptable or potentially harmful stimuli. It is worth pointing out that such radical reactions were, fortunately for my research, quite exceptional. All the same, some sort of denial did prove to be the most common reaction. Strikingly enough, 44 respondents out of 72 (61%) initially denied ever having been bored (cf. Darden and Marks, 1999, p. 28). In the course of the interviews, some of those 44 respondents changed their minds and said that they had experienced boredom in non-academic contexts or, indeed, at work. Thirteen respondents claimed that they had never felt bored by any academic activity (staff meetings, conferences, teaching, research), while many participants admitted to getting bored by at least one activity. Almost all of the respondents, however, maintained to get bored only rarely.

> You know, sir, you are asking me about this boredom, but this is not a question addressed to me, because I'm never bored. I can't imagine being bored.
> (Teacher, interview_32, female, hab., humanities)

> You know, sir, it's hard for me to talk about it, because I have never experienced boredom ... Boredom is unknown to me ... I don't know, I can only talk about it theoretically.
> (Teacher, interview_35, male, PhD, humanities)

> I'll tell you so, the concept of boredom [is] hardly personal to me. My parents said, and they were right, that "an intelligent man doesn't get bored."
> (Teacher, interview_37, female, prof., social sciences)

There may be a whole bunch of various reasons for denials and the rest of this section deals solely with them. The most general suggestion may be a semi-automatic reaction in humans who tend to keep up appearances at all times when confronted by strangers – pretending to be invariably happy, positive, and fulfilled. As Stendhal once observed: 'Everyone pretends to be happy; I know people who in good faith assure that they never get bored; but their deeds prove to the contrary' (Stendhal, 1892, p. 195, cited in Tardieu, 1913, p. 155).[2] People may not detect boredom at all, even when actually suffering from it. Moreover, it seems generally considered inappropriate to complain about it, especially to a researcher. It is a form of all too well-known methodological problem – denial of entrance to the field, i.e. limited access to data that are sensitive and meticulously hidden. In a strikingly apparent form, it happened in the study by Sandi Mann:

> When I conducted my research into workplace boredom, I struggled to get access to many organizations. And the reason? They refused to contemplate the idea that any of their staff were ever bored. One CEO told me, "My staff are never bored – they don't have time." Such people are in denial.
>
> (Mann, 2016, p. 59)

Christina Garsten (2005, p. 11, cited in Loukidou, 2008, p. 13) encountered a similar situation in her study at Apple Inc. The company did not find boredom acceptable among its employees due to its obvious incompatibility with the brand's creative and innovating profile. From the PR perspective, exposing the corporate identity onto notions that are by default negative is detrimental and, obviously enough, to be avoided. Therefore, in the above cases, the researchers had to deal with defensive mechanisms, which the companies vigilantly employed in order to avoid a risky confrontation with the reality.

This leads us back to the findings of this study which concern the respondents who proudly asserted that they never got bored. Their assertion may reflect their (intentional or not) aspiring to gain superiority over all those who do experience boredom, as if boredom afflicted the miserable, the unintelligent, the lazy, the average but never the ones who are, in a way, superior human beings. Upon gaining quite a deep insight into the phenomenon under my study, I remain sceptical towards one's assertions of never experiencing boredom in any context. Such a person would be some sort of *übermensch* ('overman'), and the gist of the argument is grasped in the following thought by Epstein: 'one cannot be [entirely – MF] human without at some time or other having known boredom' (2011, p. 43). My guess would be along the same lines as Mann's, who suspected that people denying to ever get bored 'simply have excellent coping mechanisms for boredom rather than never experiencing it' (Mann, 2016, p. 58).

To take this argument further, I hypothesized that such coping mechanisms would be mastered with time, thus be more prevalent in older participants than in younger ones. Indeed, this way of reasoning resonates with some studies suggesting that age and boredom are negatively correlated (Harju, Hakanen, and Schaufeli, 2014; van Hooff and van Hooft, 2014; Gkorezis and Kastritsi, 2017). Additionally, I guessed that older participants – due to their age and academic seniority – would be likely to have more inhibitions when it comes to confessing their boredom to a young researcher. In this respect, I put forward the hypothesis that disavowing one's boredom would

Table 1.1 Occurrences of boredom in academics in non-job-related time

Do you ever get bored out of the university context?	MA		PhD		Habilitation		Professor		Total	
	No.	%	No.	%	No.	%	No.	%	No.	%
Yes	9	75	12	55	3	15	4	29	28	39
No	3	25	10	45	17	85	14	71	44	61
Total	12	100	22	100	20	100	18	100	72	100

be in direct proportion to one's academic degree (and, by the same token, to one's age). In other words, the number of denials would increase along with the degree of the participants. My hypothesis found full corroboration in my data. It turned out that nine out of 12 MAs (75%) and 12 out of 22 PhDs (55%) admitted to being bored in non-job-related contexts. In contrast, only seven out of 38 participants with habilitation (18%) answered positively to the question (three out of 20 habilitation holders and four out of 18 full professors). The most bored/the least in denial/the most eager to share were definitely the representatives of the humanities (13 out of 24, i.e. 54%), followed by those of the social sciences (eight out of 26, i.e. 31%) and eventually those of the natural sciences (seven out of 22, i.e. 32%) (Table 1.1).

The principle of busyness and interestingness of the world

One of the most prevalent reasons given by the participants for not experiencing boredom was their busyness. In the current culture of productivity, people are constantly prompted to remain active, to get busy at all times (see Boltanski and Chiapello, 2007). In consequence, people indeed tend to do so. Within the working hours, we are driven by the culture of financial and social status achievement, and the bureaucratic requirements of efficiency. In our leisure time, we keep multi-tasking to achieve our goals set in the fields of consumption, personal development, and hobbies. We are programmed to spend time actively, with no gaps in our tight schedules and no void in our consciousnesses. It is, therefore, probably not surprising that, when directly asked about boredom, people frequently answer that they 'don't have time to waste on being bored' (Darden and Marks, 1999, p. 28). Some respondents directly connote boredom with childhood when they still had time for it.

> I associate boredom rather with some kind of school, childhood period. That is, I have the impression that at some moment in the past I stopped having time for boredom.
> (Teacher, interview_57, male, hab., natural sciences)

> [Boredom] makes me think of children, because I often hear about boredom from my children. I cannot understand it. It seems to me that

the older you become, the less often you get bored. There is even the opposite relationship: you lack time for different [things] which you would like to do and which you cannot do.

(Teacher, interview_45, female, PhD, social sciences)

All such introspections remind me of Harry Truman, president of the United States (1945–53), answering the very same question:

Oh, my, no. We didn't know the meaning of the word, and I'll tell you another thing. I can't remember being bored, not once in my whole life. How in the world can you be bored if you have things to think about, which I must say I always have?

(Miller, 1974, p. 48, cited in Peters, 1975, p. 496)

On a deeper level of speculation, one could probe into how the president and people who share his viewpoint on boredom could be so sure of not being ever bored while having no knowledge of 'the meaning of the word.' The promoters of the idea of 'no boredom possible' argue that life is too short and there are too many activities to spend time on or obligations to fulfil to get bored. This argument seems to be in agreement with Wilhelm Leibniz's 'principle of identity of indiscernibles' (Forrest, 2016), which says that the universe is astonishingly interesting because there are no two absolutely identical things in it. In the same vein, 'no two occasions in life would ever exactly duplicate each other …, no moment is ever the stale replica of another' (Barrett, 1975, p. 552). In short, every possible moment of life can bring us plenty of fresh surprising/entertaining/absorbing things. This stance is depicted by the utterance of one of the respondents:

I really find it hard to understand boredom … The world is so interesting around us, I don't know how people can get bored. There is science, cinema, theatre, art. After all, it is enough just to look around. There are so many opportunities to develop your interests.

(Teacher, interview_15, female, MA, social sciences)

Shameful vice of boredom

In the culture of productiveness, which is currently becoming more and more widespread/globalized, being active is essentially perceived as the main antidote to boredom. Boredom is rather stigmatized as an individual's vice or even a sort of social disability. In the spirit of capitalism, it evokes the notions of failure, shame, waste, idleness. People tend to avoid doing nothing, having a rest in a passive way, wasting time on feeling bored. The skills of meaningful time management and active personal development are honed throughout one's entire (private and social) life. Boredom, connoting sloth and laziness, is deemed blameworthy also in the religious frameworks of the Protestant work ethic and the Christian commandments (Boyns and Appelrouth, 2011, p. 194). In such contexts, boredom is considered a fault (Klapp, 1986, p. 20) and is 'turning into a shameful stigma, a testimony of negligence or defeat' (Bauman, 2007, p. 130).

> Boredom is associated with wasting time. At home, we would say that when you are bored, get undressed and watch your clothes so that you have an occupation. But yes, you waste time when you are bored ... Okay, you may lack creativity to find something to do, but you still are lazybones to waste time on boredom.
> (Teacher, interview_31, male, MA, social sciences)

Therefore, this state is frequently associated with a sense of shame. As Peter Toohey (2011) claims:

> Children have no shame when it comes to complaining of being bored. Adults, though never immune, are quick to deny they suffer from boredom – they're too grown up. Perhaps adults complain less, because they feel that they should be able to stimulate themselves enough never to be bored – and many will brag that they never are bored. They are almost always lying. (p. 11)

Toohey's comment brings up the more general problem of depreciation of emotions. As Keith Oatley and Jennifer Jenkins (1996) noted, emotions (including boredom, we may add) are sometimes considered primitive and childish rather than civilized and adult. Most people somehow accept boredom in their children, perceiving it as a weakness appertaining to a transitional stage in life. But boredom in grown-ups is regarded as a symptom of regression without much excuses. Thus, many people feel guilty of not being productive enough (see Martin, Sadlo, and Stew, 2006; Wechter-Ashkin, 2010). In the research questionnaire by Karolina Kabzińska (2015, p. 83), the participants were asked whether they felt remorse when bored. Interestingly, as many as 73.8% of them answered in the affirmative ($n = 198$, Polish general public).

In the light of what has been mentioned so far, it is barely surprising that many people, even if aware of their boredom, do not speak openly about it. Sometimes, the researcher can receive some actual insight only once reformulating his/her questions so that they do not sound to the respondents like accusations. Indeed, even a minor semantic/grammatical shift can alleviate the tension. For instance, by replacing the form 'somebody is/gets bored' (*nudzić się*) with the form 'something is boring' (*być nudnym*), I neatly avoided the sensitive direct question 'Do you ever get bored in your life/work?' and, instead, asked it in a more indirect way 'Do you find anything in your work/

life boring?' The second version occurred to be more acceptable to begin with, because it reassured the respondents that I did not implicitly accuse them of being unintelligent (cf. dictum 'Intelligent men never get bored'). This linguistic shift elicits a significant shift of perspective by, so to speak, shifting the blame. 'As in the grammatical properties of verbs – transitivity – the boredom of the subject (I bore myself) goes to the object, person or object, accused of causing this feeling (this is boring)' (Petry-Mroczkowska, 2004, p. 195). In other words, admitting that something bores us is usually easier than saying that we ourselves are bored, although there might be no difference in the actual state of boredom itself.

In Polish language, many verbs have the reflexive pronoun *się* as their integral part. The complex problem of reflexivity (literal, reciprocal, or figurative) in Polish happens to be relevant to the present study – the verb *nudzić się* ('to be bored') is figuratively reflexive, but some of the respondents would get somehow confused and look for its literal reflexivity (against their native language intuition). On a basic level, literal reflexivity indicates that the object of a clause is the same as the subject. For instance, in the verb *ranić się* ('hurt oneself'), the reflexive pronoun *się* signals that the doer does the action to him/herself, which is the very essence of reflexivity. Verbs with particle *się* are also used to talk about actions that are reciprocal, e.g. *szanować się* ('respect each other'). The third type of reflexivity concerns fixed expressions – the pronoun *się* is inseparable and must not be taken literally on its own. If you do so with the verb *nudzić się*, you are bound to get entangled in metalinguistic doubts: 'Does the doer actively bore themselves?' and 'Does the doer do the action of boredom to themselves?'

Another method of denial is to misattribute boredom by avoiding the term itself (using some other words instead), while actually speaking of it. The trick is to choose words/names/labels which are euphemistic, not as much morally burdened as boredom is. As distinguished Polish writer Czesław Miłosz (the Nobel Prize winner in Literature, 1980) observed: '[a]nyone who is usually bored will never admit it but will eagerly grasp at assurances that he is alienated, an outcast, lonely, frustrated, and so forth' (1982, p. 167).

Experience without qualities

When asked about their experience of boredom, people quite frequently answer in a way similar to the U.S. president Truman's statement on the issue. Namely, they claim that they 'don't remember' having been bored (Darden and Marks, 1999, p. 28; Maeland and Brunstad, 2009, p. 114), which does not necessarily mean that they have never experienced it. In this section, I would like to focus on why boredom can be deemed as underreported in the light of it being hardly memorable. As Elizabeth Goodstein (2005) put it, boredom is an 'experience without qualities,' hence easy to forget and difficult to recall. Not keeping 'nothingness' in one's memory is probably typical of human cognition in general. If what we are experiencing at present is interesting, time seems to be passing quickly and the event will be remembered as long and full of details. In contrast, when a situation is boring, we will keep virtually no memory of it. Thus, boredom is, as French sociologist and philosopher Jean Baudrillard asserted,

> a subtle form of filterable virus, of fossilized tonality, which might be said to pass invisibly across the substance of time (*durée*), without altering it. Fine particles of boredom striate time like neutrinos, leaving no trace. There is scarcely any living memory of boredom. This is why it can superimpose itself on all kinds of activities, even exciting ones since it lives in the interstices.
> (Baudrillard, 2007, p. 50, cited in Gamsby, 2012, p. 2)

Psychologists and philosophers argue that emotions (e.g. boredom) can manifest themselves in an individual's behaviour and physiology without getting revealed in a subjective experience (Sartre, 1962; Prinz, 2005). Emotions are non-reflexive phenomena, which means that people can experience them without being aware of the fact (see Raposa, 1999, p. 39; Svendsen, 2005, p. 14). By the same token, one 'can live in boredom without feeling it' (Schielke, 2008, p. 257). Jesse Prinz maintains that emotions can be either consciously felt – being thereby called 'feelings,' or go unfelt – being merely 'unconscious perceptions of patterned changes in the body' (2005, p. 17).

> It is comparable to the claim that one might be angry or jealous without being fully conscious of the fact. Indeed, we often rely heavily on others to interpret our own psychic or spiritual states. Since it is all a matter of interpretation, it is reasonable to expect that I might fail to make the correct one.
> (Raposa, 1999, p. 39)

One can be perfectly aware that he/she experiences some emotion but be unable to name/define/describe it (Mulligan and Scherer, 2012), be unskilled in characterizing it (Klapp, 1986, p. 20), or be incapable of accessing/understanding it, which in turn can provoke difficulties in identifying and communicating it (Eastwood et al., 2007).

Ultimately, some people can suffer from alexithymia, which is a kind of psychological dysfunction/personality trait characterized by limited insight into one's emotional life ('emotional illiteracy/blindness'). Alexithymics are unable to identify/process/verbalize their own emotions as well as differentiate between particular emotions and bodily sensations (Strelau and Doliński, 2011). All these problems may lead to misattributing feelings and lower the validity and accuracy of the research tools, especially self-report measures (Vogel-Walcutt et al., 2012).

Yet another possible reason for boredom to be unconscious is its pervasiveness in the everyday life. We are so familiar with boredom that we take it for granted. In contrast to vivid, dramatic, and memorable emotions such as anger, love, or fear, boredom has hardly any anchor in our recollections of the past (see Spacks, 1995, p. 27).

What also makes boredom barely detectable is the fact that, in the majority of cases, it lasts only a brief moment. It is, in a sense, a transient, situation-dependent state. Often, it is rather 'a conveyor belt' to other emotions/states of mind than a clearly recognizable/distinctive, long-term experience in its own right. Experiencing boredom signals that a particular mental/physical activity does not meet one's expectations, does not satisfy one's need for meaning and that another, more valuable engagement should be looked for (see Brisset and Snow, 1993; Spacks, 1995; Barbalet, 1999). Due to this, boredom can disappear at the very moment it emerges, as almost immediately one begins to search for another activity. Frequently, boredom is quickly replaced by other emotions such as frustration, anxiety, anger, etc. The process is, by nature, rather swift and quasi-mechanical, for emotions flow smoothly into one another (see Strelau and Doliński, 2011, p. 547). Moreover, humans almost automatically counteract boredom by distractions/entertainments (Klapp, 1986, p. 20) – in essence, by activating coping mechanisms of all kinds. This modus operandi is evident in the following self-analysis by one of the respondents:

> I would like to get bored sometimes, but I just have this kind of temperament, certain shaped attitudes, a certain way of functioning [that] I cannot, because my body automatically senses such [empty] space, begins to feel this state and introduces such activities to eliminate [it].
> (Teacher, interview_22, male, PhD, social sciences)

As a result, people tend to recognize only their immediate responses to boredom (emotional or behavioural), while forgetting about boredom itself, which is masked by those responses. This tendency had a strong influence on the level of denials noted in my research.

Poor conceptualization of boredom

Definition of boredom: respondents (general population)

The last factor that may contribute to the participants' denying the experience of boredom is the lack of one unambiguous definition of the phenomenon in question. Incidentally, this is another major issue that hinders doing research in this domain. The most crucial problem consists in oversimplifying boredom and confusing it with other phenomena. Such oversimplifications and confusions were common among the respondents (general public), but they are also present in the literature as some authors tend to follow the colloquial understanding of boredom. The vagueness of the concept of boredom was noticed by one of the interviewees. His remark provides a revealing glimpse of the crux of the issue:

> It seems to me that one of the basic difficulties you find is that it is a very imprecise term in everyday language .... In the ordinary sense it is terribly simplified and used imprecisely to situations that are very different.
> (Teacher, interview_63, male, prof., natural sciences)

First of all, boredom seems to be commonly thought of as self-explanatory, needing no verbal definition. This premise shows its strength when one is challenged to actually specify/express the meaning of boredom. Such an attempt takes place in the conversations between Dino and Cecilia – the main characters of Alberto Moravia's *Boredom* [*The Empty Canvas*]:

DINO: 'Boring—how d'you mean, boring?'
CECILIA: 'Boring.'
D: 'But what does that mean, to you—boring?'
C: 'Boring means boring.'
D: 'And that is?'
C: 'Boring.' ...
D: 'Are *you* ever bored?'
C: 'Yes, sometimes.'
D: 'And what d'you feel when you're bored?'
C: 'I feel boredom.'
D: 'What *is* boredom?'
C: 'How am I to explain that? Boredom is boredom' (1965, 290, 519).

Boredom like '[m]ost things immersed in daily life one understands fairly enough until asked to define them' (Bauman, 2000, p. 110). In this respect, boredom shows the general trait of emotions that are, for the main part, taken for granted. Everyone seems to know 'what an emotion is until asked to give a definition. Then, it seems, no one knows' (Fehr and Russell, 1984, p. 464). The state is found to be somehow inexplicable (12 of 72 respondents failed or openly refused to give any kind of explanation of what boredom is). In addition, when eventually put in words, it is prone to be simplified and confounded with other states. To illustrate the point, it is worth noting that a substantial number of the respondents (28 of 72, i.e. nearly 39%) connoted and/or defined boredom (directly or indirectly) as idleness.

> To me, boredom is not-doing; boredom equals not-doing anything. When I'm doing something, I don't get bored.
> (Teacher, interview_26, male, prof., natural sciences)

> Maybe I protect myself against boredom. I mean, against such situations when I would have nothing to do.
> (Teacher, interview_5, female, hab., social sciences)

> To me, boredom is inactivity, not necessarily in the physical sense ... boredom is something like inactivity of the mind or a low activity of the mind ... A certain celebrity said 'I try not to think, and when I am supposed to think, I think about nothing.' This would be the quintessence of boredom to me.
> (Teacher, interview_37, female, prof., social sciences)

Numerous instances of denials were probably caused by an oversimplified perception of boredom. The most common way of construing the notion of boredom was to limit it to the picture of a total inactivity/wasteful idleness. The second way, almost equally popular and strongly connected with the first one, was to connote boredom with relaxing/resting (cf. Kabzińska, 2015, p. 48). Nowadays, having nothing to do and doing nothing (in terms of either idling or relaxing) is extremely rare, as people act under the social pressure to keep their professional and personal schedules fully loaded.

> O mother, I would love to be bored for a time! [*laughs*] I mean, I sometimes think how wonderful it would be if a person could feel bored.
> (Teacher, interview_4, female, PhD, social sciences)

> This is a sort of battery charging for any further effort. I think that this is a natural phenomenon, of course as long as we understand boredom as lowered activity or relaxation before you shift up a gear.
> (Teacher, interview_8, male, prof., humanities)

> Most often it is doing nothing. 'Now I will not learn, I will not do anything, I will just rest.' Everybody needs a moment of rest.
> (Teacher, interview_16, female, MA, humanities)

Boredom is justified by some respondents as the time when one can gather energy necessary for further activities that are to come. In this sense, it is understood as a well-deserved rest after overworking.

Another justification is connected with resetting/decluttering one's mind in order to foster creativity. To some of the participants, boredom in this sense is a blissful state to be craved for at times, because of its being a defence mechanism against the constant overload of everyday stimuli and tasks to do. One of the respondents said that boredom was a kind of body response aiming at 'working overstimulation off' (Teacher, interview_51, female, hab., natural sciences; cf. Simmel, 1950). A few other interviewees voiced a similar opinion, implying boredom as a deliberately passive way of resting from an abundance of stimuli.

> Sometimes it's good to be bored, that is to have nothing specific to do – to deliberate a little bit about what to do, etc., maybe to lie down, to sleep, not to read a book at the moment... I think that this kind of

boredom, which I'd rather define as 'I don't have anything to do and I benefit from it,' is a resting time – but resting on the basis of 'staring through the window-glass.'
(Teacher, interview_60, female, PhD, social sciences)

Rest can also be a walk, reading a book ... And boredom would be a state of exclusion, a state where I reject even entertainment, I reject some nice things, so that I can deal solely with the fact that I just am. (Teacher, interview_36, female, MA, humanities)

Having said that, the findings of my research indicate that boredom has predominantly negative connotations. Many of the respondents associated boredom with doing nothing and thinking of nothing in particular out of laziness/passivity/apathy/lethargy. They would clarify their point by explaining that boredom occurs when one is unmotivated to do what one should do, or when one is too tired, or just unwilling to do anything constructive. Furthermore, as a result, one can slip into some kind of mind-numbing, passive busyness, e.g. futile Facebook scrolling, YouTube watching. As many as 40 participants (i.e. nearly 56%, or 75% – if we exclude 12 respondents who did not answer the question at all) mentioned at least one of the three notions: idleness, rest, laziness. The finding defies a straightforward interpretation as far as boredom is concerned, because what we actually learn from the data is that many academics have little/ no time even to rest/be genuinely idle, let alone to be bored.

All three notions are somehow connected with boredom, but none of them can serve as its adequate synonym. Idleness can elicit boredom, but is not synonymous with it, especially as one can be bored while performing an activity, i.e. while not being idle. As for rest, it has, by definition, positive connotations of, e.g. a desirable break, whereas boredom is intrinsically negative. Thus, it remains unsure whether the participants talked actually about boredom, since the general public's perception of boredom is not in accordance with the scientific framework thereof.

It would be, therefore, more precise to say that the very notion of boredom remained quite vague to a number of the participants. Some of them identified boredom indirectly through its causes, with idleness being the most commonly mentioned one. Others associated boredom with constraint, situations when one is unable to engage oneself in a meaningful activity due to external circumstances, e.g. illness or injury.

Such a cognitive desert. I am lying in bed and my illness or fever or other affliction doesn't allow me to read. A model example is an inflammation of the labyrinth, which once disabled me from reading for a month. And then there are very few activities that you can spend time on in a reasonable way. This is indeed an experience of boredom and it is associated with negative experiences.
(Teacher, interview_6, male, PhD, natural sciences)

Another notion mentioned by the participants was monotony, futility, routine, repetitiveness. In this context, the respondents pointed to situations that can be characterized by predictability, a sense of time dragging on, waiting (waiting rooms at hospital/clinic, a delayed train/plane, etc.), a state of suspension, or being fed up with performing some repetitive/automatic activities for a long time.

> [We are] waiting for something, which causes that we can neither relax nor start any new activity, because we know that it would be discontinued soon.
> (Teacher, interview_57, male, hab., natural sciences)

> For a long time we are forced to do a certain homogeneous activity and we cannot change this activity to another one.
> (Teacher, interview_45, female, PhD, social sciences)

> When a man acts like an automaton, he gets bored ... You, like a robot, automatically repeat the activities you are doing and you look at the passage of time and wonder and rage: 'Damn, at that time, I could have done something more useful.'
> (Teacher, interview_41, male, prof., humanities)

In this context, boredom induces, first and foremost, a sense of wasting time. Boring activities/situations are those of low usefulness and are essentially perceived as meaningless, personally unsatisfying, and non-engaging. Table 1.2 presented herein summarizes all associations with boredom that were mentioned by at least two participants. Based on this principle, the associations mentioned only by one participant are not included in the summary. All the same, I am listing those here in order to signal the scope of mental connections revealed in the research: uselessness, unfulfilled

Table 1.2 Respondents' connotation with the word 'boredom'

Connotations with boredom	Number of mentions
Idleness	28
Monotony, repetitiveness, routine	12
Relax/rest	11
Laziness	8
Waste of time	6
Disengagement	5
Meaninglessness	3
Passivity	3
Lack of communication	2
Fatigue	2
Dragging time	2

expectations, lack of attention, lack of challenge, lack of purpose, lack of interest, indifference, void, hopelessness (entrapment, no chance to avoid or get out of an uninteresting situation), impatience, burn-out. The data presented above provide us with a strong evidence of a poor conceptualization of boredom among the respondents. By implication, it can be justified to claim that the general public has no clear and unanimous idea of what boredom actually is. Consequently, the issue poses a large methodological challenge in researching the phenomenon of boredom in general and that of academic boredom in particular.

Definitions of boredom: dictionaries and literature

The conceptualization of the research subject constitutes a crucial element of any scientific endeavour. The relevant literature on boredom, however, not always employs comprehensive definitions of the phenomenon in question. Out of 572 texts analysed in the present study, only 36 (6.29%) formulate a more or less original definition of boredom, 161 (28.15%) cite definitions of other authors (more than 50% cite one of three definitions coined, respectively, by Fisher, 1993; Mikulas and Vodanovich, 1993, or Eastwood et al., 2012), 117 (20.45%) use some definitional expressions, frequently delivered in a metaphorical/poetic language, which I call quasi-definitions (cf. 'impressionistic definitions,' Spacks, 1995, p. 14), and as many as 258 (45.11%) employ no definition at all.

The above-mentioned analysis was based on the following principle. As 'a definition' I understand an intentional/connotative definition that attempts to grasp the essence of a defined object and traditionally consists of two elements: *genus* (a large category) and *differentia* (distinguishing characteristics). In my analysis, if a definition under consideration had both elements and was not cited with a reference, I coded it as 'an original definition;' if a definition was not formally correct or was not meant to be an actual definition at all (e.g. was introduced by 'boredom is...'), but still aimed at describing some essential qualities of the phenomenon, I coded it as 'a quasi-definition.' Nevertheless, the most disturbing and shocking fact, in my view, is that almost half of all analysed texts did not employ any kind of definitions at all. The term 'boredom' was employed in its common, colloquial, taken-for-granted sense (see Darden and Marks, 1999, p. 14), on the premise that everybody knows what boredom is. I am of the opinion that making such a presumption constitutes a serious methodological problem, because – as I argued in the previous sections and as I will show in the next chapter – the conceptualization of boredom is far from obvious. Because of that, I found it difficult to properly evaluate the texts where the author theorized 'about separate constructs, though each one is referred to as boredom' (Baratta, 2014, p. 2).

Having no definition is a problem, but so is having an empty/vague definition. The first issue in this regard is the self-explanatory character of some definitions, which refers to various kinds of the formal fault called *ignotum per ignotum*. Instances of explaining one unknown thing by another unknown thing can be found in dictionaries and in the relevant literature: *Webster's Student Dictionary* (2004) explains 'boredom' as 'the condition of being bored,' 'to bore' as 'to weary by monotony, dullness,' and 'dull' simply as 'boring.' Given that tedium and dullness are considered synonyms of boredom, defining one by referring to another provides no extra information to those who have not known the meaning of the words. The vicious circle is evident in the following citations:

> [Boredom is] a reactive state to wearingly dull or tedious stimuli.
> (Musharbash, 2007, p. 307)

> Boredom is the reflection of objective dullness.
> (Adorno, 2001, p. 192)

> To bore is 'to weary by tedious iteration or repetition' or 'to tire by insufferable dullness.'
> (Concise Oxford Dictionary, 1990, cited in Carroll, Parker, and Inkson, 2010, p. 1032)

The second issue is oversimplifying, i.e. reducing boredom to a traditionally identified limited set of characteristics/keywords. This pertains to many definitions coined in dictionaries. The most popular dictionary of English conceptualizes boredom as 'the state of being weary and restless through lack of interest' (Merriam-Webster, n.d.). The same practice can be noticed in dictionaries of other languages. For example, in Polish, boredom is commonly defined as 'an unpleasant state or feeling caused usually by idleness, lack of interesting occupation, lack of excitement, monotony of life' (Szymczak, 1995) or in German as 'depressing feeling of having no occupation' (Digitales Wörterbuch der deutschen Sprache, n.d.). All of these provide no information on the essence of the experience, giving rather limited information about its causes. Defining boredom by its causes instead of specifying its differentiating characteristics may constitute a more general problem (Daschmann, Goetz, and Stupnisky, 2011; Eastwood et al., 2012).

In the case of the dictionary and literature definitions of boredom, one encounters the same kinds of interpretive difficulties as I did in the case of the respondents' conceptualizations of boredom. As it has already been signalled in the course of the present argumentation, the most typical difficulties are oversimplification and confounding boredom with other states (most notably, idleness). Boredom is defined as 'the tension created by the lack of neural nourishment' (Saunders, 1996, p. 465), 'the most common emotional response to lack of occupation' (Wilcock, 2006, p. 171 cited in Martin, Sadlo, and Stew, 2012, p. 171), 'understimulation stress' (de la Peña,

2006), 'a feeling of mental weariness, listless discontent, produced by want of an occupation' (Gabriel, 1988, p. 157), 'an affective state that can be connected to low levels of arousal' (Giakoumis et al., 2011, p. 121). Similarly, '[t]o be bored is to feel some kind of emptiness of mind that does not know what to do, looking for fun, but cannot find it' (Krasicki, 1994, p. 131). In all these formulations, idleness is the main explanatory backdrop notion, while boredom is as a kind of frustration, a reaction to a dearth of occupation, a low level of arousal. This may be construed as a formal fault of excessive broadness of the definition, for indeed there are also other affective states characterized by idleness or a low level of arousal (e.g. sadness, laziness, dejection).

Boredom is often defined by reference to various connoted states. This conceptualization was observed among the respondents, but it can also be revealed in specialist texts and written artistic works. The first strong connotation concerns relaxing and sleeping. Boredom is described, for instance, as 'a yawning empty chasm between two meaningful moments' (Gabelman, 2010, p. 147). Along the same lines, Walter Benjamin famously claimed that 'if sleep is the apogee of physical relaxation, boredom is the apogee of mental relaxation' (2007, p. 91). Secondly, boredom connotes laziness. This can be aptly illustrated by quoting Erich Fromm: 'Laziness, far from being normal, is a symptom of mental pathology. In fact, one of the worst forms of mental suffering is boredom, not knowing what to do with oneself and one's life' (2002, p. 282). To some authors, boredom has direct connotations of apathy, emotional detachment or 'affective deficiency,' 'affective lack' (Ngai, 2005, p. 268, 269). In this respect, it is defined as a state of 'not having any feelings, being blocked emotionally, being frozen, feeling the self to be unreal, in a word, apathy' (Bibring, 1953, p. 28, cited in Kenny, 2009, p. 139; cf. Ngai, 2005; Schneider, 2013). To put it another way, boredom is a state of general listlessness (Csikszentmihalyi, 2000b, p. 442), 'emotional flatness and resigned indifference' (Gardiner, 2014, p. 30). Finally, there is also a discernible tendency (prevalent for decades in industrial studies) to treat boredom as a synonym of monotony (Davies, 1926, p. 473).

In all of the above-mentioned examples, boredom is presented one-dimensionally by being fallaciously deemed equivalent to something that is intrinsically similar to it yet distinguishably different from it. These examples of oversimplification in conceptualizing boredom boil down to the observation that the general public's perception of boredom is reproduced, to a certain extent, also in literature.

One more definitional problem is formal negativity of some definitions, i.e. describing boredom by enumerating what boredom is not. The definition of *ennui* in *The Great French Encyclopaedia* can serve as an extreme example of the case:

> [Boredom is] a kind of displeasure which cannot be defined; it is neither sorrow nor sadness; it is a privation of all pleasure, caused by I do not know what in our organs or in external objects, which, instead of

occupying our soul, produces a malaise or disgust, which we cannot be accustomed to.

(Jaucourt, 1772)

To be blunt, this appears to be a method to avoid defining the phenomenon rather than to explain its essence in a comprehensive way. Of course, perhaps the tendency to define boredom by negation lies in the very essence of boredom, insofar as it is deemed to be an ambivalent, obscure and shapeless experience: 'lack, void or absence, so this what can only be determined by difference' (Markowski, 1999, p. 290).

Another definitional issue is the tendency to, instead of risking a formal definition, provide some more or less general, poetic, metaphorical, or just partial expressions. One may argue that perhaps such explanations of boredom can be even more revealing and touching upon the kernel of the phenomenon, but I argue they are, for the most part, one-dimensional and limited in their explanatory capacities. The bulk of such expressions provides an important insight into the essence of boredom but cannot serve as scientific conceptualizations of the phenomenon. By way of example, boredom is described as 'another name for a certain species of frustration' (Sontag, 1967, p. 303), 'the growing awareness of nothingness' (Mijuskovic, 1979, p. 20, cited in Kirova, 2004, p. 244), 'extreme aesthesia' (Aho, 2007), 'the dream bird that hatches the egg of experience' (Benjamin, 2007, p. 91), 'a psychic anorexia' (Healy, 1984, p. 60), 'the lassitude of the soul' (Sandywell, 2011, p. 177), 'experience without qualities' (Goodstein, 2005), 'the longing for a content' (Marx, 1992, p. 398), 'a heightened awareness of the passing of time' (Raposa, 1999, p. 42), or 'a form of devastating agony' (Seo, 2003, p. 3). Some of the above wordings are strictly emphatic and poetic, with no exclusive connection to boredom (e.g. 'lassitude of the soul' may be a proper characterization of depression as well, and 'devastating agony' of many other states); others are more concrete and, arguably, more closely connected with boredom ('extreme anaesthesia' or 'psychic anorexia'). Nevertheless, none of these can serve as a proper scientific definition of the phenomenon.

Transcultural/Translingual differences between boredoms

What makes the scrutiny of boredom even more challenging is the fact that boredom may be understood differently in different languages and cultures. The language/culture-specificity of understanding a given phenomenon makes it difficult for researchers to interpret the data from various linguistic/cultural/national fields. The Anglo-Saxon 'boredom' may have a different meaning from the actual meanings of its closest equivalents in other languages. More to the point, some languages may not even have adequate terms for boredom or may adapt the English term with a significant shift in meaning (see the case of the Australian Aborigines, Musharbash, 2007). Thus, due to their specific etymologies and socio-cultural contexts, the words which in other languages are the counterparts of the English 'boredom' are likely to reveal/accentuate different aspects of the phenomenon (Ejder, 2005, p. 13). In brief, people of different linguistic/cultural/national origins may understand boredom differently. In the framework of collecting research data from respondents, this consideration reveals a significant methodological problem with reliability and accuracy of research tools and, ultimately, proves that comparative studies concerning various linguistic/cultural/national fields are, in essence, extremely difficult (Wierzbicka, 1999). The insight that some facets of a notion will not lend themselves to translation has proved relevant in countless cases of doing research in most academic disciplines.[3]

Certainly, nowadays there can be observed a gradual globalization and standardization of the meanings of various terms employed worldwide as translations of the Anglo-Saxon 'boredom.' Nonetheless, each of those words has its specific linguistic/cultural history, which, on the one hand, can be traced in dictionaries and on the other hand, is somehow kept alive in the language-users' understanding of it. In some cases, the etymologies of the two words (i.e. of the word 'boredom' and its equivalent in translation) may be parallel, and yet both words do retain their specificities, at least to a certain extent.

In the light of the above and given that boredom is a multidimensional phenomenon, it is not too surprising to notice that different languages accentuate or share distinct qualities of the experience. I have selected a few instances to illustrate the point. In Chinese (Mandarin), Japanese, and Korean, the terms for boredom highlight the meaning of having 'nothing to do' and being 'not interesting' (Sundberg and Staat, 1992, cited in Vodanovich et al., 2011). The Hungarian *unalom*, as László Földényi (2016) indicated, up to the eighteenth century used to mean 'to be satiated with,' implying 'a state of having had enough.' The German *Langeweile* ('a long while') and its Slovenian derivative *dolgčas* ('a long time') accentuate the time dimension of boredom. Originally, the word *Langeweile* was used in its literal meaning of time passing slowly, but in the nineteenth century, it fused with the French *ennui* and, consequently, included a sort of existential dimension as well (Silver, 2012). In translation, the Anglo-Saxon 'boredom' often embraces both mundane and existential facets of the phenomenon, and therefore carries a much more extended list of connotations. As Özge Ejder (2005, p. 4) noted, the Turkish *sıkıntı* means, besides boredom, also distress, trouble, difficulty, annoyance, worry, depression.

A similar phenomenon can be noticed in many Romance languages, where the terms for boredom have many different associations or where there are more than one term for boredom. In the languages spoken in the Iberian Peninsula, we may find two major groups of etymologies that serve as the basis for translating 'boredom.' The first source is the Latin *ab-horrere* ('to hold in horror'/'to abhor,' Dalle Pezze and Salzani, 2009b), which is directly traceable in the Asturian *aburrición*, the Catalan *avorriment*, the Spanish *aburrimiento*, and the Portuguese *aborrecimento*. It accentuates connotations of hate (derived from the Latin *odium*), disgust (see the Spanish *fastidio*, the Portuguese *fastio* from the Latin *fastidium*, or the Portuguese *nojo* from the Provençal/Occitan *enojo* derived from the late-Latin *inodiare* 'to hold in hatred'), horror, annoyance, fatigue (see also the Spanish *cansancio*), satiety (present in the Portuguese term), or even anger (in the Portuguese term, as well as in the Spanish *enojo*; Michaelis: Dicionário Brasileiro da Língua Portuguesa, n.d.; Diccionario de la lengua Española, 2001).

The second group of etymologies that some Romance languages employ to signify boredom is derived from the Latin *taedium* – hence, e.g. the Asturian *tediu*, the Catalan *tedi*, the Spanish *tedio*, or the Portuguese *tédio* (the Portuguese *enfado* shares similar meaning). These terms emphasize the existential dimension of boredom, i.e. its connections to depression, melancholy, spiritual displeasure, profound disgust. Both meanings (mundane and existential) are also present in the Romanian *plictiseală* (Dexonline: Dicționare ale limbii române, n.d.), the Italian *nòia* and the French *ennui*. The Italian and French terms, similarly to the Spanish *enojo* and the Portuguese *nojo*, originate from the Provençal/Occitan *noja*, *enoja* (verb *noiare* or *annoiare*) and used to have quite a different meaning.[4] In Dante, the term *noia* signified pain and displeasure. The word *ennui*, which originated from the twelfth-century troubadour poetry, meant 'profound sadness, sorrow, disgust' (*Le Trésor de la Langue Française Informatisé*, 2018). It was 'a form of moral pain particularly associated with the loss of a loved one' (Goodstein, 2005, p. 109). In both Italian and French of modern times, we can see the dichotomous meaning of the terms used for 'boredom.' The Italian *noia* is defined both as a 'sense of dissatisfaction, of annoyance, of sadness, which comes from lack of activity and idleness or from feeling busy in a monotonous thing, contrary to one's inclination, such as to appear useless and vain' and as 'tedium, painful sense of the vanity of life, considered as the habitual condition or disposition of the soul' (Treccani, n.d.). Similarly, the French *ennui* is defined in a twofold way as 'moral weariness, impression of emptiness generating melancholy, produced by idleness, lack of interest, monotony' (Larousse, n.d.) and, simultaneously, as 'feeling of weariness coinciding with a more or less profound impression of emptiness, uselessness that gnaws the soul without a specific cause or which is inspired by metaphysical or moral considerations' (Centre National de Ressources Textuelles et Lexicales, n.d.), 'dejection caused by deep pain, profound distress ... [n]ostalgia, regret for somebody or something' (Le Trésor de la Langue Française Informatisé, n.d.). As I was trying to demonstrate herein above, in the Romance languages there is a plethora of associations concerning boredom. Associations such as pain, melancholy, disgust, and annoyance signal a more profound dimension of the concept of boredom. To grasp the general significance of this conclusion, from both linguistic and methodological perspectives, one can broaden the scope of the probe by checking the word 'boredom' in a few other languages. Slavic languages seem to provide a rich ground for this analytical pursuit.

The Russian term for 'boredom' *skuka*/скука is associated with quite a different set of notions. It allegedly originated from an onomatopoetic imitation of the call made by the cuckoo, which has connotations of repetitiveness and monotony (Wangh, 1975, p. 516). Because, in translations from French, *skuka* is to mean the same as *ennui*, it has received the extra meaning that the French word intrinsically carries, i.e. mental anguish and despondency (Gramota, n.d.). To illustrate the point, the Russian phrasal verb *skuchat po*/скучать *no*, which means 'to long for somebody/something,' 'think of somebody/something with grief, longing,' does resemble the original meaning of *ennui*, brought to the fore in the poetry of mediaeval troubadours ('to feel pain of yearning'). Interestingly, the same relation is evident in the Polish [obsolete] *nudzić za kim, po kim* (Skorupka, 1967, p. 522) and the Ukrainian *nudha za kim*/нудьга за ким (Словник української Мови, 1974, p. 452). Another interesting connotation of the Russian term under consideration is the verb *dokuchat*/ докучать (see the Polish *dokuczać*), meaning 'to bother, trouble, pester.' This meaning is strikingly present in the Polish phrasal verb *nudzić o coś* (a derivative of *nuda* 'boredom'): 'to bother somebody obtrusively about something, if one wants something from somebody' (Bańko, 2000, p. 1049). In a sense, if it was to be construed literally, one could probably still guess its actual meaning by means of a wordplay 'to bore for something' by analogy with 'to ask for something.' The Polish *nuda* (similarly to the homophonic expressions in Slovakian and Czech) is believed to be derived from the Latin adjective *nudus* meaning 'nude, bare, stripped' and the Latin verb *nudo* 'to lay bare, to strip' (*Latin Dictionary*, n.d.). The connotations pertaining to the Latin words, such as being bare/stripped, being void of something, experiencing emptiness/loss of something, might resonate with native speakers of Polish, Slovakian and Czech when they think about boredom. *Nuda* is also suggested to be derived from the Russian *nuża*/нужа meaning 'misery' (Bańkowski, 2000, p. 325), which evokes the association with a shortage of something. The contemporary Polish verb *nudzić* has been known since the fourteenth century, initially in the version *nędzić*, which meant 'to oppress, harass, torment, emaciate, weaken' (Malmor, 2009, p. 291). In addition, it may be connected with the Bulgarian *nudja* and the Proto-Slavic *nudit*, meaning 'to coerce' (Boryś, 2005, p. 368). This connection accentuates the notions of constraint, dutifulness, and the compulsory, forced character of boring activities. Another association present in the Polish concept of boredom is that of disgust and nausea. It dates from the sixteenth century (Mayenowa, 1988, p. 563) and, despite 'nausea' being still mentioned as semantically related to the term *nudzić* in some modern dictionaries (Bańko, 2000, p. 1049), it seems to be preserved actually only in the word *nudności* (nausea, queasiness). Until the first half of the twentieth century, the Polish term *nuda* was also associated with melancholy (see the obsolete Polish verb *nudnieć* 'anguish of the heart;' Linde, 1994, p. 327), but it seems to have lost this meaning definitely by the end of the twentieth century. To sum up, the Slavic terms for 'boredom' are connected mostly with 'a shortage of something,' 'monotony,' 'coerce.' In contrast, the equivalent terms in the Romance languages have connotations rather of 'annoyance,' 'disgust,' and 'melancholy.' The latter set of associations used to apply (in a limited way) to the Slavic terms as well, but now they are, for the most part, obsolete.

In the light of the above argumentation concerning the complicated details of etymology and semantics, it should be clear that my respondents, native speakers of Polish, may understand 'boredom' somehow differently from native users of other languages. As far as English is concerned, it is noteworthy, in this respect, that the word 'boredom' originated from verb 'to bore' – meaning 'to pierce, perforate, make a hole, make something hollow' (Online Etymology Dictionary, n.d.-a; Pease, 2012, p. 2). As Allison Pease noted, 'the modern conception of "bore" is recorded by *Oxford English Dictionary* in an exchange of aristocratic letters written in 1766 and 1767 complaining of chamber bores, presumably men who talked so tediously as to metaphorically pierce holes in their listeners and render them hollow' (Pease, 2012, pp. 2–3).[5] Therefore, the term 'boredom' has no particular 'innate' connotations with acedia, melancholy or ennui. This existential dimension of boredom is present in many Romance languages, but English has separate terms for it: 'tedium' and (transplanted from French in the mid-seventeenth century) 'ennui.' Consequently, the English 'boredom' seems to be associated with lack of interest, fatigue (see 'weary, weariness, wearisome'), lack of content (emptiness, making something hollow), lack of pleasure/satisfaction (see 'dull' in *Online Etymology Dictionary*, n.d.-b). As Edward Peters summarized, 'boredom never acquired in English that rich set of connotations already at hand for Rousseau, Buchner, and Baudelaire' (1975, p. 508). It is a highly context-dependent phenomenon and the language/cultural dimension should be taken into account not only in researching boredom and drawing conclusions, especially in the case of international comparisons but also in translating a research from one language to another.

Lack of consensus on definition: multidimensionality of boredom

A considerable hurdle in researching boredom is posed by the lack of consensus as to its definition. It seems to have simultaneously no and many shape(s) and to hinder reaching its own essence (Markowski, 1999, p. 290). As the previous sections elaborately showed, the conceptualization of boredom is far from obvious, due to boredom having various dimensions, existing in many forms and being a complex and ambiguous phenomenon, which eludes a precise definition (Kuhn, 1976, p. 5). It would probably be even more accurate to 'speak not of boredom, but of boredoms' (Phillips, 1993, p. 82), as the term might be just a 'grab bag of a term' (Beres, 2017). Because of this, 'the only apparent consensus is that boredom is a complex phenomenon' (Caldwell et al., 1999, p. 103). The conceptualization of boredom is so difficult not because, as it is commonly believed, there is nothing to say about it, but because of its multidimensionality and complexity. For centuries, there have been forged multitudes of paradigms and theories in the attempt to interpret/unravel the phenomenon of boredom. The word cloud (Figure 1.1) shows the words which were the most frequently used in the definitions of boredom analysed in the present study. The scope of this data visualization reveals the theoretical diversity in the field. The next chapter

Figure 1.1 The most frequently used words in definitions of boredom.

Source: Data collated by Author; word cloud generated by Nvivo Software.

will be devoted solely to the presentation of various disciplinary/theoretical approaches toward the conceptualization of boredom.

———————— *** ————————

This chapter was focused on presenting various kinds of methodological problems connected to researching boredom. Studying boredom faces probably the same obstacles that are characteristic of studying emotions in general and those sensitive ones in particular. People repress/hide their emotions, have trouble naming them, do not reflect much upon them or are even not aware of the fact that they experience them (Stets and Turner, 2006). Boredom is difficult to conceptualize and operationalize, thus it is hard to observe, distinguish from other states of similar symptoms (such as fatigue or sleepiness); is oversimplified and connoted with idleness, rest, and laziness, highly vulnerable to denial, shameful, haze, perceived differently in various cultures or scientific disciplines/theories, ultimately multidimensional. All these may prompt significant methodological problems and should be taken into account both during research and analysis. This chapter aimed to be an exhaustive guideline for those who are attempting to research boredom, especially via qualitative methods.

Notes

1 Pol. *Narodowe Centrum Nauki* – one of the biggest academic institutions financing research grants for scientists in Poland.
2 Cf. 'The majority of persons who suffer from boredom never complain about it, and its latent existence can be concluded only indirectly, from the strange and paradoxical splenetic-like actions of those afflicted with boredom in their efforts to avoid it' (Bergler 1945, p. 38). We may call it 'covered-up boredom' after Sundberg and Bisno (1983), that is 'a denial of being bored despite evidence of lack of interest in the activities of life' (Kerce 1985, p. 9).
3 Cf. The case of a Chinese-Canadian research, where the results were believed to be significantly influenced by the translation of the English questionnaire into Chinese (Ng et al., 2015, p. 15).
4 It is interesting that, as noted by Barbara Dalle Pezze and Carlo Salzani (2009b, p. 9), 'French still uses the term *ennui* for boredom, and so does Italian with the cognate *noia*, whereas the Spanish *enojo* (rage, anger) and even the English *annoy* retain a signification closer to the original connotation.'
5 This may be comparable to the Polish phrasal verbs *nudzić o coś* or *wiercić komuś dziurę w brzuchu* ('to drill a hole in somebody's belly,' i.e. to badger).

Chapter 2

Theories of boredom

In the literature on boredom, the phenomenon is discussed under the umbrella term, whereas, in fact, it is complex and multidimensional to such an extent that various disciplines and theories appear to deal with a multitude of boredoms. The principal aim of this chapter is to provide a comprehensive overview of the existing theories/conceptualizations of boredom developed in various disciplines. The first part of the chapter is devoted to divisions of boredom employed in the relevant literature. The consecutive sections expound, respectively, on psychological, philosophical, and microsociological theories of boredom. However, the material presented herein is not only a review of the literature in the strict sense of the term but also my interpretation of the content. Thus, the consecutive sections do not reflect pure disciplinary boundaries but are rather focused on general approaches/perspectives. Accordingly, I occasionally cite a sociologist or a philosopher in the psychological section and refer to my own data in the sociological sections, if relevant, as illustrations of the theses or concepts under discussion.

Divisions of boredom

Despite all the trouble with defining boredom, which was shown in the preceding chapter, there seems to be a general consensus among boredom researchers – namely that two major kinds of boredom can be differentiated. For the sake of the clarity of the present argumentation, I will loosely name those boredoms as 'common' and 'complex.' There are various criteria according to which authors differentiate between those, but the main line of division is usually whether boredom is induced by/anchored in/associated with an external situation/environment or the individual. Table 2.1 summarizes the majority of the dichotomous divisions presented in the literature.

The group of 'common' boredoms is quite coherent (different classifications just accent various dimensions of the phenomenon) and boredom is described as (1) transient/transitory/short-lived, (2) normal/

Table 2.1 Dychotomical distinctions of boredom

'Common'	'Complex'	Author(s)
Task-focused boredom	Self-focused boredom	Acee et al. (2010)
Reactive boredom	Endogenous boredom	Neu (1998)
Situation-dependent boredom	Situation-independent boredom	Todman (2003)
Objective boredom [L'ennui objectif]	Boredom of the soul [L'ennui d'âme]	Tardieu (1913)
Content/transient boredom	Chronic/life/pathological boredom	Fisher (1987)
Responsive boredom	Chronic boredom (malaise)	Bernstein (1975)
Episodic boredom	Chronic boredom	Mael and Jex (2015)
Temporary boredom	Chronic boredom (ennui)	Irvine (2001)
State boredom	Trait boredom (boredom proneness)	Elpidorou (2017a) and Mikulas and Vodanovich (1993)
Normal boredom	Pathological boredom	Fenichel (1951)
	Habitual boredom	Bargdill (2000a, 2014)
Situational/situative boredom	Existential boredom	Svendsen (2005) and Toohey (2011)
	Hyperboredom	
	Profound boredom	Healy (1984) Heidegger (1995)

Source: The data collated by the author.

justifiable/'innocent'/conscious, (3) directly observable, (4) easily induced and alleviated, (5) affective/emotional state/reaction/response to, and (6) concrete/real situation/task at hand/external circumstances/objects. This state is rather superficial, almost entirely dependent on external factors and it slips away along with the removal of its causes (Kuhn, 1976; Healy, 1984; Irvine, 2001; Toohey, 2011).

The second group, albeit less consistent, can be summarized as describing boredom as (1) long-lasting/chronic, (2) pathological/non-normal, (3) abstract/not directly observable, (4) highly enduring/persistent, (5) existential state/mood, (6) endogenous/internal/deeply rooted in the individual's self (Elpidorou, 2017c; Fahlman et al., 2013). This type of boredom is understood in at least three ways (depending on discipline and approach) as: (1) a personal trait, (2) an individual attitude towards or perception of one's existence, or (3) a pathological response to or an outcome of unconscious processes.

The first understanding, the most prevalent in psychology (but used also in managerial studies, education studies and sociology), conceptualizes boredom as a trait, i.e. as boredom proneness, and describes it as a (not continuously manifested) personal characteristic associated with an intense and frequent experience of boredom, a tendency to feel boredom on a higher level than individuals who are not prone to boredom (Elpidorou, 2017a).

It is definitely the most frequently used concept in psychologically led research. While it is generally conceived as a steady individual characteristic, some studies (Martin, Sadlo, and Stew, 2006) suggest, nevertheless, that the level of boredom proneness may change in the course of one's life, which indicates that it can be something less than a personality trait.

The second understanding, mostly philosophical, accentuates the existential dimension of the phenomenon. It uses such expressions as chronic, existential, profound, metaphysical, or hyper-boredom and describes boredom not as an inherent feature of one's psychological apparatus but rather as an existential state/mood that assails all aspects of the individual's life, being the direct or indirect outcome of intellectualization or (quasi-)philosophical reflection on the meaning of one's life (Gemmill and Oakley, 1992, p. 359; Svendsen, 2005). This attitude may take a more specific form (life in general can have some meaning but mine has none) or a more general form (life as such is meaningless, empty, worthless, and nothing can change it). In this approach, boredom is described as 'an agonizing and chronically painful disease' (Healy, 1984, p. 28) that turns one's existence into a hateful burden.

The third understanding of boredom, as a pathological response to unconscious processes, is psychodynamic. It emphasizes pervasiveness of boredom and unspecified cause thereof (Neu, 1998). In this construal, boredom is compared to endogenous depression (Jackson, 1985), melancholy (Freud, 1953) or anxiety, and treated as an expression of a more general 'internal psychological disturbance' (Bernstein, 1975, p. 514) – a distinct, empirical, pathological state caused by repression of an instinctual need/action (Fenichel, 1951; Gabriel, 1988).

Apart from the above presented approaches towards the division of boredom, we can find a few more. One of these is the distinction between apathetic and agitated boredom (Fenichel, 1951) or between listless and restless boredom (Sundberg and Bisno, 1983), which divides boredom according to its most typical symptoms: listlessness, lethargy, inactivity – on the one hand, and restlessness, agitation, fidgetiness – on the other. This division may be influenced by or indirectly derived from the former tradition of reflection on melancholy, whose two main types were distinguished according to its causes and outcomes. Those were (1) apathetic melancholy resulting from chilling/cooling the black bile and manifesting itself as torpor and (2) manic melancholy resulting from heating the black bile and manifesting itself as frenzy (Klibansky, Panofsky, and Saxl, 1964). This conceptualization is still present in the current reflection on boredom (see Malkovsky et al., 2012; Fahlman et al., 2013; Goldberg and Danckert, 2013) and referred to in the rudimental traditional discussion on whether boredom is a low or high arousal phenomenon.

Level of arousal was used also as a variable in the interesting proposition of boredom distinction authored by Thomas Goetz et al. (2014). Basing

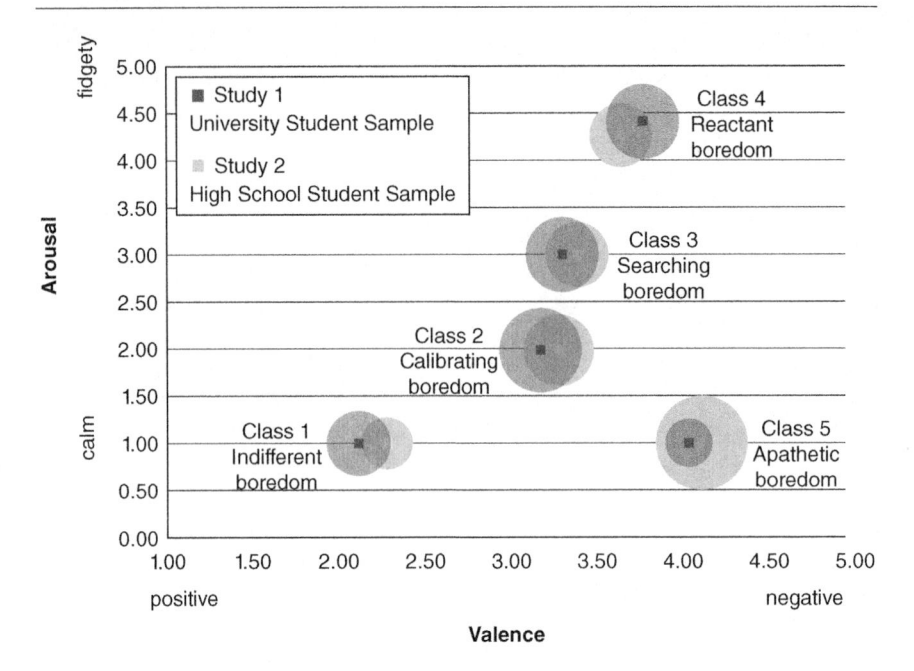

Figure 2.1 Mean values of negative valence and arousal for latent boredom classes.
Source: Goetz et al. (2014, p. 410).

on their quantitative research among German high school and university students, the researchers distinguished five types of boredom (indifference, calibrating, searching, reactant, and apathetic) according to two variables: level of arousal (from low to high/from calm to fidgety) and valence (from positive to negative, see Figure 2.1 below). The first four types were characterized by an increase in both the level of arousal and the negative valence, i.e. crescent discontent and tendency to take actions in order to alleviate boredom. The last type, not anticipated by the researchers, apathetic boredom, was defined as a state of low arousal and high negative valence and by contrast to indifference boredom was not a mild withdrawal from external situation but a state similar to learned helplessness and depression.

This research demonstrates that there are distinct types of state boredom. All the same, it actually merely (1) describes a simple mechanism of growing disconnection and readiness to employ boredom coping techniques and (2) adds to the previous division between agitated and apathetic boredom the dimension of valence.

Looking at two aforementioned divisions more closely, we can perceive them not as distinctions between different types of boredom but rather as classifications of possible responses to boredom. One can either actively counteract boredom and become restless in consequence (to a various, gradable extent), or cease fighting and become apathetic. In a similar manner, some authors create effectual classifications of boredom (in fact, boredom outcomes), which are variations of the abovementioned distinctions. For example, Sharday Mosurinjohn (2015, p. 12) distinguished three modalities (ways of being) of boredom: manic (stultifying), meditative (relaxing), and revolutionary (transformative); and Milan Kundera (1999) differentiated three types of boredom: passive (not doing anything specific), active (leisure activities), and rebel (burning cars and breaking shop windows).

In the light of these several examples of divisions of boredom, one conclusion seems to be particularly striking: there is no single general approach towards boredom. The rest of this chapter is devoted to the scrutiny of the existing conceptualizations of the phenomenon in question, in order to provide a more complex and nuanced description of boredom in various disciplinary and theoretical contexts. Figuratively speaking, what I actually aim to do is to situate boredom in the middle and, by slowly enveloping it with observations from various angles, ultimately obtain as complete understanding of the essence of it as possible. The outcome of such a procedure will be as comprehensive description of boredom as possible, which will constitute a background for reflection on definition of boredom pursued in the next chapter.

Psychological perspective

Psychology is the discipline with the richest tradition of researching boredom. It is, therefore, not a coincidence that psychological understandings of boredom are far from being coherent. Indeed, various approaches differ (at times significantly) in the way they conceptualize the phenomenon. This section shows how boredom is understood in psychology. There are at least four distinct frameworks of defining and interpreting boredom: (1) arousal, (2) cognitive, (3) psychodynamic, and (4) existential.

Arousal theories

Arousal theories basically claim boredom to be a state of an unsatisfactory level of cortical arousal due to a non-optimal stimuli intake (Berlyne, 1960; Mikulas and Vodanovich, 1993; de Chenne, 1998; Csikszentmihalyi, 2000a; Gerritsen et al., 2014). According to arousal theorists, boredom is caused by the mismatch between the individual's need for stimulation and its inadequate supply – mainly from external sources (the mismatch hypothesis). The background for this approach is the optimal arousal theory (Yerkes and Dodson, 1908; Zuckerman, 1979), postulating that everybody has their own level of mental stimulation at which their performance and well-being are maximized (the Yerkes-Dodson law). Boredom, in this paradigm, is interpreted as an emotional response to a deviation from this optimal level of arousal and 'a form of search, by which humans strive to keep up an optimal level of arousal …' (Klapp, 1986, p. 36).

The issue that has been discussed most widely among arousal theorists is whether boredom is a low or high arousal state. The majority of authors associate boredom with the lack or a low level of stimulation (Mikulas and Vodanovich, 1993; Pekrun et al., 2010; Mann, 2016), which is consistent with the common perception of boredom as a state of idleness, passive rest, or laziness. In this conceptualization, the causes of the phenomenon are attributed to occupational deprivation (Wilcock, 2006), 'exposure to monotonous stimulation' (O'Hanlon, 1981, p. 54), 'an environment which is unchanging or which changes in a repetitive and a highly predictable fashion' (Davies, Shackleton, and Parasuraman, 1983, p. 1) or constraint ('when one is forced to remain in a low stimulation setting;' Fisher, 1987, p. 4) such as waiting (Bengtsson, 2012; Lehner, 2015; Tymkiw, 2017), or the lack of challenge (Csikszentmihalyi, 2000a).

Some theorists, however, claim (somehow to the contrary) boredom to be a high arousal state – with reference to Otto Fenichel's (1951) distinction between apathetic and agitated boredom (Berlyne, 1960; Smith, 1981; Perkins and Hill, 1985; Fisher, 1993; Bench and Lench, 2013; O'Brien, 2014). There again, others assume that boredom is both a low and high arousal state or that there are different types of boredom, some of which are associated with high arousal and others with low arousal (Bernstein, 1975; Eastwood et al., 2012; van Tilburg and Igou, 2012; Fahlman et al., 2013; Elpidorou, 2014; Goetz et al., 2014).

Cognitive theories

Cognitive theories concentrate on two major notions: attention and perception. In the framework of cognitivism, boredom is generally described in terms of a deficit of attention, 'an impaired ability to concentrate' (Eastwood et al., 2012, p. 485) or the individual's attitude towards the situation/task at hand, which is seen as providing no chances for a subjectively gratifying activity. According to cognitive theorists, an essential component of boredom is the subject's inability to (or a difficulty in) focus/maintain attention on 'information required for participating in a satisfying activity' (Eastwood et al., 2012, p. 484; cf. Gibson and Morales, 1995; Harris, 2000; Laird, 2007; Martin, Sadlo, and Stew, 2012; Baratta, 2014; Hunter and Eastwood, 2016). Boredom is perceived as 'an affective consequence of effortful maintenance of attention to a particular stimulus event' (Leary et al., 1986, p. 968) or, to be more exact, as a result of the individual's failure in/exhaustion with the struggle to maintain attention (Damrad-Frye and Laird, 1989). Boredom is, therefore, a state 'where one has no strength to think of anything; and … where, in spite of oneself, one thinks of too many things, without being able to focus at will on any particular one'

(Jaucourt, 1772).[1] The subject's failure of focusing attention may be induced by (1) attentional constraint due to some individual characteristics (e.g. extrovertism) or psychological malfunctions (e.g. some attention deficit syndromes; Todman, 2003; Todman et al., 2008), (2) excess of unused mental resources, a discrepancy between one's overall mental capacities and the use of them in a given situation (Davies and Fortney, 2012)[2]; or (3) individual perception of the situation as boring, monotonous (Perkins and Hill, 1985), uninteresting[3] (Fisher, 1993), insufficiently challenging (Csikszentmihalyi, 2000a).

Cognitive theories frequently accentuate human perception and attributions given to external elements of the reality. For example, the research by Robin Damrad-Frye and James Laird (1989) showed that a moderate level of distraction is the most influential in provoking a decrease in attention and is the most frequently linked to the attribution of a task/situation as being boring. The study involved three groups of participants. Each group was exposed to the same tape recording of someone reading an article. Then, in the adjacent room, the experimenters turned on an apparently completely unrelated soundtrack of a soap opera. Each group could hear the sounds at a different level of loudness. In the quiet group, the sounds were not disturbing at all and the participants managed to remain attentive to the task. In the loudest group, the people reported being distracted but did not report being bored with reading the article, because they were aware of the source of the distraction and made an extra effort to focus their attention on the task. In contrast, participants of the middle group did attribute the article as boring – in the case of that group, the volume of the sound was sufficiently low for the persons to be unaware of the actual impact of the distraction. This experiment shows that boredom, like many other cognitive feelings, is related to the monitoring of cognitive processes (e.g. focus of attention) and, in many cases, its occurrence is a matter of the individual's perception of the situation rather than of its objective qualities.

In the context of perception, the literature provides a few interpretations of the phenomenon of boredom and its causes. The state of boredom may be a function of inadequately attributed motivation (Barnack, 1939), the lack of motivation, and the subject's perception of the task as being either too simple (Csikszentmihalyi, 2000a) or too difficult (perceiving the situation as not controllable enough or lacking in value, see the control-value theory of achievement emotions by Pekrun, 2006; Pekrun et al., 2007). Another cognitive factor possibly contributing to the feeling of boredom is failure of expectations, i.e. a discrepancy between one's expectations and the reality (Beckelman, 1995; Conrad, 1997; Neu, 1998; Darden and Marks, 1999). Boredom would, therefore, be a matter of previous attitude towards the current situation, a form of 'disappointment drawn out in time' (Krajewski, 2017). It emerges primarily when our expectations are much higher than practicable or are maladjusted to the realms of reality. We get bored with a movie/book/spectacle and we are more likely to deem it as merely a shallow entertainment – if we expected it to be rather ambitious and challenging. By the same token, we get bored with our current lifestyles if we (pre)conceived them differently or when we begin to harbour higher aspirations towards a different kind of life. In this understanding, boredom is not a derivative of some external circumstances but rather of our perception of our place within them.

Another vital issue addressed by cognitive theorists with reference to boredom is the perception of time dragging, which is believed as an essential component of boredom or a consequence of it. Therefore, either boredom itself results from 'a heightened awareness of the passing of time' (Raposa, 1999, p. 42) or the sentiment of dragging time results from the experience of boredom. In this framework, boredom is conceptualized in terms of failing to focus one's attention on the current activity, and instead – allocating it to temporal cues (Baratta, 2014; Eastwood et al., 2012). According to the scalar expectancy theory (SET, Gibbon, 1977), each organism has an internal clock, a kind of pacemaker that emits temporal pulses. Those signals are accumulated throughout a given time interval (event/activity) – the more pulses registered, the stronger the sensation that the time interval lasts longer, or in other words, that time passes more slowly. When we are engaged in something, our attention is focused on it and we do not spot all of the temporal pulses – time seems to move faster. In boredom, we are basically unengaged and we perceive more temporal pulses, because we experience the passage of time more consciously. In consequence, the time seems to drag on.

The significance of subjectivity in people's assessing the flow of time and evaluating the duration of specific time intervals was shown in the experiment conducted by Harvey London and Lenore Monello (1974; cf. Laird, 2007; Bench and Lench, 2013), who explored how boredom affects one's sense of time. In that study, the participants were divided into three groups and asked to perform a task in front of a clock. The task lasted 20 minutes, but in two groups the clock had been manipulated to go slower or faster so that it would show, respectively, 10 or 30 minutes instead of the time that has actually passed. The highest level of boredom occurred in the group where the clock showed 10 minutes – the participants felt as if time was going more slowly than normal. This subjective time deceleration is what psychologists refer to as 'protracted duration' (seen Evans, 2014). London and Monello's findings indicate that the individual's feeling of boredom is deeply influenced by the perception of time and that, in consequence, it can be induced by manipulation of external measures of time passage. Thus, according to the cognitive theory, we tend to feel boredom when the amount of the accumulated time cues significantly exceeds its expected value in a given interval of time (calibrated by our previous experiences stored in our memory).

Psychodynamic theories

Although psychoanalytically oriented, theorists do recognize the 'normal,' 'innocent' kind of boredom that arises provisionally when 'we must not do what we want to do, or must do what we do not want to do' (Fenichel, 1951, p. 359), they are primarily interested in the 'abnormal,' persistent form of the phenomenon, which they treat as something pathological. In the most basic sense, this theory interprets boredom as a sort of inhibition of the life drive (Freud, 1961), which translates into a rudimental need for health, safety, or sustenance and as the sexual drive. In other words, boredom stems from the individual's incapacity or the lack of opportunities to assign mental energy (libido) to an external object. It is 'a feeling of displeasure due to the conflict between the urge for intense psychic occupation and the lack of stimulation or the incapacity to allow oneself to be stimulated' (Lipps, 1904, p. 477, cited in Fenichel, 1951, p. 349). In the most common conceptualization, boredom is the result of 'an intrapsychic struggle' (Wangh, 1975, p. 543), 'a drive-tension' (Fenichel, 1951, p. 351), the inner conflict between the individual's libido (personal desires) and super-ego (the society's values and morals), which eventuates in a repression of drive – aims, desires, emotions – most commonly identified as aggressive or sexual impulses (Esman, 1979) – which do not fit in with the broader, dominant cultural/social order (tribe/family group, religious commandments, etc.; see Bernstein, 1975). The objects of such a repression may be emotions (e.g. uncontrolled anger, despair, grief) or forbidden desires (e.g. homosexual, see Greenson, 1953). A striking example of boredom conceptualized in this manner is hysteria quite commonly diagnosed among women in the nineteenth century. Understood as some kind of paroxysm of women's repressed rage triggered by the lack of the sense of agency and the failure of satisfying their aspirations (women's ambitions to gain the right of self-determination and to achieve gender equality in the male-dominated society were incompatible with the reality of the rigid social order), the hysteria of that time can be interpreted in terms of feminine boredom resulting from unfulfilled desires and 'self-castration that leaves [nothing but] loss and emptiness' (Pease, 2012, p. 108).

Ralph Greenson (1953) described boredom as a state characterized by dissatisfaction, a feeling of emptiness, and 'a sense of longing and an inability to designate what is longed for' (p. 7). In boredom, not only instinctual aims and/or objects themselves are repressed but also fantasies and thoughts. In this context, boredom is associated with inhibition of imagination ('inner inhibition of voyeurism,' Bergler, 1945), which 'often occurs because of an unconscious fear that fantasy might lead to action of libidinal or aggressive nature' (Wangh, 1975, p. 543). Upon shunning one's fantasy world, a bored person is, therefore, left without an access to a cognitive domain, which could serve as an effective defence against the feeling (Todman, 2003; Steele et al., 2013). In the consequence of such 'self-administered deprivation'

(Greenson, 1953, p. 19), the individual experiences a sense of emptiness and tension that appears in a form of stimulus hunger (restlessness) or paralysis of will (apathy) – 'not having any feelings, being blocked emotionally, being frozen, feeling the self to be unreal' (Bibring, 1953, p. 28, cited in Kenny, 2009, p. 139). What is crucial, the individual is not aware of the repressed desires,[4] which may eventuate in the inability to determine what is actually desired and to understand his/her emotions altogether (low emotional awareness). In this framework, boredom is a feeling of conscious discomfort resulting from an unconscious inner tension between desires and constraints in fulfilling them. More to the point, boredom can be, thus, perceived as a powerful defence mechanism against unconscious fears, needs, and desires, which may threaten the stability of the subject (de Chenne, 1998; Dalle Pezze and Salzani, 2009b). It might be also a means of defence of the ego against attacks from the super-ego resulting from external defeats – put simply, a means of defence against the feeling of failure (Bergler, 1945, p. 46). For example, when someone cannot solve a problem, 'the narcissistic ego denies the defeat felt in not finding the solution' (Bergler, 1945, p. 47) and the person begins to feel bored to mask/negate the failure and not to pay psychological consequences of it.[5]

In this paradigm, boredom has been medicalized. What used to be conceptualized as subjective and spiritual (if we assume melancholy as a precursor of serious boredom) is now reduced to objective physiological categories (Goodstein, 2005; Dalle Pezze and Salzani, 2009b). Some psychodynamic theorists perceive boredom as a pathologic, neurotic 'disease entity in itself' (Bergler, 1945, p. 40), others suggest that it is a concomitant of other psychological disorders (e.g. Goldberg et al., 2011).

Existential psychology

In psychology, the existential approach towards boredom, despite its strong connection to the psychodynamic paradigm (see e.g. existential psychotherapy), perceives the phenomenon in a distinctly different way. In psychoanalysis, the individual is basically the object/victim of his/her internal, unconscious processes. Existential psychology stresses man's sense of agency, the fact that humans are rather makers than observers of their own lives. In a way, it de-medicalized boredom (Berra, 2019). In the centre of this approach lies the premise that the process of sense-making is essential for human beings, that humans 'are addicted to meaning' (Svendsen, 2005, p. 30). In normal, everyday-life conditions, people usually manage to successfully satisfy their urge for meaning, but when they fail to do so, boredom emerges as a signal of 'the inability to realize this desire' (Misztal, 2016, p. 102). Thus, in the existential paradigm, boredom is conceptualized as an absence of meaning (Barbalet, 1999; Baratta, 2014), 'a meaning withdrawal' (Svendsen, 2005, p. 30). At least two conceptions in the domain are associated with such a notion of boredom: (1) noogenic neurosis (Frankl, 2000) and (2) habitual boredom (Bargdill, 2000b, 2014).

The first conception was created by Viktor Frankl, Austrian psychiatrist famous for his *Man's Search for Meaning*, firstly published in 1946, where he described, apart from his internment in a Nazi concentration camp, the concept of noogenic neurosis (from Greek νόος meaning 'mind,' 'spirit,' 'will,' 'sense'; Thesaurus Linguae Graecae, n.d.) and proposed the method of its psychotherapeutical treatment called by him logotherapy. Noogenic neurosis refers to the spiritual dimension in humans and is provoked by the subject's frustration of the struggle for establishing meaning to one's existence. The main symptom of this suffering from a sense of meaninglessness and existential vacuum is chronic boredom (Frankl, 1988, 2000), seen as a much more important psychological problem than those identified by classical psychoanalysis. A powerful description of noogenic neurosis was provided in the case study by John Maltsberger (2000). This is how the analysed individual characterized his own state:

> I feel like I'm not alive in this moment in time, as if I am a spectator to life and to myself. I feel detached from others around me. I feel I lack a sense of purpose, and completeness. Most of all, I feel extremely bored. Bored of everything – work, friends, hobbies, relationships, music, reading, movies, bored all the time. I do things [merely] to occupy my time, to distract myself from trying to discover the meaning of my existence, and I would gladly cease to do anything if the opportunity arose. No matter what the activity is, it leaves me feeling unfulfilled. I'm bored of thinking, of talking, of feeling, bored with being bored. What possible difference does it ultimately make whatever I do? What difference does anything make? What does it even mean to make a difference? Who cares?
> (Maltsberger, 2000, p. 84)

As a crucial element of the aetiology of noogenic neurosis, Frankl pointed out a loss of belief in the future. Man feels that his life is devoid of opportunities for a meaningful fulfilment (see Brisset and Snow, 1993) and of prospects for any change, which ultimately renders him confronting the void. Thus, boredom blocks the process of becoming (Straus 1980 and Knowles, 1986, cited in Bargdill, 2000b) – people cease to set goals and are unable to imagine meaningful life scenarios for the future. For that very reason, logotherapy is concentrated mainly on the future and the meaning of the subject's life. As Frankl (2000) succinctly explained, the most significant difference between psychotherapy and logotherapy is that '[d]uring psychoanalysis, the patient must lie down on a couch and tell you things which sometimes are very disagreeable to tell, [while] ... in logotherapy, the patient may remain sitting erect but he must hear things which sometimes are very disagreeable to hear' (Frankl, 2000, pp. 103–4). According to Frankl, the most powerful motivation in human life is not pleasure (Freud, 1961) or will to power (Adler, 1917), but will to meaning. Frankl believed each epoch to have its own kind of massive neurosis, and suggested existential vacuum to be 'the mass neurosis of the present time, [which] can be described as a private and personal form of nihilism; for nihilism can be defined as the contention that being has no meaning' (Frankl, 2000, p. 131). In addition, Frankl predicted that noogenic neurosis would play a more and more significant role in the society as masses would have fewer predefined meanings and more spare time at their disposal. He interpreted many of human actions as mere compensations for frustrated will to meaning and boredom as a main symptom of existential vacuum – so prevalently experienced in the current times.

The second notion of boredom conceptualized within the framework of existential psychology is habitual boredom, advanced in the series of papers by Richard Bargdill (2000b, 2014, 2016). This kind of boredom is a habituated, settled, long-lasting experience, which stems from giving up on/relinquishing/compromising one's personal life-projects and replacing them with others. After some time, people realize they are actually bored with the new project and, in consequence, begin to feel ambivalent towards themselves: being ashamed and angered for giving up the previous one(s). They start to question their identities, which leads to the feeling of emptiness – their pre-bored identities are lost and nothing can make up for the loss. In view of no belief in any meaningful future, the habitually bored sense the futility of pursuing any long-term goals in life, and – eventually – they stagnate altogether. As specified by Bargdill, the crucial characteristic of the habitually bored is passive hope – hope that somebody else will change the situation for them, since they have become unable to initiate anything by themselves. They are helpless, stuck with the life-projects that they find futile/unsatisfactory/boring, unable to set meaningful goals. While fantasizing about their situation getting miraculously changed by others and passively waiting for such a miracle to happen, they painfully experience time dragging on. Bargdill claims that habitual boredom sometimes (after many years) can mutate into depression. It happens when the emotional ambivalence implodes and the individual can no longer deny his responsibility for squandering his life-projects. Blaming others/external situation for the failure is no longer an option. In that perspective, boredom can be perceived as a defence mechanism against depression as it keeps self-guilt at bay.

Philosophical perspective

Philosophy has a long and rich tradition of reflection on boredom. Throughout the ages, many thinkers have touched upon the phenomenon in one way or another. The philosophers who have significantly contributed to the reflection on boredom are Blaise Pascal (1623–1662), Arthur Schopenhauer (1788–1860),

Giacomo Leopardi (1798–1837), Søren Kierkegaard (1813–1855), Martin Heidegger (1889–1976), Jean-Paul Sartre (1905–1980), and Emil Cioran (1911–1995). They can be loosely described as representatives of two strands of philosophical reflection: pessimism and existentialism (some of them became associated with these approaches posthumously). This section is a summative overview of the main philosophical concepts of boredom.

In the literature, there are various approaches to the subject under discussion, but they seem to converge at several points. First of all, philosophers are preoccupied primarily with the 'complex,' existential form of boredom, understood as a malaise of the ontological or metaphysical (in the philosophical sense of the term) character, deeply rooted in the situation of human existence in the world in general. It is an endogenous experience, whose causes are internal and independent from situational/social circumstances. Secondly, philosophers commonly perceive boredom as a human-specific phenomenon. It is believed not only to be unique to humans but also, by the same token, to distinguish us from animals (Nisbet, 1983; Kołakowski, 1999; Svendsen, 2005; Dienstag, 2006; Leopardi, 2015). Giacomo Leopardi claimed that 'perhaps all our ills can find their analogues among animals except boredom' (2015, sec. 2220). In the same vein, Friedrich Nietzsche wrote in his essay *On the Advantage and Disadvantage of History for Life*:

> Consider the herd grazing before you. These animals do not know what yesterday and today are but leap about, eat, rest, digest and leap again; and so from morning to night and from day to day, only briefly concerned with their pleasure and displeasure, enthralled by the moment and for that reason neither melancholic nor bored. It is hard for a man to see this, for he is proud of being human and not an animal and yet regards its happiness with envy because he wants nothing other than to live like the animal, neither bored nor in pain, yet wants it in vain because he does not want it like the animal.
> (Nietzsche, 1980, p. 8)

Humans are simultaneously jealous of the simplicity of animal life (as opposed to the misery of man's dilemmas) and proud to be a higher form of creatures, to transcend their bestial nature. From this perspective, boredom is a consequence of (self-)consciousness – an animal might feel boredom theoretically, but only humans can actually experience it because they are capable of self-reflection. Animals can appear bored but, in fact, they are able merely to be apathetic, which is something completely different from boredom in the philosophical sense of the term. 'Animals cannot suffer a loss of meaning' and such an attribution would be a form of anthropomorphism (Svendsen, 2005, p. 128). Man is the only creature conscious of his 'continuous existence in time' (Dienstag, 2006, p. 30). Human beings are 'thinking reeds' (Pascal, 1910, sec. 347, 348) – weak in flesh but powerful in mind, with a superabundance of attention that can be devoted to concerns other than the mere sustenance. Some thinkers go even further, claiming that boredom is an affliction that can be experienced only by 'the highest and the most active animals' (Nietzsche, 1924, p. 225), 'in whom the mind is of some relevance' (Leopardi, 2015, sec. 4306) – in brief, by the chosen ones (Leopardi even claim that boredom is unknown to primitive peoples and children, 2015, sec. 175). Boredom, in this perspective, is not a common phenomenon. It increases proportionately to the level of consciousness – the higher the (self)consciousness is, the more severe feeling of existential despair it prompts (Kierkegaard, 1980).

According to this conceptualization, boredom is first of all a mood, which is long-lasting and lacking a determinate object (in opposition to concrete and transient emotions). There is no possibility for us to be without any mood. We can only replace one mood with another, because moods constitute the basic structure of our being-in-the-world (Heidegger, 1995, p. 176). Being existential orientations rather than some particular emotional states, moods situate us in/connect us with the world. In a nutshell, they 'are the most fundamental means by which human being actually dwells in the world' (Svendsen, 2005, p. 110). In everyday life, they are hardly noticeable because our attention is directed externally. However, we can clearly see how our perception of the life/world/circumstances differs when we are in a joyful or gloomy mood. Indeed, we see through moods rather than experience them directly – and boredom is one of such existential orientations.

To all philosophers who devoted a piece of reflection to it, boredom seems to constitute some kind of 'the baseline mental condition from which we can only be distracted' (Dienstag, 2006, p. 30), 'a black hole in man that can only be covered, but never removed' (Markowski, 1999, p. 298), 'an essential characteristic of man as such' (Svendsen, 2005, p. 53), a part of human own nature that can only be fallen asleep, shaken off (Heidegger, 1995, p. 79), feature that defines man as a human being (Pascal, 1910, sec. 127), 'the profound heart of existence, the very matter [man is] made of' (Sartre, 2000, p. 148). Leszek Kołakowski (1999) claimed even that our capacity to feel bored is what makes us humans. According to Leopardi,

> ... boredom is like the air here below, which fills all the gaps left by other objects, and hastens immediately to take the place that they have vacated, if other objects do not replace them.
>
> (2015, sec. 3715)

In Leopardi's view, boredom is experienced whenever man does not feel pleasure or pain, which corresponds with Schopenhauer's perception of life as 'a pendulum to and fro between pain and boredom' (1969, p. 312). To fully understand this perspective, we must pinpoint what vision of life those philosophers (primarily pessimists) represent. According to them, life is a burden, a curse, a constant pain, and displeasure.

> Each of us in entering the world resembles a man on a hard and uncomfortable bed. As soon as the man lies down, he feels restless and begins to toss from side to side and change his position momentarily, in the hope of inducing sleep to close his eyes. Thus he spends the whole night, and though sometimes he believes himself on the point of falling asleep, he never actually succeeds in doing so. At length dawn comes, and he rises unrefreshed.
>
> (Leopardi, 1882, p. 122)

Human life is something that is hard to be integrated with (Cioran, 1999), a constant feeling of insufficiency, unfulfilled 'desire for pleasure' (Leopardi, 2015, sec. 3622), moving from one desire (and some gratification) to the next – without achieving a sense of happiness, which is impossible to achieve or can last only for a brief moment. Life constitutes an aimless and infinite pursuit, and people 'are like clockwork that is wound up and goes without knowing why' (Schopenhauer, 1969, p. 322). Human existence 'is only in the present, whose unimpeded flight into the past is a constant transition into death, a constant dying' and 'the alertness and activity of our mind are also a continuously postponed boredom' (Schopenhauer, 1969, p. 311), constituting a vain attempt to provide a distraction from the consciousness of life's meaninglessness. In this existential perspective, boredom is the basic state of human beings, which can be distracted only by pleasure (the less efficient palliative) or pain (the more efficient one). According to Schopenhauer, when man struggles for his sustenance – he experiences suffering,[6] but as soon as he has his needs fulfilled – boredom emerges.

> The striving after existence is what occupies all living things, and keeps them in motion. When existence is assured to them, they do not know what to do with it. Therefore the second thing that sets them in motion is the effort to get rid of the burden of existence, to make it no longer felt, "to kill time," in other words, to escape from boredom.
>
> (Schopenhauer, 1969, p. 313; cf. Pascal, 1910, sec. 55)

However, all attempts to get free from boredom of existence eventuate in subsequent sufferings – human beings are doomed to thrash around between different kinds of pain and boredom, sharing Sisyphus's lot – struggle, pain, disappointment, and futility are definitional features of human existence.

Boredom, therefore, is the realization of the very nature of human life and the place humans occupy in the universe. Man turns out to be, eventually, as Pascal famously claimed, 'a Nothing in comparison with the Infinite, an All in comparison with the Nothing, a mean between nothing and everything' (Pascal, 1910, sec. 28). He is unaware of the aim of the world but is conscious enough to need/seek for some form of purpose – he occupies a tragic position between animals and God. In boredom, man becomes aware of 'his nothingness, his forsakenness, his insufficiency, his dependence, his impotence, his emptiness' (Voegelin, 1999, p. 282, cited in Avramenko, 2004, p. 118; cf. Heidegger, 1995). In a sense, boredom is a philosophical phenomenon par excellence, a powerful tool enabling the human being to leave the Platonian cave, i.e. the world of illusions, imitations, falsity, and inauthenticity; it constitutes 'the moment of vision,' in which we are able to see the truth of our existence, our *Dasein* ('being-in-the-world,' Heidegger, 1995). In boredom, when one is not occupied by anything or oneself, one encounters/becomes aware of nihility and, from that standpoint, nonexistence (death) becomes obvious as an alternative to *Dasein*. Thereby, man transcends his being, due to which Heidegger (2013) included boredom into the domain of metaphysics.

Boredom reveals the tragedy of man's finitude against the world's infinity, his insignificance, smallness (Pascal, 1910; Brodsky, 1995), and his homelessness in the world (uncanniness, not-being-at-home [*Unheimlichkeit*], 'being a stranger in the world,' Heidegger, 1995). According to Pascal, man is 'a dispossessed monarch' (Kuhn, 1976, p. 112), banished from the Garden of Eden, being nostalgic for the paradise (where everything had a meaning, and death was neither present nor even conceivable/'invented' yet), longing for the sense of being at home, feeling an unbearable boredom – a deeply kenotic[7] (Markowski, 1999, p. 300) and vanitative experience. Upon his expulsion from Eden, man becomes painfully aware of the vanity of earthly things, which is unequivocally expressed already by Ecclesiastes, probably the first pessimist *avant la lettre*. All things are futile and nothing can change that, 'all potentialities have been realised' (Gadacz, 2002, p. 184), all what has been left is a void. Ecclesiastes' vision was conjured up by Kierkegaard in the following passage: 'I lie prostrate, inert; the only thing I see is emptiness, the only thing I live on is emptiness, the only thing I move in is emptiness' (Kierkegaard, 1843). Kierkegaard referred to boredom as a 'demonic pantheism' or a 'reverse pantheism,' because – unlike pantheism – it is founded on emptiness instead of fullness. In this connection, he argued that '[b]oredom depends on the nothingness which pervades reality; it causes a dizziness like that produced by looking down into a yawning chasm, and this dizziness is infinite' (Kierkegaard, 1971, p. 287). Boredom, therefore, is a form of nihilism, an axiological void, a spiritual insatiability, an unspecified sense of lack (Bizior-Dombrowska, 2016), whose exemplary manifestation is, for instance, Goethe's Faust.

From this standpoint, human existence seems to be totally absurd, unjustified, random. As long as we perceive our life as a realization of some plan (divine/ideological/individual), boredom is kept at bay. But when we realize our facticity (as Sartre would call it) – that is when we begin to be aware that our life is nothing more than a set of random circumstances limiting our freedom and agency – a sense of boredom/absurdity/futility is bound to emerge promptly. Sartre connected boredom also with disgust towards life as such (see Finkielsztein, 2016).[8] Since existence seems to be absurd, unjustified, and one cannot find a sufficient reason for living, having been 'thrown into the world' (Sartre, 1989) without any explanation, one may experience disgust and/or satiation with one's own existence (*nausée*), *taedium vitae* (Seneca, 1917) – some kind of existential burnout.

Another crucial category in the philosophical understanding of boredom is time. Boredom is perceived as 'a paralyzing encounter with pure passage of time' (Safranski, 2017, p. 13) – it painfully reveals/highlights the existence of time. Boredom, therefore, is 'only possible at all because each thing ... has *its* time' (Heidegger, 1995, p. 105) – genuine boredom has its source in the temporality of *Dasein*.

> Eventually boredom concentrates on time – the horror of time, fear of time, anxiety of time, revelation of time, consciousness of time. People who are ignorant of time are not bored. Life is tolerable only when we are not aware of every passing moment, otherwise we are doomed. The experience of boredom is the awareness of an irritated time.
> (Cioran, 1999, p. 241)

Boredom, in a sense, annihilates/repeals time, condemning one for entrapment in a shapeless, endless 'now' which is not able to actualize itself. Time stands still, turns into a dead/empty eternity in which one ceases to differentiate between past, present, and future – all three temporal dimensions merge 'into an unarticulated temporal unity' (Slaby, 2010, p. 115). Boredom, according to Cioran, is the most essential form of suspended time (Cioran, 1995). Our everyday life consists in its inclusion into time, whereas boredom, in opposition, consists in falling out of time. In other words, boredom is the situation where time detaches from the existence. (Cioran, 1999, pp. 58–59)

Philosophers who take boredom seriously and devote a significant reflection to it are preoccupied primarily with 'complex' boredom. Yet, there is one important exception – Heidegger's classification of boredom. He distinguished three types of boredom: (1) boredom by something, (2) boredom with something, and (3) profound boredom. The first form is illustrated by waiting for a delayed train at a deserted provincial railway station, where one is confined to a situation that renders him hollow and leaves him empty. This kind of boredom has its clearly identifiable object – one is bored by something external (a boring interlocutor, film, lecture) that fails to provide him with content/fulfilment. The second form is introduced with the example of a party that one finds entertaining while it is happening and yet realizes, in hindsight, that he was actually bored during the event and this realization, in turn, makes him feel the weight of time wasted at the party, the opportunity cost of time spent there. As Heidegger suggested, this kind of boredom is easily 'suppressed' by the first form, so that it may go undetected (1995, p. 234). This type of boredom is rather self-inflicted, one is, as a matter of fact, bored with oneself – 'the subjective component of mood takes precedence over the objective component' (Biceaga, 2006, p. 145). To reiterate, this boredom is an outcome of one's disappointment with oneself for having wasted time on trivial, futile activities. Illustrating it with an example, A person can be bored by a film (feeling bored while watching it and realizing, at the same time, that it is boring/not entertaining enough/not valuable enough) or be bored with it (not feeling bored while watching it but realizing, after the screening, that the movie was, actually, boring/worthless, etc.). The third type, profound boredom, is beyond subjectivity or objectivity, 'it is boring for one,' where 'it' is an expletive subject like in the phrase 'it is raining' (Heidegger, 1995, p. 203); it 'holds us in limbo and yet leaves us empty' (Heidegger, 1995, p. 87). This kind of boredom (or its variations) is basically what was described earlier in this section – a sort of existential boredom.

Existential boredom is at the centre of philosophical analysis of boredom and this subchapter was aimed at providing a summative description of the subject, irrespectively of numerous differences between particular authors. The overview was based on the premise that when one scrutinizes their views collectively, it becomes quite clear that they are actually compatible to a substantial extent in referring to a similar kind of experience (characterized by a list of concrete features). Existential boredom would be a state of a void resulting from the individual's encounter with nihility upon realizing man's insignificance in the world, life's meaninglessness and the futility of all actions. Such a concept shows a strong connection with *taedium vitae, acedia,* or melancholy. It is an 'absolute,' 'pan-ontological' boredom (Witkiewicz, 2005, p. 246), 'an anesthetizing mood' (Thiele, 1997, p. 502), 'emptiness that makes everything of equally great and equally little worth' (Heidegger, 1995, p. 137). It is a notion 'constructed from a union of boredom, chronic boredom, depression, a sense of superfluity, frustration, surfeit, disgust, indifference, apathy, and feelings of entrapment' (Toohey, 2011, p. 142). Toohey claims existential boredom to be a phenomenon more of the intellectual than experiential nature – to be strictly theoretical. However, Svendsen (2016) strongly disagrees, presenting himself as an example of the malaise. I would hypothesize that existential boredom intercepts and continues a long tradition of reflection on melancholy (in all its historical manifestations from acedia to spleen and ennui), which in the nineteenth century was medicalized, and nowadays has been reduced to some sort of depression, with its erstwhile spiritual, metaphysical, deeply existential dimension blurred, neglected, or totally cut off (see Földényi, 2016).

The existentially bored are totally disengaged, disaffected, indifferent, and paralyzed (Tardieu, 1913; Thiele, 1997). They are held in limbo of their own emptiness and worthlessness. Life seems to have no meaning and value whatsoever. Nothing has any merit any more. Such boredom is a state of a profound axiological crisis, connected with the annihilation of any possibility of accessing meaning. Bored is Shakespeare's Hamlet lamenting: 'How weary, stale, flat and unprofitable/Seem to me all the uses of this world' (I,2,133). The emptiness of the world reflects the inner void of the bored individual, who is totally sterile and disgusted with life in general as well as with his own existence.

> Tedium ... To think without thinking, but with the weariness of thinking; to feel without feeling, but with the anxiety of feeling; to shun without shunning, but with the disgust that makes one shun – all of this is in tedium but is not tedium itself, being at best a paraphrase or translation of it.
>
> (Pessoa, 2002, sec. 263)

Such boredom is virtually unspeakable. Kierkegaard (1843), describing the monstrousness of boredom, pointed out the impossibility of finding expression equivalent to 'boredom' that could explain this affliction adequately. Frequent also are claims of the incurability of the state (e.g. Chateaubriand's *René*), which would make it the most radical and extreme kind of boredom among all presented in this chapter.

Microsociological perspective

Presented from the vantage point of microsociology, boredom is perceived, in the first place, as a social emotion that emerges when an interaction between social actors lacks qualities necessary to arouse engagement, flow, and/or effective communication. Social world is a place of constant interactions and acts of communication with others (Berger and Luckmann, 1991). Boredom is a strictly relational and relative concept, being a matter of interpretation and relationship established between people, or people and objects (Raposa, 1999; Mansikka, 2009). In this approach, there is no such concept as an intrinsically boring situation, because boredom is constructed in the process of interaction and results from one's malfunctioning interaction with the environment. Boredom occurs when there is no meaning in the interaction (Barbalet, 1999) or when meaning is totally unanimous (it leaves no room for ambiguity or conflicting points of view), which makes the situation entirely predictable (Darden and Marks, 1999).

Boredom is primarily the experience of one's disengagement from an interaction. This is the situation where 'an individual experiences being out of synch with the ongoing rhythms of social life,' 'being disengaged from the ebb and flow of human interaction' (Brisset and Snow, 1993, p. 239, 241), and 'not being involved in or engaged by events or activities' (Barbalet, 1999, p. 634). Boredom is 'a longing to engage in an unspecified satisfying activity' (Baratta, 2014, p. 13), a longing for 'making a connection with it' (Conrad, 1997,

p. 471). 'When we are bored, we cannot bring ourselves to care about something in particular (or anything at all), we do not feel that this thing that – or person who – we are confronted with is important enough to actually *connect* and *interact* with' (van Leeuwen, 2009, p. 178). Boredom 'frequently ends an interaction' (Darden and Marks, 1999, p. 27), and throws the individual 'in a kind of social limbo' (Kenny, 2009, p. 9).

Role distance

Another conceptualization that may be extracted from sociological theories is the one that interprets boredom as 'role distance' (Darden and Marks, 1999, p. 25). In everyday social interactions, each individual has a role to play and sets of such roles define who we are, form our identity. On the one hand, there are social roles of a general nature that tend to be hardly changeable (e.g. the roles of parents, children, etc.). And on the other hand, there are many casual roles played during particular everyday micro-interactions with other people. Some of such roles may be strictly defined with a traditional set of qualities (e.g. the role of a student), others are more flexible. Usually, people are expected to perform a role in every social situation, be it a careful observer, a good listener, an active interlocutor, etc. According to Goffman's (1956) self-presentation theory/dramaturgical approach, social life can be described as a constant presentation of self to other people. In this perspective, boredom would constitute a fracture in one's performance of his/her role (called by Goffman 'face'). When bored, one feels distant from one's role and finds no other role to replace it with, for either there is no particular role to play instead or none of the available roles 'measure[s] up to our standards' (Darden and Marks, 1999, p. 24), satisfies us. Boredom, therefore, would be a visible sign of one's discontent with the situation at hand, usually eventuating in 'leaving the scene, either physically or through fantasy' (Darden and Marks, 1999, p. 18). In Goffman's terms, boredom is the domain of 'backstage,' when the individual descends from the scene, is free from interactions and can display his/her emotions freely without damaging his/her reputation. Thus, boredom breaks the standard course of social rituals, i.e. everyday interactions that confirm the moral order of society. Symbolic interactionists claim that ordinary reality of everyday life is far from being automatic, but it is constantly under construction in the ever-ongoing process of mutual interactional work (Goffman, 1956; Blumer, 1986; Collins, 2004). However, it becomes difficult/impossible to conduct a ritual in an effective way, when boredom comes into force, because it destroys one's performance. Once boredom breaks in through the facade of tact, social graces and savoir-vivre, one's face is compromised and, in time, one ceases to even pretend to be interested in participating in the interaction. Boredom is 'a way of disqualifying oneself from participation in the situation' (Brisset and Snow, 1993, p. 242) and by showing it, the individual signals that he

> will make no effort to terminate the encounter or his official participation in it but that he will no longer give as much to it. The initiation of side-involvements, such as leafing through a magazine or lighting a cigarette, are instances. Other symptoms of boredom suggest that the individual is about to terminate official participation and function as a tactful warning of this.
>
> (Goffman, 1982, p. 127)

In Goffman's view, boredom would be, therefore, a form of disengagement from interaction, a situation where the individual is uninterested/uninvolved in what he is expected to be interested/involved in, and becomes busy with some 'external preoccupation.' In sum, formally, one still participates in the interaction but, mentally, one is (entirely) elsewhere. Goffman seems to associate boredom with 'ways of not quite concealing tactfully concealed misinvolvement' (1982, p. 127). To reformulate, bored people generally tend to mask their reluctance to adhere to the official definition of the situation, but they still signal their disapproval, albeit in a discreet manner (e.g. talking with the interlocutor and discreetly watching the clock).

Low emotional energy

Another conceptualization of boredom may be derived from Randall Collins's theory of interaction ritual chains. According to Collins (2004), each person constitutes an interaction ritual chain and is charged up with emotional energy (i.e. self-confidence, excitement, enthusiasm and initiative to take action), because of having successfully participated in chains of previous encounters. An interactional ritual takes place when (1) two or more people occupy one space, (2) there exist unambiguous boundaries between the participants and outsiders, (3) people focus their attention on a shared object or activity and, via communicating, are reciprocally conscious of their attention, and (4) people share their mood or emotional experience (Collins, 2004, p. 49). In Collins's view, rituals play a key role in shaping both individual character and group boundaries. To be more specific, outcomes of such rituals include social solidarity, emotional energy, shared symbols representing a group, and sense of morality, sense of pertinence in belonging to a group. The essence of social life consists in exchanging emotional energy through interactions. Once accumulated enough, such energy nourishes collective emotions (most notably – solidarity) and empowers a sense of group identity. Thereby, it becomes a foundation for social group formation.

In the light of the above, boredom can be explained as a lack of emotional energy, momentum (Adler, 1981), or flow (Csikszentmihalyi, 2000a).

As David Boyns and Scott Appelrouth (2011) suggested, Collins's idea of emotional energy resembles Mihalyi Csikszentmihalyi's concept of flow (optimal experience). Flow is an experience of 'loss of ego,' being totally involved in, giving one's entire attention to, having a sense of control over the activity that one is performing. In addition, when in the flow state, the doer perceives the very act of doing as intrinsically rewarding or even autotelic (having a sole purpose in itself). Emotional energy would be social counterpart of flow, which is strictly psychological/individual in nature.

Collins analyses emotional energy in the context of cultural capital, which has an affinity with Csikszentmihalyi's understanding of skills. In the theory of flow, a balance between challenge and skills is one of the characteristics of the state. In the case where one's skills are high and the challenge provided by the situation is low (to put simply, the activity is too easy for one), flow does not occur, but boredom does. According to Collins, a similar situation takes place when one's cultural capital is higher than the demands of the interaction in which one is participating. The person is likely to find such an interaction tedious, unchallenging, and alienating. Collins, therefore, translates Csikszentmihalyi's discrepancy between skills and challenge into discrepancy between cultural capital and possibilities to use it in order to gain emotional energy. The incongruity discourages the individual from fully participating in the interactional ritual, and his/her withdrawal blocks the energy that was meant to be exchanged/magnified through the interaction. In this connection, boredom would be a feature of unsuccessful interactional rituals, characterized by low level of emotional energy, the feeling that the ritual is dragging on, sense of coercion, fatigue with the interaction, even a kind of disgust at the ritual and desire to escape (Collins, 2004, p. 51).

***

As this chapter meant to present, boredom is far from being an unambiguous phenomenon and its conceptualizations have varied quite vastly among disciplines and researchers. Boredom is certainly a multidimensional – it may take various forms, depending on the situation at hand, individual characteristics (e.g. personality, cognitive capabilities), culture, or one's social position. First of all, there can be distinguished two general groups of boredom: simple boredoms (situational boredom) and complex ones (chronic, trait, existential boredom). The former would constitute rather a reaction to external factors, and the latter – an individual inner disposition (inborn or acquired).

In psychology, four conceptualizations of boredom, based on the criterion of indispensable qualities, appear to have been at the core of the discussion: (1) arousal theories (non-optimal level of cortical arousal), (2) cognitive theories (withdrawal of attention, or the perception of a situation as boring and of time as dragging on), (3) psychodynamic theories (an unconscious struggle between desire and possibilities to fulfil it), and (4) existential theories (a deep sense of meaninglessness). From the philosophical standpoint, boredom is conceptualized in its existential dimension, in terms of the human condition, as an overwhelming experience characterized by one's lack of agency, axiological crisis, sense of meaninglessness, worthlessness or even absurdity of existence. An utterly different approach has been developed in sociology. Here, boredom treated as a social construct is conceptualized as a relational phenomenon, a matter of interactional disengagement, and of communication obstruction.

Notes

1 Some authors maintain that such attention problems are prompted directly by the character of contemporary work and culture, which adversely affects human capacity to concentrate and vastly contributes to the growth in acquired attention deficit syndromes in the population (Schnabel, 2014; Ringmar, 2016).
2 This explanation of mechanisms standing behind the emergence of boredom is called the Menton theory of boredom. According to this conceptualization, each person has limited mental resources that can be allocated to particular actions. Boredom is the state which occurs when one's attention capacities are not fully employed, and it constitutes a valuable signal that some additional activity should be looked for. The authors of the research on doodling (Andrade, 2010) evidenced that it can improve the attention of students during boring lectures (such students recalled more facts from the lecture). Doodling is believed to provide necessary additional mental occupation that optimizes the usage of the individual's overall mental capacities and, therefore, improves the focus of attention. As an example of this theory may serve the fact that, as reported by James Gleick (1999), an average person speaks at the speed of about 150 words per minute, but an average listener is able to understand speech of the speed of 500–600 words per minute. The discrepancy between these two numbers constitutes the primary cause of boredom in lectures.
3 Cf. Klapp's (1986, p. 36) assertion that boredom 'occurs when we are forced to give attention to a situation providing too little of what we are interested in – or too much of what we are not interested in'.
4 'If fantasies or other derivatives of forbidden impulses would break through into consciousness, there would be no boredom but either frustration, anxiety, depression, or obsession, as we see in other neuroses' (Greenson, 1953, p. 20).
5 This explanation appears to be applicable to certain cases of boredom in the academic milieu, when students mask their failures by the feeling or just the label of boredom. Apparently, it is far less threatening for one's self-esteem and easier to say 'I'm bored' than 'I'm not smart/intelligent enough'. This mechanism might be an unconscious or conscious strategy to handle the experience of failure without bruising one's ego (Larson and Richards, 1991).

6 Schopenhauer's understanding of pain/suffering is quite broad, including – apart from physical pain (e.g. due to hunger, poverty, illness) – also emotional disturbances, like passionate love, envy, hate, fear, ambition, greed etc.
7 From Greek *kenosis* (κένωσις) meaning emptying, depletion, emptiness of life (Liddell and Scott, 1940).
8 This association is present in the literature of the whole nineteenth century (Kuhn, 1976, pp. 167–278), where 'loathing' became an integral component of 'ennui' (see e.g. Byron, Goethe, Flaubert, de Musset, Stendhal, Wilde).

Chapter 3

Conceptualization of boredom

The aim of this chapter is to provide a summative reflection on defining boredom, in the attempt to reduce boredom to its essence and, thereby, propose a 'gist' conceptualization that will serve as a point of reference in subsequent, empirical chapters. Thereby, it constitutes an attempt to offer a new approach towards the conceptualization of boredom, which thus far has received relatively scant attention from boredom researchers. The chapter is based on the analysis of both the relevant literature and my field data. In consequence, the definition of boredom that I propose at the end stems from these two sources of inspiration. It is construed to serve as the concluding point of previous analytical reflections and, at the same time, as the background for further analysis. The structure of this section will be as follows: (1) listing the elements of boredom's definitions, which have been accentuated in the interdisciplinary literature on boredom as particularly important and which I, on the contrary, deem insufficient, irrelevant, or just not essential for defining the phenomenon; and providing a justification of my stance; (2) presenting the definition components, which I reckon essential, and justifying my choice; (3) proposing an original definition of situational boredom; and (4) giving an analysis of the applicability of the proposed definition and providing original conceptualization/redefinition of the term 'chronic boredom.'

Non-essential elements in defining boredom

Idleness

As shown in Chapter 1, boredom is frequently associated with idleness. Yet, I argue that it is not at all equal with boredom. In my view, inactivity is only one of many circumstances under which boredom arises. Clearly enough, if it were an essential feature of boredom, work would be the most effective remedy for it. Admittedly, such a solution was suggested, for instance, in the Enlightenment era (Helvétius, 1810; Krasicki, 1994; Voltaire, 2006).

However, as indicated by the findings of countless research dealing with work and employment, many people experience boredom while performing their jobs. On the most fundamental level, two types of boredom can be distinguished: (1) non-occupation-related boredom, when one remains in a state of subjective inactivity and/or non-productiveness and (2) occupation-related boredom, when one performs an activity that bores him/her. In brief, work cures merely idleness but not boredom (Kierkegaard, 1843).

Rest

In the cases where one perceives one's idleness or low intensity activity as beneficial and purposeful (e.g. resting, meditating), boredom is not in the picture at all. The state of low arousal and satisfaction constitutes a state of relaxation and peacefulness (Mikulas and Vodanovich, 1993; Kroes, 2005). Boredom does take place when one is inactive and, at the same time, does not want to stay inactive any longer. In this context, it is connected with dissatisfaction and functions as a universal signal that something needs to be changed in the current situation (Elpidorou, 2017a). In other words, it 'is not the disease of being bored because there's nothing to do, but the more serious disease of feeling that there's nothing worth doing' (Pessoa, 2002, sec. 445). What proves crucial, therefore, in defining boredom is the subject's negative perception of the feeling (Macklem, 2015).

Laziness

Also frequently associated with boredom, laziness constitutes a state of generic slowness, inactivity, and disinclination towards activity. To many authors, it is a synonym of boredom (e.g. Gurycka, 1977; Fromm, 2002) or a cause of it (Krasicki, 1994; Kabzińska, 2015). However, since boredom leaves the individual craving stimulation, with a host of mental and behavioural consequences, which include – in some cases – hyperactivity/restlessness/fidgetiness (e.g. Phillips, 1993; Kenny, 2009; Burn, 2017), laziness cannot be a *sine qua non* of the phenomenon.[1] To my mind, it is rather one of possible outcomes of boredom (Rothlin and Werder, 2008) or of its anticipation – we usually get lazy when we are not willing to do something that we expect to be boring, unpleasant, difficult, and/or wearisome (see more in Finkielsztein, 2018).

Apathy

Some equal boredom with apathy (Bibring, 1953; Knabb, 2006; Ngai, 2005). Nevertheless, it is evidently well-distinguishable from it as apathy constitutes a total lack of emotions, lack of motivation, and 'a failure to seek alternatives' (Bench and Lench, 2013, p. 463), whereas boredom spurs one's motivation to change the current activity and to pursue an alternative set of actions. As Ralph Greenson noted, in patients suffering from apathy, in contrast to those afflicted with boredom, 'there is no more longing and a far greater inhibition of the ego's thinking and perceptive functions' (1953, p. 12). Apathy is, thus, a more radical state, whose scope overlaps that of boredom but lacks many other qualities of it. It may also be one of possible outcomes of boredom.

Repetition/monotony

Many researchers and theorists have claimed that one of the essential qualities of boredom is repetition and monotony (Davies, 1926; Hill, 1975; O'Hanlon, 1981; Drory, 1982; Brodsky, 1995). However, the findings of a large number of studies indicate that these features not necessarily induce boredom. The following three examples clarify the point: (1) students can get bored also in lectures, which are far from being monotonous (Finkielsztein, 2013), (2) some industrial workers express even a preference for routine tasks, arguing that those provide them with an opportunity to focus their thoughts elsewhere, typically on more pleasurable activities (Watt, 2002), and (3) artists who, like musicians or dancers, need to regularly or repeatedly practise some basic exercises do not get bored with the routine (except from some children musicians, Wagner, 2015). When, in the eyes of the person who has settled down into a routine, it is meaningful and purposeful, the routine does not cause boredom and may even provide him/her with a sense of security and belongingness (Klapp, 1986; Barbalet, 1999; Winter, 2002). Therefore, monotony is rather one of possible causes of boredom (Hill and Perkins, 1985; Harris, 2000; Daschmann, Goetz, and Stupnisky, 2011; Vogel-Walcutt et al., 2012) and is not at all essential to the feeling.

Lack of interest

Another common statement is that, firstly, boredom is characterized by lack of interest, and that, secondly, interest is, perforce, its ultimate antithesis (Spacks, 1995; Bruss, 2012; Chapman, 2013). Yet, boredom has a multidimensional character and significantly differs from a simple lack of interest. Lack of interest is affectively neutral, implying neither the wish to engage in the situation at hand nor to escape from it (Preckel, Götz, and Frenzel, 2010, p. 454), whereas boredom conveys a clearly negative affective message. One can be not interested in classical ballet yet not bored by it, because he/she is never to go to the ballet performance (Svendsen, 2016). Boredom constitutes rather 'a state of strong counterinterest' (Healy, 1984, p. 58). Lack of interest, therefore, is not essential to boredom, either.

Dragging time

While many theorists have eloquently argued for a close connection between boredom and the experience of time dragging (e.g. Heidegger, 1995; Zakay, 2014; Safranski, 2017), I, after Patricia Baratta (2014; cf. Mikulas and Vodanovich, 1993), treat it rather as a consequence of boredom, a significant concomitant thereof. This conclusion is strongly favoured by the very premises of the cognitive theories on time perception. According to the scalar expectancy theory (Gibbon, 1977), perception of time is a consequence of attentional processes. When a person is not engaged in an activity that he/she is doing, he/she allocates more attentional resources to the passage of time, which creates the impression that time is moving slowly. The experience of boredom is, therefore, fontal to the perception of the slowness of time passage – we get bored with something and our boredom makes us perceive time as if expanding, passing slowly.

Essential elements in defining boredom

Emotion/feeling

Many authors define boredom by using the amorphous word 'state' or the general term 'affect,' which includes all affective states (emotion, feeling, and mood; Zhu and Zhou, 2012), others simplify boredom to be a drive (for novelty, stimuli, etc.). All the same, the most frequently used genera are 'emotion' and 'feeling,' whose differences in meaning seem rarely to be analysed. Upon confronting boredom with psychological definitions of emotions, one comes to the conclusion that it perfectly fits into those conceptualizations and can be successfully defined as an emotion. Accordingly, boredom is a short-lived, subjective, psycho-physiological affective state that can be described as having five components (see Macklem, 2015): (1) affective (an unpleasant, negative feeling), (2) physiological (a non-optimal level of arousal), (3) cognitive (a low level of attention, the perception of time dragging on), (4) motivational (disinclination towards the activity/situation at hand), and (5) expressive (a slumped posture, drowsiness). Emotions are also described as 'hot,' which applies to boredom as it includes an experience of restlessness/agitation (Fenichel, 1951).

However, a definitional problem begins with the term 'feeling,' which is frequently used interchangeably with 'emotion' (Mulligan and Scherer, 2012, p. 353) and is used as an integral part of its definition (many definitions of emotion start with the phrase 'emotion is a feeling…'). Here, I follow the strain of the theoretical reflection, which interprets 'feeling' as a conscious experience of emotion, one of its symptoms (Frijda, 1986; Damasio, 1999; Prinz, 2005). In this conceptualization, emotions are merely 'unconscious perceptions of patterned changes in the body' (Prinz, 2005, p. 17), 'a physical response to change that is hard-wired and universal,' and feelings are 'mental associations and reactions to an emotion that are personal, acquired through experience' (Meyer, 2012). Thus, emotions are conceived as being generally unconscious and feelings – conscious. To reiterate, a feeling constitutes the conscious mode of an emotion, its extension towards the realm of awareness. In the present conceptualization, therefore, boredom is treated as either an emotion – if unconscious or a feeling – if conscious.

Negativity/aversion

As has been mentioned many times throughout this work, boredom is commonly perceived as a negative, aversive, and unpleasant state. This conclusion was drawn by Vogel-Walcutt et al. (2012) in their review of the literature, and by Baratta (2014), with half of the definitions under her analysis including the component of negativity/aversion. My textual analysis of definitions of boredom in the literature corroborates the findings of those studies thoroughly. Boredom is frequently associated with the feeling of dissatisfaction and is reported to be positively correlated with the occurrences of other negative affective states and emotions, like loneliness, anger, sadness, worry (Chin et al., 2017), and frustration (Hill and Perkins, 1985). This is not to say that boredom is negative per se, as it may have many positive outcomes and serve various functions, but rather that its perception is basically negative. I am of the opinion that boredom as such is neither positive nor negative, but it has positive or negative consequences. Thus, what is essential in defining boredom is the negative perception of it rather than the negativity of the phenomenon itself.

Listlessness/restlessness

I argue that boredom is a distinctive state characterized simultaneously by both listlessness and restlessness, which are oppositely directed and each of which is indispensable and essential to the experience. Listlessness alone would constitute the state of apathy, and restlessness – merely a kind of nervosity. On the one hand, there are innumerable testimonies connoting boredom with a sort of freezing, lack of energy, weariness, lethargy, stagnation, paralysis, anaesthesia, indifference, emotional flatness, or lack of care (Gabriel, 1988; Beckelman, 1995; Thiele, 1997; Bargdill, 2000a; Kenny, 2009; Wechter-Ashkin, 2010; Gardiner, 2014; Frederiksen, 2017). This view was corroborated also in my research among university students (Finkielsztein, 2013), who described boredom as, among others, 'freezing/spacing out,' 'hibernation,' 'sleep mode,' or 'quieting the mind.' On the other hand, boredom is connected with a high motivation for stimulation (Burn, 2017), a constant search for novelty (Mosurinjohn, 2016), agitation (Fenichel, 1951; Wechter-Ashkin, 2010). In this context, boredom implies 'a longing to engage in an unspecified satisfying activity' (Baratta, 2014, p. 21) and is defined as the state 'of diffuse restlessness which contains that most absurd and paradoxical wish, the wish for a desire' (Phillips, 1993, p. 68). Putting it in terms of arousal, there are some evidences that boredom is both a high and a low arousal state as it has been found positively correlated with both restlessness and sleepiness (Danckert et al., 2018).

This duplicity is reflected in the distinction between apathetic and agitated boredom (Fenichel, 1951), or between restless and listless boredom (Sundberg and Bisno, 1983), which specifies two major possible manifestations of boredom. One can become either lethargic or overactive. In other words, one can react to the core experience of boredom by further deactivation or by attempting to re-engage. From this perspective, listlessness and restlessness are basically outcomes of the feeling rather than ingredients of its essence. However, I argue that both are always present in boredom, with one of them prevailing over the other. Accordingly, to be bored is to experience listlessness and restlessness at the same time, from which the former is directed towards the situation at hand and the latter is focused on a prospective activity, thus, on escaping from the anesthetizing experience. As Wendell O'Brien puts it, when speaking of his boredom: 'I am weary with one thing and restless for another' (2014, p. 239).

In this context, I endorse a position close to Baratta's (2014), who described boredom as simultaneously lethargic/deactivated and restless, and Andreas Elpidorou's (2016), who defined boredom as a state of dissatisfaction, restlessness, and weariness. This coexistence of such opposite states is also corroborated by some empirical data derived from the field of existential psychology. A patient analysed by John Maltsberger (2000, p. 84) described his boredom in the way that clarifies my point: 'I feel discontented, restless, and anxious, yet at the same time lethargic, indifferent, unmotivated, unmoved, an automaton' (cf. Martin, Sadlo, and Stew, 2006, pp. 207–8).

Disengagement/attention withdrawal

In my conceptualization, I apply the basic principles of the relation/interactional perspective on boredom. In this framework, I indicate that essential for boredom is some form of lack of engagement (Goffman, 1982; Brisset and Snow, 1993; Darden and Marks, 1999; Eastwood et al., 2012), disconnection, and withdrawal of attention (Healy, 1984, p. 58; Klapp, 1986, p. 105), which is, to my mind, the psychological term describing substantially the same experience (disengagement is always the case of inattention). Boredom constitutes withdrawal from interaction with social and/or physical environment (e.g. when one is alone). It is a relational state characterized by lack of involvement in any kind of social and non-social activity, neglect of or withdrawal from active and genuine participation in the interaction with other people or objects. Boredom is a form of disconnection, zoning out, switching off, inattentiveness. As described by one of the interviewees:

> To me, boredom in class is when a professor is speaking and I – at some point or at the very beginning – start thinking about something completely different, and despite the fact that I do try again, I catch myself thinking about something completely different. I try to start listening to the professor yet again, but it takes me just a few minutes to switch off again and to start thinking about something else. And this makes me realise that the lecture is boring me or the seminars bore me.
> (Student, FGI_2, sociology, female, graduate)

Meaninglessness

If there is one unique feature of boredom which could be broadly perceived as central to the experience, it certainly is a sense of meaninglessness. Many boredom researchers appear to have developed convergent views, at least in part, with this regard (Martin, Sadlo, and Stew, 2006; van Tilburg and Igou, 2012; Elpidorou, 2017a; Chan et al., 2018). Meaning deficit (Svendsen, 2005), the perception of the activity as meaningless (van Tilburg and Igou, 2012) proves quintessential for boredom. Firstly, out of a number of important elements of the experience, it is the one that knits all of them together and, secondly, is not shared with any affective state (depression is a mood). There are other aversive and unpleasant affective states (e.g. anxiety, disgust, worry, irritation), some that can be associated with disengagement, listlessness (e.g. sadness), or restlessness (e.g. impatience, frustration). Some researchers, especially psychologists, indicate that the lack of meaning is a cause of boredom (Hill and Perkins, 1985; de Chenne, 1998; MacDonald and Holland, 2002; Fahlman et al., 2009), with which I generally agree. However, to be more specific, I claim that an atrophy of meaning is a distinctive and essential feature/cause of boredom. What I mean by this is the subject's personally perceived lack of meaning in a concrete situation – not meaningfulness in general, in some kind of activities. There is no possibility for one to be bored and simultaneously to perceive the situation as personally meaningful. If one feels bored, it means that one does not assess the particular situation as personally valuable, and would prefer to do something else instead. If one truly finds meaning in one's occupation, one never gets bored by it. If one feels bored, it means that, at this very moment and in the specific circumstances, one does not evaluate the task/activity/situation as meaningful. The task as such may remain 'objectively' meaningful to somebody who performs it, but carrying it out can be, at times, boring – under certain conditions, in particular situations. To illustrate the point, a teacher who likes his/her job and finds it generally meaningful and rewarding, may, in some situations, feel bored with his/her teaching performance, when its actual meaning becomes questionable to him/her due to adverse conditions (e.g. he/she feels exhausted, the students are not engaged in the learning process).

Frustration

Associated with disappointment, frustration is defined as 'irritable distress after a wish collided with an unyielding reality' (Jeronimus and Laceulle, 2017), or 'failure of expectations' (Conrad, 1997). It can be either a cause or a consequence of boredom (Baker et al., 2010; Wechter-Ashkin, 2010; Vogel-Walcutt et al., 2012), but boredom can be as well 'only another name for a certain species of frustration' (Sontag, 1967, p. 303). I claim that boredom is a kind of meaning frustration, i.e. an emotional reaction to the unfulfilled need for meaning or to the unsuccessful construction of meaning. If we assume, after Viktor Frankl (2000), that humans constantly 'search for meaning,' which I find correct, as people never willingly perform activities they perceive personally meaningless (i.e. without some rationalization, imagined functionality), boredom constitutes the situation where this pursuit fails and the individual is left with the frustrated need for meaning. Therefore, contrary to what existing theories of emotions have indicated, I argue that if boredom were to be primarily associated with a single emotion, it would be frustration – and not disgust (Plutchik, 1991) or disappointment-sadness (Turner, 2000).

Liminality/transitionality

The last essential feature of boredom is its liminal/transitional character. It is described as a kind of captivity, entrapment (Martin, Sadlo, and Stew, 2006; Wechter-Ashkin, 2010; O'Neill, 2014), stuckness in-between, in some transitional state of suspended present, un-realization. The situation in which the past is 'no more' and the future is 'not yet' (Frederiksen, 2013, p. 6). Boredom is a state of suspension between engagements – one involvement has ceased but another is not yet to begin. I conceive boredom as 'a conveyor belt' to other emotions or activities. If the individual quickly manages to transit into a new activity/mental engagement/emotion, the transitional state can take just a moment, and, thus, go undetected – as it actually often does. This interpretation seems to be reinforced by the fact that situational boredom is frequently unaware. All the same, when the conveyor belt goes on and on, with no conceivable destination, the sense of being stuck in the transition can become a mood or a steady disposition (chronic/existential boredom). In this sense, boredom is characteristic of any on-going transitions that inhibits the process of becoming. It may emerge in situations of major activity changes in life – when the old pattern has expired and a new one has not got established yet. It is, therefore, a matter of a sudden drop in the individual's activity level characterized by the feeling of indeterminacy. A few typical situations to illustrate the point are: losing one's job, graduating from school/university, transition between army and college (Fisher, 1987), or parents' experience of an 'empty nest' after the children 'suddenly' left home (Rogge, 2011).

The plight of being 'stuck in-between' is the leitmotiv of Saul Bellow's (2007) *Dangling Man*. Joseph, the protagonist of the novel, experiences a long-term boredom, caused by the fact that he has been drafted, but not yet taken into the army. On the one hand, his civilian life has ended up, and on the other hand, the conscription has not been realized yet. For this reason, Joseph is trapped in the quintessentially boring situation. One commitment has expired, whereas the other has not yet appeared – what remains is only anticipation, filled with tension, uncertainty, and boredom.

The long-term liminality under discussion, a kind of suspension, is described by Alfred de Musset in his autobiographical novel *The Confession of a Child of the Century*. Written in the Romantic era, it depicts the painful experience of striving desperately to burst through old and cramping patterns, and yearning for unachievable goals. The pain pervaded the whole generation of romantics, who spent their adolescence in the frivolous, adventurous times of the Napoleonic era and reached adulthood after the Congress at Vienna, in the times of stagnation: 'That which was is no more; what will be, is not yet. Do not seek elsewhere the cause of our malady' (de Musset, 2006). That 'malady' was, vastly influenced by boredom, 'the Great Ennui' (Steiner, 1971).

Yet another illustration of the indeterminacy of protracted transition is the case of young Native Americans in the Grass Creek Reservation (Jervis, Spicer, and Hanson, 2003). At present, their native tradition (the cultural inheritance) is losing its significance and is endangered of extinction. At the same time, new culture patterns (the mainstream culture) are, as for now, out of reach. In consequence, there opens up a void which breathes boredom and unease. That the high likelihood of the void becoming, after a prolonged period of time, their deeply internalized everydayness is evidenced, among others, also by the homeless in post-communist Romania, who live 'at the margins in limbo, between a nostalgia for a brutal past and a resignation toward a hopeless future' (O'Neill, 2014, p. 24).

Boredom, in this sense, may be metaphorically compared to the situation of a rite of passage, which has got stuck in the middle – one is already deprived from the attributes of one's former position but not yet included into the realm of one's new status – a bored individual is marginalized and his/her status is ambivalent (Gennep, 1960). To sum up, a bored person is imprisoned in a kind of limbo, stuck between activities, statuses, experiences, engagements and, in this sense, I define boredom as a liminal/transitional emotion that constitutes the moment of suspension, 'betweenness.'

Definition and its applicability

Taking into consideration all of the above described essential components of boredom, I define situational boredom as follows:

> Boredom is a transient, negatively perceived, transitional emotion or feeling of listless and restless inattention to and engagement withdrawal from interacting with one's social and/or physical environment caused distinctively by an atrophy of personally-valued meaning, the frustrated need for meaning.

Therefore, I construe boredom essentially as a state of inattention/disengagement prompted by a sense of meaninglessness, being a suspension between two activities/engagements in which one is simultaneously listless in the current situation and restless to find a relief from it. Furthermore, I interpret boredom also in terms of interaction withdrawal and claim that it is relational in character, as it always emerges in the context of some interplay between one's personal attitude, perception, characteristics, etc. and something external (activity, object, one's social position, institutional ambience, one's life from which one is alienated, etc.). One's relationship or connection with other people, one's environment, the performed task, or – ultimately – with oneself, erodes. Thus, I argue that every manifestation of boredom somehow breaks or ends an interaction, and each case of boredom implies its negligence.

Frequently, such emotion is just momentary, being quickly replaced by other emotions – the relation with social/physical environment is re-established and one is free from the sensation. This is why I have called it 'a conveyor belt.' A simple yet representative example of such a process is students' boredom during university classes. 'Pure' boredom (inattention and lack of engagement manifested by idleness, sleepiness, glazed look, supporting one's head with one's elbow) appears there quite rarely, because students' disengagement from the interaction with the teacher and with the content of the course quickly becomes replaced by their engagement in alternative activities (Finkielsztein, 2013, 2020). In the case where a student perceives particular classes as personally meaningless, he/she disengages from them by directing his/her attention to something else. In this sense, the student does not feel bored. All the same, his/her boredom in class is dormant, latent – ready to erupt as soon as the sideline engagement expires. There again, in my conceptualization, it would not be treated as boredom. To be more specific, I argue that one's cognitive appraisal that something is boring is not equivalent with one's feeling bored, but it constitutes only one of the predictive factors of boredom. In brief, one is bored with a boring activity only when he/she is actively 'exposed' to it. In this connection, a student may attend a boring lecture and yet feel even excited in class – because of him/her being absorbed in some non-class related, exciting preoccupation during that time (see more in Finkielsztein, 2020).

I am convinced that the above definition can have potentially universal applicability. Firstly, if one is inattentive to the situation at hand and disengaged from it, we call this 'situational boredom.' Secondly, if the state is recurrent, it can become transformed into a mood of the same qualities and, accordingly, be called 'chronic boredom.' Thirdly, if it embraced one's life in general (one is disconnected/alienated from one's life, which he/she regards as meaningless), it would be called 'existential boredom.' Therefore, depending on the scope of boredom occurrence in one's life – from the most limited to the broadest – different kinds of boredom may be distinguished. From this perspective, situational and existential boredoms may be considered as definable by generally analogous features (such as the sense of meaninglessness, engagement withdrawal and listlessness/restlessness), but there is a crucial difference, which makes the two types of boredom clearly distinguishable. To be specific, existential boredom is not a short-lived emotion/feeling but a mood, which lasts usually for a longer period of time, is low in intensity and is object-less/undirected (Thoits, 1989). It is rather a background sensation, or – as Heidegger (1995) stated – rather a standpoint colouring our perception of the reality. Somebody who suffers from existential boredom (1) assesses his/her life, or life in general, as worthless, (2) lives without much genuine involvement in it, and (3) is generally somehow lethargic. Nevertheless, he/she yearns for meaning – as it remains his/her point of reference and something that he/she wants to gain in life, even if not believing much in the success of the pursuit.

Chronic boredom

Most researchers and theorists have been preoccupied with situational boredom (limited to a particular situation), trait boredom (personality characteristic, psychological proneness to experiencing boredom), or existential boredom (embracing every sphere of one's life). The relevant literature virtually lacks an intermediary concept, as the notion of chronic boredom usually resembles trait or existential boredom. Yet, my empirical data have shown that it is indispensable that an intermediate kind of boredom (between situational and existential) should be conceptualized. This kind of boredom affects only one sphere of the individual's life, leaving the rest of it untouched. One can be extremely bored, for instance, with one's job or studies, and still not be existentially bored, as one finds his/her leisure time or family life enjoyable and rewarding. Such boredom, which I would still call 'chronic,' is a consequence of the accumulation of situational boredoms due to its frequent repetition in similar circumstances associated with a particular sphere of one's activity. In support of such a new construal of boredom is the case of some senior university students' attitude towards their studies. As can be seen from my interviews with them, they feel disheartened, fatigued, and extremely bored with their studies in general. Students affected by this kind of boredom are definitely not entirely/existentially 'paralysed' by it, for they do get satisfaction from activities, which are not related with their studies (e.g. their hobbies and/or jobs). Nevertheless, they deem university classes/activities – lock, stock, and barrel – as meaningless and unequivocally boring by default. Importantly enough, their opinion is impregnable – no matter whether the given classes/activities are, in fact, boring or not. To reiterate, the vast majority of activities that are connected to the university education seem to automatically receive the label 'boring,' merely by association with that particular sphere of life. This is not classes that are boring, but the education process itself and everything that goes with it. The case under discussion is paradigmatic of the state of suspension, stuckness in-between. The students' engagement in their studies has already ceased and the formal end of the university education process is not yet to come, the unavoidable outcome being that the sense of meaninglessness reigns supreme. In this connection, some of the students who participated in my study on boredom (Finkielsztein, 2013) said that they 'served classes,' waiting impatiently to gain the diploma – implying 'serving their sentence,' seeking to regain their freedom. The connotations of the phrasing (i.e. imprisonment, punishment) illustrate the students' perception of the situation (see 'educational burnout,' Finkielsztein, 2020).

This permanent state of dissatisfaction, disengagement, and fatigue, if not considered in its university context, could indeed resemble a state of existential boredom. However, it is not the case here, given that, just after leaving the classroom, the majority of the students evidently revive – the lack of meaning and their sense of fatigue do not apply, therefore, to their entire life but only to the specific sphere of it. This kind of boredom I shall call 'chronic boredom.' Along with situational boredom, it shall constitute the object of the subsequent empirical chapters.

Note

1 Admittedly, some authors (Petry-Mroczkowska, 2004) associate hyperactivity with laziness – as its outcome (i.e. one can get hyperactive because of one's laziness). Yet, I argue that it is not inherent to laziness in the same way as it is to boredom.

Part 2

Work-related boredom of academics

Chapter 4

Academic boredom as a systemic issue

As many researchers have noted, workplace boredom remains a kind of taboo (e.g. Mann, 2016) yet being still common in the post-industrial era. Work-related boredom is defined as 'a negative, deactivating emotional state experienced while performing work-related activities' (van Hooff and van Hooft, 2014, p. 349) and is characterized by passiveness, a lack of interest in tasks, an inability to concentrate (Harju, Hakanen, and Schaufeli, 2014), 'vigilance decrement' (decrease in readiness to detect and respond to certain small changes in the environment; Cummings, Gao, and Thornburg, 2015), a lack of perceived meaning in work tasks (Rothlin and Werder, 2008), the perception of work as insignificant, or not worth the effort (Campagne, 2012), demotivation (van Hooff and van Hooft, 2014 found negative correlation (–.45) between motivation and boredom), and disengagement (Parkinson and McBain, 2013). William Kahn (1990) claimed that work-related boredom is a kind of defence mechanism against the meaninglessness of work assignments and a means of distancing/withdrawing from the work role. The opposite of such a feeling is job involvement/engagement which is characterized by vigour (high levels of energy and resilience), dedication (strong involvement in, enthusiasm for and sense of significance of one's job), and absorption (a state of total immersion in one's work; Maslach, Schaufeli, and Leiter, 2001, p. 417; cf. the state of flow, Csikszentmihalyi, 1997). Two kinds of work-related boredom can be distinguished: one associated with the situation or experience being sometimes boring (episodic/situational boredom) and one characterized by the regular and recurrent occurrence of the feeling (chronic boredom, Mael and Jex, 2015). Both of them, in accordance with the conceptualization presented in Chapter 3, will be the object of interest in this part of the book.

Academic work as a job, and academic institutions as a workplace are usually perceived as settings where outstanding professionals constantly perform creative activities, discovering new scientific facts and inventing new theories (see the role of the 'explorer of the truth;' Znaniecki, 1940). Consequently, such working places tend to be conceived as incompatible with the experience of boredom. The outcomes of my research, however, stand in contradiction to this common perception and clearly show that even in this prestigious, and in a way, distinctive vocation, some activities bear a clear potential to prompt the feeling of boredom, at least in some academics – some enclaves of boredom exist. Ultimately, all academics are human beings, and thus, are prone to occasionally feeling bored with every possible aspect of their work.

This chapter aims to provide a detailed description and an analysis of the boredom present in the work of academics in general, and Polish research-teaching university employees specifically. Although the analysis involves Polish academia, its applicability may be broader, as many characteristics of university life are common to various national institutional systems. In this part of the book, I will focus on systemic factors that may contribute to the feeling of boredom. As such, I will consider all those factors that may have an effect on disengagement/inattention and role distance (Kahn, 1990; Darden and Marks, 1999) irrespective of whether they are usually labelled boredom-inducing or not. As Fisher (1993) suggested, boredom may be provoked by organizational constraints, rules, and specific procedures that institutions impose which limit activities and behaviours within the work setting. Boredom will thus be treated as a social construct, an emotion/feeling emerging as a consequence of the interaction between an individual and their social and institutional (organizational) environment. This feeling will thus be analysed as a possible outcome of functioning in a social, vocational, institutional reality.

Although boredom, unsurprisingly, is not perceived as the main problem of academic life (unsatisfactory levels of funding, lack of university autonomy or academic frustration seem to be far more frequently raised), it still constitutes a useful analytic tool in raising and/or highlighting the unambiguously far more 'serious' issues concerning academic work in general, and the well-being of academics in such a system specifically. I do not employ the category of boredom as an accusation of any kind, and this is what, I hope, the previous chapters have shown through translating boredom from colloquial to scientific understanding. Of course, all that is to be described in this (and the next) chapter, applies to only a limited number of academics, however, the major issues derived from this analysis have a much broader scope of applicability.

As mentioned in Chapter 1, some respondents denied feeling boredom altogether, others admitted to occasional ailments, and a few experienced it more regularly. The general tendency seems to be a casual occurrence of the sensation at least in one or two areas of academic activity. For some, the issue and the word itself came as a prompt response to my general questions about academic work, for others it was the interview that made them realize the boredom of various academic activities that they undertook. At times, after an initial denial of ever being bored, some participants finally admitted (upon being asked one of the more detailed questions) that they had indeed experienced boredom, for example at scientific conferences or in faculty meetings. Nonetheless, for most respondents, boredom did not constitute a major problem in their academic life thanks to advanced and perfectly applied coping techniques. Some respondents also drew the distinction between things being boring and one feeling bored. Many things are perceived as boring, but one does not necessarily feel bored by them. For the purpose of this chapter, however, I treat all boring things as potentially boredom-inducing – thereby all following issues are only described as risk factors, possible contributors to academic boredom, especially boredom that is chronic, which in one person may be realized and in another may not. In this way, boredom in academic work is always merely a possibility, a matter of interpretation shaped by individual characteristics (personality), an individual's personal and/or vocational trajectory (socialization), social relations in the workplace, working conditions, power and career dynamics (the place in the institutional structure and the amount of individual agency), or skills in finding balance between personal needs and institutional demands.

(Post)modern academia and (post)modern boredom

Secularization – academic work as a job

Boredom is frequently presented to be one of the characteristics of modernity (Spacks, 1995; Goodstein, 2005; Dalle Pezze and Salzani, 2009a). Consequently, it can be perceived as a characteristic of modern academic work as well. All processes that have been shaping the modern reality, sooner or later and to a various degree, have affected the academic world (Shapin, 2008). Despite science being still mythologized by many scientists and philosophers of science, in its everyday practice it does not solely embrace the Platonic contemplation and pursuit of pure knowledge, the glorious ambition of discovering rules governing the world in its myriad aspects and it rarely resembles Raphael's *School of Athens* (Siegel, 2017). Modern scientists, as a conglomerate of various vocational groups, have become less the melancholic men of genius, the 'children of the Saturnus' (Klibansky, Panofsky, and Saxl, 1964), elevated magicians (Perlow, 1995) or isolated noble 'explorers of the truth' (Znaniecki, 1940) than their ancestors saw themselves and/or wanted to be seen in previous eras. Instead, modern scientists nowadays often play the role of artisans, technicians, and/or bureaucrats. The science in all of its aspects is now secularized, which deprives it of its semi-sacred status (see 'sacral schools' in Znaniecki, 1940). Aspirations for the absolute truth are no longer conceived as legitimate and possible in times of relativity and uncertainty. It makes science a decreasingly sacred mission, less of a calling where the scientist was primarily 'the original discoverer,' and more frequently viewed as 'a job, not significantly different from other high-level occupations, a way of earning a living which offers money, prestige, and satisfactory working conditions' (Reif and Strauss, 1965, p. 305). This shift in self-perception and general attitude to science, is an essential prerequisite for experiencing boredom. Due to its secularization and professionalization, scientific work is no longer perceived as a calling but rather as career with pros and cons, working conditions, and prospects (Hermanowicz, 1998; Shapin, 2008). Some people enter their field with passion and an idealistic approach but over time lose their self-perception as an original discoverer and begin adjusting to the actual conditions of their working environment. Others enter academic work lacking any philosophy of passion, treating it less as a 'labour of love' (Freidson, 1990), and more simply as a partly creative and partly clerical knowledge job. This attitude was noted by respondents complaining of the decline of the academic ethos and calling, especially in the domain of teaching duties.

> Now it's probably more of an approach to come [and] whip through classes, to give just a short test at the end and that's it. There are fewer and fewer lecturers who really want to have this contact with students, to teach them something.
> (Teacher, interview_5, female, hab., social sciences)

As one respondent noted, a few decades ago there was a limited number of scientists, and academic work was conceived more as a privilege and an honour, a calling and mission of sorts. Today, however, university 'is treated by many as a work place, you come at 8 a.m. or whenever your classes start and you leave at 4 p.m. or whenever your classes finish, full stop, goodbye' (Teacher, interview_33, male, hab., natural sciences).

Rationalization

Another facet of modern academia is the standardization and specialization caused essentially by technological progress and a general increase in knowledge. In many disciplines this makes scientific methodology more and more technically-based, routine, and laborious. Standardization imposes many routine and repetitive tasks, and specialization encompasses dealing only with a small piece of the scientific enterprise, which can result in repeatedly pursuing similar procedures in a specific, very narrow field of expertise. These very processes, however, are simultaneously responsible for the great efficacy of modern science in comparison to pre-modern science, in terms of the significance of its outcomes for general society. The growth of scientific boredom is an inevitable consequence, and one of the side effects of its success. As Kevin Donnelly (2013) points out, boring science, characterized by 'the strict division of labour' (specialization), and 'impersonal and meaningless routine' (standardization) turned out to be 'the most direct path to success' (p. 489), both in terms of scientific recognition and making a valuable contribution to the development of scientific knowledge. Bruno Latour and Steve Woolgar's (1986, p. 31) study is one example of this tendency – work in the laboratory they researched was found to include a great deal of 'routinely dull work,' and yet still its members were awarded the Nobel Prize in Medicine. This shows, then, that tasks which may be perceived/interpreted as boring (as they frequently substitute meaning with mere function; Zijderveld, 1979), may often become significant contributors to scientific achievements.

Another boredom-inducing organizational factor is the general tendency towards the imposed rationalization of academic work described by the principles of McDonaldization (efficiency, calculability, predictability, and control; Ritzer, 1983), which constitutes an amplification and extension of Weber's theory of rationalisation (Ritzer, 2011). This theory can be applied to academic work at a few levels (Parker and Jary, 1995; Hayes, Wynyard, and Mandal, 2002). The most apparent one – teaching – has been restructured to the market-defined goal of an efficient 'production line' of graduates, educated with packages of predictable, uniform content within the 'calculable' formula of 'knowledge transfer' (Garland, 2008). A parallel process haunts scientific work, which is now expected to take the form of 'science production,' and to be: (a) efficient in terms of 'publishability,' both in quantity (number of publications) and quality (measured by the impact factors of journals, etc.), (b) predictable in terms of content standardization, for instance, in the form of uniformly-structured journal papers, and (c) calculable in order to enable easy reporting and control. Currently, scientists are less engaged in time-consuming, risky projects, as they have no time to determine whether their courageous hypotheses can be supported or not. They need to perform predictable work in order to publish in highly ranked, prestigious journals and to satisfy grant givers. This predictable and secure research may be a source of boredom, for it frequently implies the lack of challenge, novelty, and risk which previously made scientific work so attractive. The principle of control results in the intensification of bureaucratization and creates work conditions that may induce boredom, turning academics into bureaucrats and labourers (Kubiak, 2019).

Diminishing enthusiasm, passion, and job involvement (or at least such a discourse) may thus be prompted by organizational constraints enforced by new public management philosophy and practice, all imposed by the neoliberal reforms of higher education (in many Western countries gradually introduced from the 1960s, in Poland brought in 2011). New Public Management has opened universities to consumer society, along with the introduction of capitalistic values, and the principle of commodification, among others (Schuster and Finkelstein, 2008; Slaughter and Rhoades, 2004; Couldry, 2011; Rhodes, 2017). Universities 'are being turned into corporate research departments. No longer may they pursue knowledge for its own sake: the highest ambition to which they must aspire is finding better ways to make money' (Monbiot, 2009, cited in Shore, 2010, p. 22). By all means, there are still some exceptions, institutions, and subdisciplines that, to an extent, avoided inclusion into the current system of 'entrepreneurial/ corporate university' (Clark, 2002; Etzkowitz, 2008; Shapin, 2008), but as voices in environmental debate in Poland (e.g. Dąbrowski, 2012; Pieniądz, 2017; Kubiak, 2019) and the relevant literature alike suggest (Wagner, 2012; Wagner, 2014a; Kowzan et al., 2015; Kwiek, 2015; Nagucka and Zawadzki, 2015; Kwiek, 2016), the vast majority of Polish universities operate in a system resembling many universities in Western countries, as they were forced to implement some version of neoliberal management principles (e.g. Shore and Wright, 2000; Sievers, 2008; Shore, 2010; Lorenz, 2012; Halffman and Radder, 2015).

This is reflected in the responses of many study participants, who noted that university is more and more frequently treated as an institution that serves to 'pass grants along' and produces graduates on a massive scale (the state subsidy for universities in Poland had for many years depended on the number of students) who are meant to receive customized, market-oriented quasi-vocational education. The brave new world of the academic market thus creates stressful, desensitized, and potentially demotivating/disengaging work conditions that tend to turn an academic's work into that of a subordinate clerk rather than the work of a free-spirited discoverer of the truth. Academics twist and turn around managerially imposed constraints simply to maintain the sense of doing 'real' science/teaching, or their academic identity. Others succumb to the system's demands, and are its active supporters (Barry, Berg, and Chandler, 2006). In fact, it can be said that many important achievements are made in spite of this system rather than because of it, with academic work now led more and more by bureaucratic procedures and an administrative/managerial way of thinking instead of what has traditionally been identified as academic one.[1] Below utterance may illustrate this point:

> Describing learning outcomes, which is a complete waste of time and basically such a circular threshing of this information, I am generally critical of the logic of the outcomes. I think that the old system, which focused on content, was much better and gave more academic freedom ... The university should be a school of thought, and we cannot even use the word "to think" in these outcomes, because it is not a term that undergoes operationalisation, we have to use rational, mostly behavioural descriptions ... It requires us to define a person that we want to release from the teaching [assembly] line, instead of showing what content we want to convey to this person ... Learning outcomes are such factory logic, in my opinion ... Certain values, ideas related specifically

to university education, at least in the rhetoric, they are supplanted by the administrative ideal, that is the ideal of quality management ... I see here at best a monstrous nuisance, which does not make sense, and at worst simply the end of freedom, or a strong restriction of academic freedom, the freedom of education, freedom of research and teaching.
(Teacher, interview_68, female, hab., social sciences)

The ideal to which the above respondent referred was probably never fully realized, constituting rather a kind of ideal type, however, it clearly represents the discursive opposition to the newly introduced system with its set of regulations over academic activities, and is an important anchor for identity and normative sign-post for many academics, in which 'academic' seems to denote all positive, noble, and commendable qualities of academic work, and its ethos, which is currently perceived as being under intensive siege by neoliberal managerial reforms, reinforced by technological advances (predominantly digitalization).

As the above respondent noted, this new administrative approach dangerously resembles Fordist assembly-line production. This may result in similar outcomes as observed in factory workers, inter alia, alienation, and boredom. As Oskar Szwabowski (2014) claimed, academic workers can be alienated in almost all dimensions specified by Marx. They are alienated from their work, for instance, they are forced to teach what students should know according to market-oriented managers, and should customize their interest, research subjects, and writing style to the externally-led demands of the system. An example of such a process is choosing a research subject not according to one's scientific interests but to the fashions and directives dictated by grant institutions. As one of the respondents noted:

I observe the lack of general discussion, which would go beyond the framework defined by the financing institutions [what do you mean?], I mean that if, for example, some assembly, let us assume, having resources for science will show the goal, we focus our interests on this goal, no matter whether we were interested in this earlier.
(Teacher, interview_24, male, hab., social sciences)

Replacing steady research funding (hard money) with a competitive grant system (soft money, Couldry, 2011) frequently leads to transforming meaning into functionality, which is described as one of the main mechanisms of modern rationalization processes (Zijderveld, 1979), making many academic activities more money-oriented.

Academic capitalism in Poland seems to be led by the principle of social Darwinism – thus, it is quintessentially modern with its emphasis on speed, quantity, and a ferocious race for limited resources (academic positions, research grants, scholarships, etc.). Performance management, i.e. control practices concentrated on output (Zawadzki, 2017), in the situation of excessive/inadequate production of PhDs in relation to scarce/limited employment opportunities, creates ratopolis-like circumstances for academic work (Therrien, 1973, cited in Wagner, 2018). Rats (academics), operating in a cage (system) that is overpopulated, demonstrate a plethora of pathological behaviours that are not characteristic of rats in the natural environment (e.g. they are highly (auto-)aggressive). Academia seems to resemble such a ratopolis, treated as a metaphor, which may contribute to many negative consequences, such as cynicism, lack of cooperation, lack of the real exchange of ideas, lack of belongingness, lower academic ethos, sense of social anomie, etc. Academics are alienated from their colleagues, frequently being perceived as rivals rather than collaborators and from the products of their work (the results being taken over by the sponsoring companies, limited access to academics' own publications and limitations to the right to disseminate the results of their research, see Szwabowski, 2014). This vision of Polish academia was shared by many of my respondents – they frequently spoke of their doubts and concerns about the challenging work conditions created by the recent regulations introducing neoliberal reforms. Boredom, especially chronic boredom and burn out reaction, seem to be a spectre haunting that vision.

All this fits nicely into the concept of an achievement society (Han, 2015). Several respondents observed that many conversations among academics are focused on the mutual reassurance of how busy and active they are.

> I have the impression that when we talk we are persistently convincing each other of how advanced we are in our work, here someone has got a grant, someone else is writing this grant, someone else just released an article and it is such a mutual drive to be active.
> (Teacher, interview_54, female, MA, natural sciences)

Junior staff[2] in particular is subjected to these requirements produced by achievement paradigm of performance-based science. Many authors and respondents claimed that this intensification forced by the 'publish or perish' system may be detrimental to both the quality of scientific research and publication, and to the well-being of academics. As Jeff Ferrell (2004) observed for sociology, '"mainstream article sociology"—the efficient, routinized production of article-length research reports—has over time displaced the deeper intellectual and temporal commitments of "book sociology" as the measure of professional success and achievement' (p. 295). Long-term, intense, ambitious projects with a high risk of failure in the realm of indicators fetishism, a regime which 'does not really care about high-quality results, which it cannot judge, but rather about performance: the tactically well thought-out and cleverly buffed-up illusion of excellence' (Halffman and Radder, 2015, p. 167), are superseded by relatively fast, concrete, and/

or preferably market-oriented projects. As Csikszentmihalyi (2000a) stated, 'under the pressure to "publish or perish" it is not unusual for scholars to forget their dreams and instead put their minds on projects that are fundable. In this way, many independent scholars turn into academic mercenaries with bustling labs but a rather cynical view of the intellectual enterprise' (p. xvii) – many academics turn to treat science instrumentally as a means to rather earthly ends, meaning more money in the form of tenure positions, more grants, and so on.

In the Polish context, commentators have even coined the special term for such an instrumental attitude – **'punktoza**,' which is still very popular in environmental discourse (probably first used by Agnieszka Graff, Polish scholar and activist, just after the introduction of the new regulations in 2011, see also Wagner, 2012). 'Punktoza' is defined as a pathological syndrome associated with science evaluation system that is characterized by excessive publication activity led by the principle of quantity over quality. In the Polish evaluation system, the value of scientific production (publications) is measured in points as specified by the Ministry of Science and Higher Education: each scientific journal, both national and international, has a specific point value which each researcher (and their employing institution) is awarded for publication in a given journal (Rozporządzenie Ministra Nauki i Szkolnictwa Wyższego z dn. 12 grudnia 2016 r., 32, 1–2). The same system has been introduced in 2019 for book publications as well (publishers have been divided into two groups according to their recognition, and a different point value has been specified for each group; Komunikat Ministra Nauki i Szkolnictwa Wyższego z dn. 18 stycznia 2019 r.). In such a system, some academics adopt a strategy aimed at maximizing the point value of their scientific output, frequently with a minimal involvement of time and energy possible. In a situation of duty overload which prevents many from doing new and ambitious research, some academics produce publications with the sole goal of meeting the demands of periodical evaluation (Kulczycki, 2017). Under conditions of duty overload and deadlines specified by the evaluation system, 'reheated chops are made, the same thing for the third time, once in Polish, once in English, once in English, but differently' (Teacher, interview_71, female, PhD, natural sciences).

Such a system may negatively affect the sense of job meaningfulness, making some parts of the job perfunctory, superficial, and deceptive.

> In such more creative professions, it kills that, when you can see that what you're doing does not make sense, you have the impression that you simply publish something to publish and to exist at this university, and what you're doing there does not make sense, so then, when the subject you are dealing with bores you, because you do not see the point in it, you simply do it because you have to work somewhere, you have to release a paper from time to time, then it's obvious that you do it with a

> minimal amount of work and ... I would say that this boredom originates as a side effect of other problems that are troubling the academic milieu.
> (Teacher, interview_44, male, PhD, natural sciences)

This demonstrates how the institutional environment, with its set of constraints and pressures may result in separating/emaciating of academic work from meaning and replacing it with mere function. As a kind of knowledge job, it is more than ever open to periodical or chronic deficits in engagement and enthusiasm. Boredom, therefore, may be a symptom and side effect of problems prompted by institutional/organizational (post)modern changes in academic work.

Bureaucracy – clerk academic

> Will not this reform, we asked, cause employees to spend a lot of time filling in these various forms? - You know, the dignified person said angrily, all civil servants of the Ministry of Internal Affairs spend their whole lives, from morning till evening, filling in various forms and no one complains. And what is it, are university employees made of different clay, or what?
> (Kołakowski, 2017, p. 200)

> The name research-teaching employee is very misleading because he is ACTUALLY an administrative-teaching employee accounted for the results of the scientific work done when the administration for the faculty and university will be done in the first place .... In Poland, no one has enough free time, after galloping through the university administration, for scientific work.
> (Adiunkt polski, commentary to Zawisławska, 2017)

Like every other modern institution, academia has currently succumbed to the principle of over-organization, and excessive managerial control (Siegel, 2017; Sułkowski, 2017). What came as a great surprise to me was that the majority of respondents did not connect bureaucratic duties directly with boredom (only seven respondents explicitly described them as boring), which seems somehow contrary to the literature on workplace boredom which suggests that bureaucracy and extensive control are the primary causes of white-collar job boredom (Gemmill and Oakley, 1992; Harju, Hakanen, and Schaufeli, 2014). Perhaps because, so far, administrative work is not the main goal/activity of academics, my respondents did not usually use the word 'boredom/boring' but instead 'frustrating' or 'irritating,' sometimes adding the notions of anger, time-wasting, opportunity cost, meaninglessness, or bitter but inevitable duty. As my data suggests, however, bureaucratic load, seen from a long-term perspective, may greatly contribute to the chronic boredom/burn out of academics, and so it is worth mentioning in this analysis.

The term 'bureaucracy,' as introduced in this section, denotes all the tasks that are somehow connected with administrative procedures, excluding staff meetings (discussed in the next chapter). Academic activities of that kind may include: (1) reporting – filling out tables/forms serving for controlling purposes (achievements/grant/finance reporting), (2) financial work – preparing contracts (specific-task or mandate contract), accounting for expenditure associated with grants, research or conference trips, and so on, (3) teaching-related paper work – filling out syllabi forms (expected learning outcomes), entering student grades into electronic systems (USOS[3]), and so on, (4) work associated with law matters – adjusting, editing, writing statutes of institute/laboratory, or their parts, and so on, applying for certificates (e.g. enabling work with genetically modified organisms), and (5) the organization of various events (conferences, seminars, unit meetings, etc.), inviting guests, and so on.

Admittedly, the majority of these tasks have not been recent inventions at all, however, as many respondents claimed, their amount has increased significantly in the last decade since the new law was brought in (Ustawa z dn. 18 marca 2011 r.) introducing a neoliberal management philosophy, already well-known in Western countries (Clark, 2002; Shore, 2010; Slaughter and Rhoades, 2010; Couldry, 2011), into Polish academia. The most differentiating feature of this new audit culture is a general mistrust towards academics resulting in 'the regime of tables,' 'tablogy' (table+l-ogy, science of making tables, Kulczycki, 2016) and the imperative of proving and justifying each and every action of an academic (Wagner and Finkielsztein, 2014). The system that was introduced under the expectation of increasing efficiency and 'excellence' (both of scientific production and university organization), has turned out on numerous occasions to be simply turning academic work into work under the dictation of administration.

> Everything is done so that when someone comes to monitor us, they will know just where they should be looking. We are now doing everything so that someone can finally check us in fact. And we do more bureaucracy because of that.
> (M1, cited in Kowzan et al., 2015, p. 42)

What was initially meant to save time and resources prompts more and more bureaucratic duties that academics are compelled to perform (Halffman and Radder, 2015). As Dimitar Todorovsky (2014) noted, analysing his own working time budget calculated based on his 45-year academic career, he spent about 52 per cent of his work time on broadly understood bureaucratic tasks (teaching weighted only 19 per cent and research 22 per cent). Despite some respondents claiming that administrative duties were not heavy, the majority find them at least excessive and redundantly multiplied.

> Bureaucratic duties are such that when you open the mailbox, every day you could just don't turn up here to work but only remotely deal with these receipts that fall into your mail.
> (Teacher, interview_52, female, hab., social sciences)

The issue seems to be equally relevant for PhD students with grant projects (Wycisk et al., 2018, p. 14) and professors being unit leaders:

> We used to complain, when I started to work, about excessive bureaucratisation, but we didn't expect that we would remember it as a time of unbridled freedom in comparison to how it is now, when more and more papers, signatures have to be gathered, there are a lot of various formal restrictions.
> (Teacher, interview_37, female, prof., social sciences)

> I remember old times, where ... there were no computers, yet there were typewriters, there were no cell phones, and then we were complaining about the amount of bureaucracy, because we at X [discipline] have to have archives, unlike other institutions, so from time to time we have to look through these archives, which things go to the actual archiving, which simply go to throw away. Some have to be kept for years and when I compare these files with those papers I had to write they are about a tenth of what I do now when I have computers, when in theory this bureaucracy should not stick to me.
> (Teacher, interview_41, male, prof., humanities)

As Mark Fisher (2009, p. 40) observed, neoliberalism, presented as anti-bureaucratic, actually re-emerges bureaucracy that has significantly proliferated under this new organizational regime. Administrative tasks can periodically occupy vast amounts of time for some academics, and are a nuisance that makes many feel like bureaucrats, scholars 'trapped in a bureaucrat's body' (Graeber, 2015, p. 54), a new category of academic employee, which I would call a **'clerk academic'** (administration overload, see e.g. Wagner, 2014a; Kowzan et al., 2015; Siegel, 2017). All these bureaucratic duties are primarily a result of overregulation due to a systemic mistrust towards academics. As one of the respondents noted, it seems to be an implicit assumption that

> ... we, scientists are cheaters and that as we take money ... for some scientific research, so we should be checked to the last zloty [Polish currency], on what we spend it on, and if we don't spend this zloty as it should be spent. These are inflexible programs, it means that we are gadabouts and we need to be pushed, that is the bureaucratic system that

at every step implies a lack of confidence in those it gives money to ...,
which results in increasing reporting.
(Teacher, interview_41, male, prof., humanities)

This bureaucratic system can be interpreted as a kind of 'structural violence,' which is 'actual violence that operates in an indirect form' (Graeber, 2015, p. 61), that is imposed on conquered population (academics) being a way of 'organizing stupidity' (Graeber, 2015, p. 81). Such a structural stupidity producing a lot of absurdities and according to Graeber creates 'dead zone of the imagination,' i.e. 'areas so devoid of any possibility of interpretive depth that they repel every attempt to give them value or meaning' (Graeber, 2015, p. 102), and thus is quintessentially boring.

Many respondents had the impression that they are forced to do a job that should be done by administrative staff and that it does not fit the role of an academic to be a clerk. Some respondents also had the impression that the main principle of the administrative staff in general is bulldozing things onto someone else, including academic staff, with the 'let George do it' attitude.

> Research-teaching employees not only have to do research, they must do teaching, they still have to produce things for administration, which the administration only collects and processes nicely later, while it should produce these things and from the beginning to the end be responsible for them. No, we have to deliver everything, give them everything, and they simply stick [it] into the binders.
> (Teacher, interview_25, male, PhD, humanities)

> We still have so many administrative things to do which I think it should not be my job, but the job of a lady from the dean's office, and I get information that I have to prepare some document, and I should emphasise this, do that in italics, here from dots and here ... I'm sorry, let this lady do it herself, I can provide the information that is necessary, but I think that this should be done by the people from administration, because it is a waste of time for me.
> (K15 in Kowzan et al., 2015, pp. 18–19)

> On the other hand, some of the duties that the administration used to carry out were bulldozed onto scientific staff, including everything connected with the USOS. Once someone filled out the records, I was simply signing the protocol and filling things in, but it was already at the exam, [grading student in] the index and today I have to put it all in the USOS and keep an eye on it in the USOS.
> (Teacher, interview_50, female, prof., humanities)

Many respondents reported feeling that the administrative input was excessively demanding to the extent of reversing the initial relationships between scientists and administration – where administration exists to fulfil the needs of academics and not the opposite, where academics are meant to serve the administration. Some respondents thought that it is administration that holds the real power over the university (cf. Lunsford, 1968; Slaughter and Rhoades, 2010). Something that may partly confirm that conclusion, and simultaneously makes things more frustrating in the eyes of some, especially junior, respondents, is the fact that the administrative staff work on permanent contracts, benefiting from much safer positions than many academics. What frustrates, or makes many academics anxious, is also the fact that irrespective of their position they still appear to be enslaved by the administration and at times bereft of real help in that kind of work. Many also feel that they are not the most adequately qualified persons to do the work that administration requires them to perform, both due to tasks being excessively difficult or not complicated at all.

> I mean, I have the impression that it is a waste of time, that the university pays me to fill in various documents, tables, that someone [else] would do it better, faster, and probably for a lower price …. I don't like [it] and I can't deal with filling in papers, I don't like to do it, I can't do it, I find it boring and unnecessary, and there is still a lot [of it]. I have the impression that if there were employees assigned to do it at the university, I would not have to fill out the same contract five times because I can't do it well because I don't know it; I know other things.
> (Teacher, interview_21, male, hab., humanities)

The paradox of the situation seems to lie in the fact that due to these issues, some academics are required to do tasks outside their expertise, to 'have all these ridiculous amount of skills none of which we are trained for' (respondent in Osbaldiston, Cannizzo, and Mauri, 2019, p. 10), becoming more and more distracted and side-tracked by the constant need to learn things outside their specialty (e.g. law and administration, finance and accounting, or management) only for the sake of bureaucratic duties or perform time-consuming but mildly complicated tasks for which they are definitely overeducated. In such a situation the cause of potential boredom may be poor person-job fit (Rothlin and Werder, 2008), incongruence between one's skills/expectations and the demands of the job, in the most cases, situations where one's skills/knowledge overtake the demands of the job (Harris and Segal, 1985; Fisher, 1987; Csikszentmihalyi, 2000a; van der Heijden, Schepers, and Nijssen, 2012). Situations where workers are employed in jobs for which they are overqualified/overeducated, and which 'are substandard relative to their goals and expectations' (Maynard and Feldman, 2011, p. 1), are defined as underemployment or inadequate employment (Dooley and Prause, 2004). This can denote either a situation in which one is employed in a position with requirements that are below one's education/qualifications, or when one is theoretically employed in a position suitable for one's qualifications, but where they are underutilized.[4] Such situation can be quite prevalent among knowledge workers (Costas and Kärreman, 2016, p. 18), like academics.

Respondents also mentioned the situations when they were forced to duplicate documents and the work of administrative staff, perform work for administration, even if it seems to be perfectly possible to do the work without much involvement from an academic, and maintain their engagement in administrative work throughout their academic career: there is virtually no degree/position that can release one from such work (rare exceptions seem to prove the rule) – as one of the respondents observed:

> This is the charm of this work and it can be seen that the further [you are] in your career, the more time unfortunately has to be devoted to such administrative, organisational and representative activity, ... when someone is a professor, there is a huge expectation that they will continue to publish, ... it turns out that there is paradoxically less time for this creative work, there is much less and it also changes over the course of a career.
> (Teacher, interview_70, female, prof., social sciences)

The general overload of academics' time budgets is a critical issue (Jacobs, 2004). Bureaucracy affects each area of academic activity and vastly contributes to the feeling that a great deal of time is being wasted. The many little things necessary to do one's job tend to grow into complicated and time-consuming operations. An example may constitute obtaining/arranging the papers necessary for any trip financed by extra-salary funds – when one frequently finds oneself 'going from pillar to post.'

> Most things are paper, because I'm here on the Ochota campus, wanting to pick up some certificate ..., then first I have to go to Krakowskie to one lady, then to Karowa to another lady, then with one sheet three floors lower to another lady then to return back to Krakowskie Przedmieście ... there is no way to generate such a document, certified by clicking and then going and [picking it up] in one place, ... as I call there, ask for it to be prepared, so that I will only take it, because the circulation of documents is such that I have to physically move it [document] from building to building, because I need a set of stamps, so this administration is very, at least I see it like this, very extensive ... which means to me that I need to spend three hours the least on the central campus, so to get here is the fourth hour, so four hours lost to running after signatures.
> (Teacher, interview_71, female, PhD, natural sciences;
> cf. Szwabowski, 2019, p. 166)

The same situation was also experienced by another respondent who wanted to buy a licence for some advanced software for research purposes, for which the university did not have access. As she said 'it took me a week of walking, ringing, searching ... I just lost a week looking for [it], and buying this software' (Teacher, interview_62, female, PhD, social sciences). This case is corroborated by another participant who noted: 'in order to buy toner I have to fly around the floors, to buy a pencil I have to fill in a pile of papers ..., you need to squabble over everything and you need to take care of everything by yourself' (Teacher, interview_55, female, hab., natural sciences). Of course, much depends on the department, institute, and attitude of particular administrative employees, but the facts may be summarized as follows: (a) many documents are still required in paper form, (b) some of them need many signatures and stamps (the less important document, the more stamped it should be as the vocational saying goes) which are time-consuming to obtain, (c) few institutions have administrative staff dedicated to helping academics arrange the bureaucratic tasks,[5] (d) general requirements of the control and distribution system at the university are definitely overdeveloped, which is particularly severe for more than averagely active academics (attending more international conferences, applying and obtaining more research grants, etc.).

The most common reactions to administrative duties among my respondents were frustration, anger, irritation, and/or a sense of meaninglessness, which in the long-term may grow into a kind of habitual/chronic boredom due to the frustration of significant life-goals (Bargdill, 2014). Many academics feel that such a substantive amount of bureaucratic tasks constitute art for art's sake, having no sense, no real effect on things that matter to them, and are only a waste of time. As an example of such tasks perceived as meaningless academics mentioned the process of creating the syllabus. The issue of greater importance for academic teachers is writing down the content program of classes itself, but except for this, further procedures are required, such as specifying the outcomes of learning or translating all syllabi into English regardless of the fact that classes are solely for Polish students and are to be held in Polish. Respondents had the impression that students rarely read the syllabi at all and that adequately determining the actual program and/or learning outcomes is frequently near to impossible. This is because, firstly, classes follow their own pace and logic, and the teacher often has to improvise, so the sequence of subjects and the content of classes may require some adjustment during the semester; and secondly, because what students actually will learn, and the knowledge they will gain varies from student to student and is difficult to be verified precisely. What is written in the syllabi is therefore only a wishful estimation and on numerous occasions, some of it, the most bureaucratic parts, are filled out using set patterns, and frequently with the copy/paste method. Some respondents explicitly found it meaningless, futile and in some cases even absurd, and had no idea why they were forced to do such things.

> Learning outcomes, it's something so 'beautiful,' clerical gibberish for clerks, and I don't know why I'm supposed to do it, because it does not mean anything and only takes time, it's unnecessary, because the students are not better taught, nor do I will feel greater professional satisfaction from this, but I have to do such things I don't know why.
> (Teacher, interview_30, female, hab., natural sciences)

> Comic learning outcomes, learning objectives, ... really nothing that is written there, almost nothing, translates into real teaching in the room, it's creating newspeak, linguistic tumours, curiosities that don't make any sense.
> (Teacher, interview_25, male, PhD, humanities)

> 'Paperology' is advanced to the limits of the absurd. For example, the requirements for USOS, that all classes must be described in English, except in Polish ... so my description of these activities has not passed, was not passed by some official, because there was no English text there, so what I did, because I thought it was absurd, completely pointless to be sitting and translating exactly what I wanted there, so I threw it into the Google translator and copied the text, the description of English classes to the appropriate table, and sent it to an official and it's gone, I have peace until today.
> (Teacher, interview_46, male, hab., humanities)

Many respondents shared their opinion that such administrative duties are utterly pointless, having no added value and sometimes being simply formal and empty rituals required by the law or administrative practice.

> In order to get money for teaching something, I have to fill in the ZUS [Social Insurance Institution] questionnaire, because this is what our finance department wants, although I know that from the legal point of view I am insured in ZUS elsewhere, so this form doesn't make sense. I mean, I know that the finance department will send it, and ZUS will not use this form anyway, because it will see that I have this insurance from another place.
> (Teacher, interview_19, male, MA, social sciences)

At times, such apparently senseless requirements are employed as preventive methods against the external assessment of which central university administration is afraid. It may also be, at least partially, a convenient excuse to gather more documents ('the more papers the stronger position we have when we are monitored/audited') and lengthening the whole procedure to buy some time (the more delayed payment/reimbursement is, the longer money is in university account making interest). It is also possible that sometimes it is an excuse on the part of the department/institute administrative staff for their mistakes. From my own observations, I got the impression that such staff constantly struggle with central administration which constantly find more obstacles to completing procedures. Depending on the institution, local administrative staff may serve as mediators between central administration and academics, who are expected to do the lion's share of the work, or as their defender against it, trying to minimize the bureaucratic input and, if impossible, preparing many documents for them. Seeing central administration as a villain seems to be, nevertheless, a common narrative.

Another frustrating and meaningless bureaucratic duty is reporting one's own achievements, which is found problematic mainly due to the poor organization of the administration, in that many academics recalled being asked to report the same achievements many times for different purposes, despite the existence of a central database in which academics are now obliged to register all their achievements.

> Sometimes it is pointless that we have to, for example, report publications that we have published in several different formats, we sometimes enter the title, names and some other data, then some other data is needed for another type of reporting, so another table is filled in, and this is such a waste of time to rewrite exactly the same data, when this data is in the database, so easily available, one could take it from there. The point is that at this time computerisation has not moved forward enough to relieve us, and sometimes we actually just rewrite the senseless papers.
> (Teacher, interview_38, male, PhD, natural sciences)

What makes all this so annoying for many respondents is its high opportunity cost. Time budgets of academics are usually very tight and administrative duties can be time-consuming, such as reporting grant realization (achievements and finances) or changing study regulations, which were described by some respondents as 'time thrown into the mud' (Teacher, interview_42, female, hab., natural sciences), and 'one of the most unproductive and wasted periods in my life' (Teacher, interview_25, male, PhD, humanities). It is perceived as even more frustrating when it is performed at the cost of research (teaching is usually less disturbed, as it has recurrent, regular, and more interactional character). Some participants suggested that 'being a bureaucrat,' (Teacher, interview_52, female, hab., social sciences) is detrimental to scientific work and constitutes something that I would call a kind of **hidden employment**. Scientists understand the necessity of some bureaucratic duties but their workload is hard on them making them put their scientific work in both a metaphorical and literal drawer.[6] Another danger of administrative work may be that such work can be engrossing in terms of the direct gratification received from it. As one of the respondents noted:

> Often it is easy to fall into such a trap. For example, for a week I deal only with administrative matters and I feel satisfied, I fill out some paperwork every day, I sign [it], I feel that everything is going forward, but no, research simply stands still, because I'm dealing with papers.
> (Teacher, interview_38, male, PhD, natural sciences)

Dirty work

In the most radical view, a few respondents spoke of bureaucracy in terms of dirty work, treating it as an occupation of degrading character that undermines their sense of personal dignity (Hughes, 1958; Simpson et al., 2012). Originally, the concept was primarily associated with occupations and roles dealing with actual dirt and being perceived as disgusting and degrading (e.g. domestic cleaners, waste collectors, care workers, nurses, prison guards, mental hospital attendances) but as Everett Hughes highlighted 'dirty work of some kind is found in all occupations' (1958, p. 50) and it does not have to be associated with dirt in the strict sense of the word. Dirty work may be something that has to be done but hardly anyone does it willingly because it would violate their self-respect and dignity. As Hughes claimed:

> It may be dirty work in that it in some way goes counter to the more heroic of our moral conceptions. It is hard to imagine an occupation in which one does not appear, in certain repeated contingencies, to be practically compelled to play a role of which he thinks he ought to be a little ashamed. Insofar as an occupation carries with it a self-conception, a notion of personal dignity, it is likely that at some point one will feel that he is having to do something that is *infra dignitate*. (1958, p. 50)

The occupations that do not fit the self-conception of an academic may be those administrative ones that, if possible, are delegated to people lower in the academic hierarchy who usually are not in a position to refuse (Hughes, 1958; Bourdieu, 1984; Wagner, 2011a; Kowzan et al., 2015) as 'the last in the food chain'[7] (Doctoral student 1, cited in Zawadzki, 2017, p. 76). If one views research as something superior to other duties, a person may perceive some administrative tasks as dirty, however, they often see it also as an inevitable requirement to be promoted or simply retain any chance of staying in academia, and thus surrender to that kind of work (substitute teaching or the most reluctant classes, especially introductory ones, writing grant proposals for the chair, etc.).

The most visible and significant distinction seem to be that of junior, non-tenured academics and senior, tenured academics. In that kind of (semi-)feudal structure, some tasks will be perceived as dirty work and are likely to be performed by junior staff who, as the respondents in Marek Kwiek's study (2017, p. 18) suggested, are 'half-human beings' and frequently serve as errand boys. As one of my respondents noted:

> PhD gives a person the power to do everything, and on the other hand, if [a person] is young enough by age, but also by degree, if you are a PhD to the end of your life, well, you are still at a low stage compared to everyone with a higher degree who will make use of a person with a PhD. If, for example, a part of the PhDs from the University of Warsaw were fired, the university would collapse, because the majority of things are done simply by PhDs.
> (Teacher, interview_3, female, hab., social sciences)

It is needless to say that the duties that are thought of as 'dirty' are usually tedious, strenuous, and sometimes boring. The crucial result of that research, however, is that boredom is not the most adequate description of academic feelings associated with bureaucratic duties – instead it is frustration. Some of those duties can be boring at times but boredom is not felt at all or is immediately superseded by others, 'hotter' feelings. There can also be other explanations for that the respondents rarely used the term 'boredom.' Some treat administrative tasks merely as a duty, an inner part of the job, the inevitable reality of academic work that must be done even if not always intrinsically pleasant.

> It's simply a job to do and it's done, this job, irrespective of whether it's administrative, whether it's research, whether it's teaching, either we accept it or not, well then we go to other activities, for example, to breeding hens, to digging ditches, or to other such activities.
> (Teacher, interview_23, male, prof., natural sciences)

The job has to be done and one is compelled to accept it and there is no point moaning about it – which is, from that perspective, futile, immature, and unprofessional.

One respondent noted that administrative duties performed from time to time can be a form of rest from other academic activities that require more intellectual effort. Others believed that an overload of such duties keeps boredom at bay because there is no time to be inattentive and disengaged. Some did not feel boredom thanks to one of three prevention techniques that seem to be highly effective for those employing them: (1) delegation, (2) procrastination, and (3) avoidance. The first embraces bulldozing unwanted/potentially boring and time-consuming work onto someone else, usually in a lower position (see dirty work above). The second means postponing the moment of doing a task to such an extent that potential boredom is superseded by stress, hurry, and overload, because procrastinated duties eventually have to be done quickly, at the last moment and in excessive amounts due to delay. Some respondents tried to ignore bureaucratic demands as long as possible, obeying the unwritten rule not to jump the gun/to keep one's head down as in an anecdotic rhyme:

> My advice to you all –
> papers into drawer fold.
> If important – I shall say –
> It'll return at second date.[8]
>
> (Tokarczyk, 2009, p. 38)

The last, most radical prevention strategy is avoidance. Many academics are constantly trying not to absorb excessive amounts of administrative duties, but some, based on their experiences with bureaucracy, if possible, try to avoid/ not to provoke any unnecessary contact with university administration. There are two modalities in this technique: (a) self-sufficiency and (b) negligence. The former relies on, for instance, not settling the cost of research/conference trips, i.e. paying the cost of the journey and attendance themselves, which constitutes a kind of sponsoring the university as it gains some credit for the outcomes of such trips. The latter embraces avoiding involvements in any kind of scientific activity that would require much administrative work (not attending international conferences, not applying for external grants, etc.).

Workload

Another way to conceptualize various possible causes of work-related boredom of academics is the notion of workload, i.e. the amount of work assigned to and/or done by an individual during a given time period. It can be categorized according to (1) the relationship between one's abilities to do the tasks in a given period of time and the amount of work assigned (underload and overload), and (2) the character of such a relationship (qualitative – referring to the difficulty of tasks, or quantitative – referring to the sheer number of them, see Fisher, 1987, 1993). Depending on these two factors four types of workload that may prompt boredom can be distinguished (Table 4.1).

Table 4.1 Workload typology (collated by the author, source: Fisher, 1987, 1993).

	Underload	Overload
Qualitative	**Qualitative Underload** (easy tasks – routine, repetitiveness, tedium)	**Qualitative Overload** (excessively difficult tasks)
Quantitative	**Quantitative Underload** (too few tasks to perform – waiting, idleness)	**Quantitative Overload** (too many tasks – satiety, weariness)

Two kinds of workload were the most prevalent among participants – qualitative underload and quantitative overload. Quantitative underload was mentioned less frequently and only in limited areas of activities (field and lab work). Qualitative overload was not found relevant for academics except for rare occasions of excessively difficult content at some scientific conferences (see Chapter 5).

Qualitative underload

Routine and repetitive simple tasks that are frequently bereft of creative and challenging components are an inevitable part of academic work, not only in administration, which has been described in the previous section. Qualitative underload, the underutilization of one's capabilities, or the occasional, tedious 'fool's job' which could be done by virtually anyone (Teacher, interview_5, female, hab., social sciences), often constitutes the everyday experience of many academics. Many interesting and creative activities are mixed with those which almost anybody could successfully perform after a short training; after an exciting interview dull transcription-making must follow; after days of introducing numerical data into tables there is the thrill of data analysis; frustrating and boring, yet highly important, grant application preparation is mixed with classes with active groups of students, and after boring faculty meetings there is the joy of reading of a new paper in one's area of research. Moreover, many modern scientific methodologies are also based on predictable and highly formalized procedures that essentially make them scientific (Ferrell, 2004).[9]

According to Csikszentmihalyi's theory (2000a), boredom is caused primarily by the discrepancy between one's skills level (high) and the complexity of the task (low). Many interviewed academics face exactly this kind of situation – they are highly trained both theoretically and practically and at times compelled to pursue quite simple and repetitive tasks for hours, days, or years. Pipetting, a manual task that involves introducing the small tips of pipettes into narrow tubes in order to place a tiny drop of liquid into the tips, is an example of such a situation in the work of scientists in the laboratories, and teaching the same course for many years in a row or to many groups on the same subject in one week is another. Many respondents admitted occasionally performing such simple, and not intellectually demanding, tasks; for some it was a kind of repose after more challenging activities, for others frustrating and/or boring moments in their generally fulfilling job, for others occasional drudgery that marks their everyday work experience. Sometimes it constitutes a vital part of significant work procedures (field or lab work), at other times it is not a desired feature of their core work duties (repetitive teaching or faculty meetings) and occasionally includes whole activity areas perceived as futile and inherently meaningless (bureaucracy).

Such qualitative underload is frequently prompted by the delegation of work that used to be, or should ideally be, done by other vocational groups (administrative or technical staff) to academics. It is due to the change in politics of ministry and, in consequence, university governance towards employing technical staff, especially at natural sciences departments. According to new regulations, universities were discouraged from employing such staff (by financial factors), and so tedious and repetitive tasks that are not intellectually challenging that could originally be delegated now have to be performed by the researchers themselves and they do not always manage to outsource it or delegate it to PhD students, thanks to grant financing.

Another example of qualitative underload, and occasionally qualitative overload, is pursuing a research grant. Many respondents complained about a lack of administrative support in everyday grant processing, which results in performing many potentially boredom- and frustration-inducing activities. This problem mostly involves junior staff (PhD students, PhDs) for which grants are frequently the only opportunity to pursue research and/or manage to provide for their families. In fact, many academics perform many tasks on a daily basis that they hardly, if at all, conceive as 'core' and/or 'proper' for their role as academics (see clerk academic) – boredom as an experience of role distance may thus constitute a justified emotional response.

Quantitative underload

In the majority of cases, boredom is a highly transitional emotion that emerges between activities, during the inactivity of waiting for the next occupation. In some disciplines an inherent part of work is waiting for something to happen, which may provoke a transient feeling of boredom among researchers. It is common in prolonged research projects and is frequently inherent to the research method itself and/or organizational proceedings (e.g. forced breaks in the research process due to technical reasons). What unites all these research situations is waiting – and repeatedly, the possibility of boredom, even if immediately mitigated as in the case of one of the respondents describing a clear example of presenteeism (being physically at work and somewhat absent from it, pursuing non-work-related activities at work; D'Abate, 2005):

> For example, when I am on duty [office hours for students] and no one comes to me, and I sit and scroll the Facebook, so it's not that I'm bored at work, because I simply don't work at the moment, I do what I do in my free time, I'm sitting here alone, if someone comes, I start to work, and then I was not bored at work, I was in a normal time.
> (Teacher, interview_66, male, PhD, humanities)

In that situation the potential for boredom, inherent in such a situation of waiting for students to come, is masked by an immediate, semi-automatic coping mechanism. Yet, without proper coping opportunities that could be a quintessentially boring situation and such moments are, if not frequent, still visible.

Quantitative overload

As one of the respondents explained to me when informed about my research subject: 'it's multi-job, so there's no boredom, there's a danger of burn-out' (Teacher, interview_35, male, PhD, humanities). In fact, many academics operate in the situation of constant overload, stress, strict deadlines, and deep exhaustion, yet boredom, especially chronic boredom, in the understanding adopted in this work, can be a significant outcome of such a situation and contribute to burn out (Campagne, 2012; Schaufeli and Salanova, 2014), because, as some authors have suggested, boredom may be associated with overload (Klapp, 1986; Mosurinjohn, 2015). As many respondents admitted, academic work is frequently unscheduled in terms of steady working hours (this depends greatly on the department, discipline, and culture, the kind of work performed and work space quality) making it difficult to distinguish work time from leisure time. Many respondents take work home (evenings, weekends) and on vacations (cf. Jacobs and Gerson, 2004), and as some research showed, working hours in higher education frequently exceed the standard 40-hour-a-week job and even the 48 hour maximum set by the EU Working Time Directive (Jacobs, 2004;[10] Kinman and Wray, 2013). Academics teach students every week, have administrative and organizational duties/tasks, and are obliged to produce scientific output in the form of publications or other activities aimed at communicating science. Many academics reported that they felt overworked, chronically exhausted, frequently bereft of enthusiasm, unable to find the time to rest properly, and full of remorse when inactive. This is a prime example of the internalization of the main principles of an achievement society, with its auto-exploitation and inside work camp mentality (Han, 2015) – this is why they so 'vigorously' denied having been bored. Many respondents felt exhausted by the constant compulsion to hurry, which is especially crucial in the case of junior staff. They need to hurry to write their PhD thesis (4 years), then to write their habilitation (8 years), alongside writing publications and reports for research funding institutions and in the meantime teaching on a regular weekly-scheduled basis (frequently on subjects not related to their scientific interests) and to meet administrative deadlines associated with bureaucratic requirements (see Wagner, 2011b; Kowzan et al., 2015). Exhaustion, i.e. the chronic state of tiredness, not prompted by one concrete activity but satiety and weariness due to life and/or vocational situation, constituting a kind of 'existential scepticism' (D'Hoest and Lewis, 2015, p. 8), may be the justified outcome of such a working style. Chronic boredom or burn out may follow. As one of the respondents explained:

> We actually burn out, this burnout comes ... perhaps from the fact that we need to know everything, for research and teaching, and administration alike, and all these three areas are so pressing, breaking into life, it's impossible to loosen anything, because if you fail when teaching you will get the wrong feedback from students in the final poll. We are called to the management, for example, [and asked] "here you have worse grades from students this year, what happened?" I had such a situation ... I cannot have a year without publication, explaining that "sorry, I have no inspiration, I am burned out, I am unable to write an article," ... The administration I cannot muck up either, because when I have to write something to someday, to fill in a syllabus in USOS, report on something, there are deadlines, ... I have to do it all, if I take the line of least resistance, I have the stress that I took the line of least resistance, and that this is a sham and false action, and if I work hard, I have the stress that I have to work hard, and here and here and here and I simply cannot close my eyes, so there's something like that, like burnout, and it really gets people around forty, people who should simply habilitate ... When we should want the most, we become cynical, we know that we will not overcome difficulties and that the system is simply like it is and we start to rush through a little, take the line of least resistance, it happens.
> (Teacher, interview_62, female, PhD, social sciences)

Over-exploitation, especially significant in the case of junior staff, is a consequence of organizational settings – laws and regulations, the underfunding of higher education, employing fewer employees than needed – and individual attitudes of self-exploitation in the hope of gaining a tenure position, which is conceived to mean a 'sacred peace/serenity' and 'becoming somebody' (Kowzan et al., 2015, p. 144). Some academics therefore intensify their efforts to boost their career advancement, a consequence of which can be intellectual barrenness, deeply-internalized exhaustion, cynicism, a lack of passion and intrinsic curiosity. As one of the respondents noted:

> Research in such highly competitive education cycles, that you need to learn a lot, in medicine, for example, to work and work, and work. And it is very noticeable that when someone exerts so much pressure for a few years, they burn out so much that when they advance to the next level, they don't have any mental space to be impressed by anything because they are simply exhausted.
> (Teacher, interview_1, female, hab., social sciences)

If emotional exhaustion, cynicism, and lower efficacy are the definitional feature of burn out (Maslach, Schaufeli, and Leiter, 2001), some academics certainly experience such a state. Many feel overloaded with work, stressed by the demands of the highly competitive academic system, at times have a cynical approach to some of their duties, as there is no sense of meaning in performing them, and frequently do not feel acknowledged for their work, in either a pecuniary or emotional form (Jacobson, 2016). In fact, the most frequently mentioned disadvantage of academic work was low salaries (for instance, the take-home salary of an adjunct, the most common institutional position in the Polish higher education system, amounts to approximately 700 euros a month). The burnout experienced by a few respondents was also due to the lack of support from senior and/or administrative staff, and a lack of recognition of their achievements (e.g. good teaching, prestigious publications, grant holding), and as research show the lack of recognition can be detrimental for job involvement (Parkinson and McBain, 2013) and contribute to the feeling of boredom. One distinct factor possibly contributing to burnout may also be the lack of status change after obtaining habilitation. At the university in this study (but not all Polish universities) many PhDs were still employed in their adjunct positions after obtaining habilitation, and thus, scientific advancement was separated from work promotion (see Rodzik, 2016; Godlewicz-Adamiec, Łuczyńska-Hołdys, and Opalińska, 2019). The outcome of such a situation may be a temporary lowering of motivation, as salary and position were not significantly bettered and more duties and responsibilities were added. A side effect of the factors listed above may also be a feeling of chronic boredom, as there is less job involvement, the start of procrastination and less motivation, resulting in a disinclination to do one's work (at least some of it). An overload of duties without proper recognition impairs engagement and a sense of meaningfulness, which may contribute to both burn out and chronic boredom.

Lack of belonging

Another contributory factor to lowering engagement in work in general is a lack of sense of belonging to the workplace (cf. Lodahl and Kejner, 1965; Maslach, Schaufeli, and Leiter, 2001; Parkinson and McBain, 2013). Some respondents, especially junior staff, reported problems fully identifying themselves with their employing institution, its goals and future. Some academics do not feel an integral part of their institution, group, unit, and so on, feel alienated and lack valuable and meaningful social relationships in the workplace, such as mentorship and support from senior academics.

Low levels of personal attachment to the workplace are significantly affected by the individualistic, instrumental attitude towards it that is encouraged by the current evaluation system, which does not acknowledge scientific discussion, engagement in institutional life or social bonds with colleagues, unless it results in international collaborations and their products. The currently enforced regulations (e.g. grant system) encourage academics to perceive others in their fields primarily as rivals and as colleagues only additionally, if it matches career advancement/opportunities. Few academics seem to be actually interested in the work of others in their institution, unless it is connected to their projects – many said that they feel that nobody is interested in their work and they know little about the projects of others (cf. Kowzan et al., 2015). The stress and rush associated with the publish or perish system efficiently changed the attitudes of many, especially junior, academics. Many institutions, unless they employ people through networks (employing (former) PhD students, collaborators or private colleagues, etc.), are usually interested in academics who, apart from fitting into the teaching needs of a unit, are highly productive in terms of grant acquisition and publication output. Many precariously employed academics, always on a kind of 'trial period' are primarily focused on mere survival. Social bonds, unless with somebody holding real power, will not help to win the next employment contest – publications and grants may. This encourages a highly instrumental, monetary, attitude to academic work, which can be epitomized by the not unknown situations when PhDs abandon an institution just after obtaining their habilitation, because they will receive a much higher salary and permanent position as university professor immediately at another (predominantly private) institution. If the sense of belonging to the institution was high, this situation would be associated with much higher personal and emotional costs and, in consequence, be much less prevalent. Although the system of competition and international migration (frequently a basic requirement of many research grants and favourably treated in the process of employment) may be beneficial for science development in a short-term and be suitable for some groups of academics, however, it may be highly detrimental in terms of the sense of rootedness and belonging which are connected to overall higher engagement in work. There are many factors that contribute to a lack of dedication and sense of responsibility to the employing institution, including (1) precarious employment with a highly competitive evaluation system, (2) not being socialized as an integral part of an institution/workplace, (3) poor work space quality resulting in limiting one's time spent at the workplace, or (4) a strict hierarchical order causing a strong agency deficits.

Precarity

The context of research work in Poland has changed tremendously in the last three decades, not only due to the technological shift (including digital revolution) but equally because of modifications in the financing system, moving from hard to soft money, which means a shift from steady financing and permanent positions to the grant system and short-term employment contracts (Couldry, 2011). This kind of employment policy and organization setting significantly affects not only a form of academic career but also the approach to the work itself and an individual's well-being. The precarious form of employment characterized by uncertainty, lack of stability, and regular evaluation at the end of each short-term contract creates a very peculiar mindset in those who are subjected to such a system. One possible outcome is the perception of academic jobs as lacking a future, with no or little prospects of long-term career development (a lack of career prospects and few opportunities for promotion may also be significant causes of work boredom; Kass, Vodanovich, and Callender, 2001). Some respondents were dubious about whether their actions will have any positive consequences for their career, and when 'the future seems devoid of opportunities for possibly making a personal difference' (Brisset and Snow, 1993, p. 240), boredom may emerge. In the Polish academic system, an official contest for the position has to be opened for each full-time short-term position. In fact, many such competitions are fake – the specifications of a position are fitted to only one particular person, or information about the contest is displayed only for a very short period of time (e.g. during a long weekend between national holidays). Yet, as one of the respondents said:

> It is not entirely certain that this contract will be extended, because there are contests here each few years ... so we have such a perspective, that maybe our research or work will be for nothing, because we won't be employed again, ... there is always a risk that someone will have better papers.
> (Teacher, interview_64, female, PhD, social sciences)

Competition for positions, of course, may result in higher motivation to work, especially measurable output, as evaluation is based on it, however, a lack of security and feeling of instability may also result in 'periods of doubt in the chosen career path, which in turn results in a lack of deep involvement in the work [which is] difficult to maintain in the context of the struggle for another contract and the next two-year employment' (Wagner, 2014a, p. 57). The situation of such casual academics being employed on short-term contracts, for instance, on grants positions, such as post-docs (Ivancheva, 2015; cf. Slaughter and Rhoades, 2010; Wagner, 2011a; Montoya and Perez, 2016) is frequently also significantly affected by the fact that for many this is the time for raising a family, child-rearing (which is even more challenging for women, see Wagner, Finkielsztein, and Czarnacka, 2017), and establishing oneself as an academic, i.e. forging one's academic identity. If one fails to accommodate to a system of precarious employment, the outcome may be boredom due to a lack of perspective and hope for the future in a particular institution. As one of the respondents said:

> I have such a malicious devil, who tells me, "basically, why the hell should you make an effort if you will not get a job anyway ... why put more heart in this department, why put more heart into this university or teaching anyway, if you will not be here in two-three years' time?" And if I had a temporary contract or some two years, I would have a shorter research grant, I don't know what is going on at all, I am a wage worker, you don't offer me stability, why should I be associated with this institution? Why engage?
> (Teacher, interview_19, male, MA, social sciences)

Precarious employment schemes may result, therefore, in lowering one's engagement with the institution – short-term contracts in either regular research-teaching positions or in research grants may lead to exhaustion and dispiritedness. The situation is exacerbated by generational inequality (Ivancheva, 2015) – junior staff are subjected to a very competitive system based on performance with little employment stability while the 'older and oldest generations can feel safe – they can participate in an ongoing game with changing rules, and many participate in it, but they do not have to participate' (Kwiek, 2016, p. 225; cf. Zawadzki, 2017). These 'double standards' may significantly affect the attitudes of junior staff, lowering involvement with the institution, heightening indifference, and concentration primarily on individual achievements (measurable ones, i.e. prestigious publications in the first place) at the cost of overall work engagement. In the more stable employment system many personally meaningless but institutionally vital tasks are less likely to prompt frustration and boredom. Yet, as Pieniądz (2017) incisively noted: 'the older generation of scholars – pursuing their scientific path in conditions other than today's – design for the young the kind of university in which they would not want to start a career themselves' (p. 306). Generationally-divided standards of evaluation are therefore highly demotivating. Some junior respondents complained that the scientific output of many senior academics, frequently holding important positions in their institutions and/or grant committees, measured by currently imposed 'objective' performance assessment methods, would not win the competition with many younger colleagues who publish and present at the international level. The sense of unfairness produced by such a policy may be one of many possible contributors to chronic boredom and/or burn out. Polish universities have been under constant transition in the last two decades, and are still suspended between old and new employment schemes. There are still academics without habilitation employed in permanent positions (so-called 'permanent PhDs') who are not being oppressed by the eight-year deadline for obtaining habilitations. The existence of such positions is frustrating for those on short-term contracts with constant deadlines and evaluation stress.

A highly competitive employment system has yet another consequence that is not obvious. Because '[w]hat is to be the object of desire [academic employment] turns out ultimately not very attractive,' many young academics, who are 'condemned to a struggle for a poor salary, high workload and a short contract' (Pieniądz, 2017, p. 306) decide to withdraw their engagement from such a system: they drop out. Many prospective PhD students or PhDs in market-competitive disciplines turn to private companies providing job security and much higher salaries, others choose to migrate to other academic systems or simply abandon academic ambitions altogether. In a way, this may turn out to be a kind of negative selection to academia, as many out of the most intellectually capable, creative, and unconventional ('forerunners' as Wagner called them) drop out of the academic world permanently (Wagner, 2011a; Wagner, 2014a, 2014b, p. 62). Precarity may lead to turnover intentions, actual drop outs, and decreases in well-being. Many PhD students have symptoms of depression (Levecque et al., 2017) due to uncertainty and the lack of prospects for an academic career, which leads many to drop out. Boredom, in this case chronic boredom, may therefore be a significant selection mechanism, as a precarious employment policy may turn out not to be an efficient way to stimulate, boost, or sustain initial passion and enthusiasm for research. Those who eventually win the permanent position campaign are frequently extremely exhausted, demotivated, cynical, chronically bored – there is a possibility that they have not been selected primarily according to their intellectual capacity and passion but due to mere persistence and a strong survivors instinct (cf. Baghdadchi, 2005).

Recruitment system

One of the primary causes of a lack of belonging is the recruitment system for academia. As my data clearly shows, narratives about initial employment at university differ significantly between senior and junior staff. What was striking in many senior staff narratives is that although it was not easy to start and establish a career at the university (jobs were also scarce), new academics were recruited during or just after finishing their MA studies and they were almost automatically (after a half-a-year trial period as an intern-assistant, for instance) an integral part of the institution, unit, and/or research group. Some were initially employed in administrative or technical positions to keep them in academia, which was up to professors (chiefs of units and/or research groups, who were frequently their MA thesis advisors), and obtained regular academic positions over time, when positions became available. As one respondent recalled:

> [My MA thesis advisor] asked me to become an employee at the university, although what he initially suggested was a secretarial, or administrative position, but he said then that it is not enough money, I may not

be satisfied [and] that I must think about it, that he don't know what the future would be like, but [that] basically everyone who is here at the institute he had worked, so they used to start in some kind of administrative function, so basically everything is still ahead of me. And that's how it really was, after six months an academic position became vacant and six months later I had full-time research employment.
(Teacher, interview_3, female, hab., social sciences)

Young academics, even if they were officially called PhD students, were treated as employees with all the consequences – they had regular hours to teach, some organizational duties and eight years to defend their PhD thesis. Each newly employed academic was included in ongoing projects and the life of the institution, integrated into it from the very beginning. As long as they did not totally fail to meet expectations, their contract was extended until they obtained a permanent position, which was granted much earlier than it is now. Obtaining a degree (PhD, habilitation) was also (almost) automatically connected to advancement in their institutional position (which meant a higher salary). Units were often organized as research groups directed by chief professors, which may sometimes have been an obstacle in terms of academic freedom, but provided junior staff with support and the transmission of knowledge from senior colleagues. The system was in many ways far from ideal, but in terms of encouraging a sense of belonging to an institution, unit, or group, it played a significant integrative role. Recruitment to academia happened at an earlier stage, stability of employment was much higher and identification with an institution much stronger.

Although this kind of system, to some extent, still seems to function in many institutions, and employment is directly dependent on social capital – at the same time, the current system creates the conditions in which certain groups of young academics, who do not manage to be co-opted via networks, operate independently, as freelancers without strong ties to any scientific community, and on the margins of the institutional system. Selection to academic positions is now postponed from MA to PhD obtaining and perhaps even habilitation as postdocs frequently serve as an academic precariat *sensu stricto* in many disciplines (Kwiek, 2016). Moreover, the massification of PhD studies[11] frequently means eliminating the idea of an academic apprenticeship and deflating the significance of the PhD title. What was once a means to reproduce academic personnel now merely reproduces academic unemployment, as the majority of PhD students never gain a position in academia. The structure of employment has been significantly changed – there are fewer opportunities for a position (such as technical, administrative positions) than before, and all grant positions are by definition precarious, providing no stability or sense of attachment. Many young academics are used as a mobile and relatively cheap work force, employed on a short-time basis in research grants whose subjects are frequently far from their scientific interests, though perfectly compatible with their competences (Zimniak-Hałajko, 2012). PhD students are no longer treated as employees and an integral part of an institution, its future personnel, but rather as students from whom money can be made – as institutions receive a ministerial subsidy for each PhD student. As research by the University of Warsaw's Laboratory of Education Quality Evaluation (Zając et al., 2014, p. 10) shows, PhD students at the University of Warsaw do not feel like fully-fledged members of their units or departments, and are treated most of all like students instead of academics. The current system is so preoccupied with so-called 'scientific excellence' (see Wagner, 2016 for a revealing analysis of the concept of 'excellence') that regular academic work, which by definition constituted a conglomerate of very different roles, is lost from sight. A freelance researcher does not belong to an institution, they are merely affiliated to it – this is the case for PhD students and post-doc researchers. They can be compared to wage workers chained to an assembly-line of scientific production. As some respondents noted, PhD studies have been disconnected from the university ecosystem, and the new bill introduced in 2018 (Ustawa z Dn. 20 Lipca 2018 r. Prawo o Szkolnictwie Wyższym i Nauce) that created so-called 'doctoral schools' with a system of steady finance for four years is far from solving that problem.

Non-Place

Spending little time in the physical space of a university may be both a cause and symptom of a lack of belonging for some academics. As I observed, and as some respondents confirmed, many academics, mostly from humanities and social sciences, visit university buildings only to teach classes, take a one- or two-hour duty for students, or arrange administrative matters, and they leave as soon as possible without further engagement with the community or institutional life. As one of the respondents noted:

> Most people ... only come to [teach] classes, to some duty once a week and for the rest they don't give a damn, they rarely get involved in any kind of, let's say, life of the institute, of some collective ... [the institute] is the point of passage through which one only passes, whips through teaching, attends some meeting, signs some applications and comes out immediately. The sooner it will be settled ... it can simply be seen how people only stop by these offices, quickly, intensely settle [things], take something and leave, they're gone, from eleven to twelve, twelve sharp, thank you, bye, I'm gone.
>
> (Teacher, interview_25, Male, PhD, humanities)

University, for many academics, is thus only a transitional space with which they do not have a close relationship, do not feel any particular attachment to, and which is not closely associated with their identity – simply, it becomes a place that dangerously resembles a non-place described by French anthropologist, Marc Augé (1995). Many institutions become spaces in which one stays only temporarily in transition to other places, and to which one does not attach, and which are only the means to certain ends and can be seen as a quintessential example of the principle of replacing meaning with mere functionality. Many humanities and social science institutions can be lined beside such non-places as hospitals and clinics, airports and train stations, motorways and oil stations, hotels, supermarkets, and malls. All these places are merely a transitory step to another destination, one attends these places simply to arrange business – have an operation, wait for a means of transportation, spend the night in foreign city, buy necessary products, or pursue leisure activities. University ceases to be a community space for some group of academics, an anthropological place inherently associated with social relationships, personal identity, and a sense of belonging (the same may apply to students as well). As one respondent observed for his institution:

> It has changed, let's say, within the last decade, because I myself was like a witness. I observed how from such a place of meetings, exchange, intense contact, within the last decade it has changed in just such a non-place, a platform or trampoline for the realisation of ambitious, private goals.
> (Teacher, interview_25, male, PhD, humanities)

Non-places are also spaces in which people do not want to, or cannot, feel at home. One respondent compared his unit's space to the waiting room before a boxing match or backstage at the theatre, where people simply drop in to leave their coats and chat non-committally for a while before going on stage (e.g. to teach; Teacher, interview_21, male, hab., humanities). A non-place is a place in which one should not feel at home as it would be inappropriate, bizarre, and/or dysfunctional. One respondent recalled his mentor warning him never to leave any books in the unit, because it was like a train station where anybody can come in and out.

Possible reasons for not domesticating university space may be (1) an instrumental, functional attitude towards an institution that is virtually encouraged by the evaluation system, (2) multi-employment, i.e. being employed simultaneously in many institutions (including outside the academic world) and/or occasional moonlighting due to insufficient/unsatisfactory financial conditions, or (3) the poor quality of space in many departments of the university. The last issue seems to be rare in natural science departments, where a substantial percentage of academics cherish their own rooms (especially professors) or share them with only a few people, but the general landscape of humanities and social science departments is quite different. Many employees share a room with 10–15 co-workers, lack their own desk and chair (not to mention a stationary computer), and thus, have no conditions in which they can work (rare exceptions only corroborate this tendency). Some are even ashamed to invite students or respondents (in the case of conducting interviews) to their unit. A consequence of that situation is the limitation of one's presence at the institution. There is not to say that improvements in the quality of space would automatically increase the presence of academics in university buildings and improve social capital, as functional attendance seems to have become an inherent element of organizational culture in some institutions. Being a part of some abstract collective such as unit or institute, means there is the possibility of not seeing or talking with many colleagues for a prolonged periods of time, unless one has classes at the similar time as others as not all units have regular meetings or they are infrequent.

This is not to say that physical presence in the university space is by definition commendable and indispensable for academic work, as many academics prefer to work at home (although some find it very difficult). My data suggests, however, that although such presence does not automatically result in higher job involvement and a sense of belonging, its lack as a result of poor working conditions can both contribute to and be the outcome of poor provision. Social capital, which is usually produced by meaningful interaction with colleagues, plays an important role in creating commitment to the institution and preventing boredom and burn out. Treating university space as a non-place only highlights the general character of relationships between (precarious) employees and employment institutions, in which 'they become temporary, non-permanent' (Wagner, 2014a, p. 57). Regular presence in the workplace may, although it does not have to, result in one's closer integration with the institution and co-workers, which may build a protective shield against the kind of (chronic) boredom that may plague isolated, detached, and self-preoccupied academics in a system of overwhelming insecurity and temporality.

Hierarchy

Another issue that may be detrimental for job involvement and sense of belonging of academics is the hierarchical order of Polish academia. Some respondents noted that work at university is associated with recurrent feeling of being submissive, remaining in a state of forced immaturity and lacking agency. As one respondent noted:

> This is an unpleasant place to work, if you are not passionate about this place. It is still a feudal institution, someone can always be found who is more important than us, by age or by degree, position, or whatever. In fact, until retirement, a person never feels, I mean I don't know, because I'm not retired, but I suppose that until then one always feels like a little

child ... And this is a terrible feeling. At some point you want to be a grown person, and at university you are not, so you have to really like this job, because from an ambitious point of view, it simply rolls over a person, that's something terrible.

(Teacher, interview_3, female, hab., social sciences; cf. Bourdieu, 1984)

In the long-term, a constant lack of agency (the sense of having a real effect on institution functioning), and lack of control over oneself 'may result in less and less involvement in the attempt to change or even lack of identification with your own university' (Kowzan et al., 2015, p. 144; cf. Zawadzki, 2017). Some academics have a sense of wasted potential, good will, and opportunities for improvement. Some claimed that this situation was mainly characteristic for those before obtaining a habilitation, yet others indicated it was a continual problem for many tenured employees. One cause of this situation is perceived as a specific kind of professor with a peculiar mindset (Bourdieu, 1984 called them 'mandarins'). Such academics feel that they are 'somebody,' a kind of VIP with 'excessively good well-being ... such a professor's bubble,' and who likes to make an impression that they are omniscient (Teacher, interview_28, female, prof., humanities). They frequently cultivate their professorships as a pompous ritual, are bossy, apodictic, not willing to openly discuss things with others holding lower institutional positions, always feeling compelled to articulate their opinion and, if possible, impose their standpoint. Some are also very sensitive about grandiose 'nominal/titular' rituals. A professor to whom I sent an e-mail message with a polite request to participate in my study is an example of this. In the first message I used the opening 'Szanowny Panie' (Dear Sir) and formal ending 'Z poważaniem' (Best regards). I received a negative answer to my request with the comment: 'Actually, one should not respond to a letter formulated like this, but I ascribe it to the general brutalisation of customs.' Out of curiosity I sent the professor another message with an enquiry about his reasons for such a reply. It turned out that instead of 'Dear Sir' I should have used 'Dear Sir Professor,' and as to the closing honorific expression, I was informed that

> [t]here is a difference between the impersonal and somewhat offensive expression "Best regards," which ends a non-personal letter to the office, and "With respect" – this is how you should write to public figures, especially if you expect something from them.

It is equally interesting that the second message was ended with a much less formal expression 'Łączę pozdrowienia' ('With greetings'). As some respondents suggested, this kind of figurative professors dominate at some institutions, forming the establishment, a 'group holding power' (Teacher, interview_56, female, hab., social sciences) which treats those lower in the hierarchical structure in a paternal and demeaning way, which may vastly contribute to job disengagement, a lower sense of belonging and result in leaving the institution (I heard about several situations when academics quit the unit or institution for such reasons).

Identity disturbance

Boredom may also constitute an emotional response to identity disturbance, which is characteristic of two kinds of situations: (1) when the roles that are offered are not perceived as 'core' to one's identity, and do not meet expectations of one's imagined role, or (2) when one is in a transitional state between two positions/statuses, thus retaining an old self-perception which is no longer valid and is incompatible with one's new position. Boredom is likely to emerge when someone's ideal vision of themselves and/or their work is at odds with the realities of their occupational role/life. People become bored with all those tasks that are conceived to be incongruent with their core identity (the inner definition of what the term 'real work' embraces). The vast majority of my respondents declared to have a primary research or, less frequently, teaching identity. Boredom can be thus experienced more often during tasks incompatible with those identities. For instance, the feeling is more likely to occur during bureaucratic duties for people who do not identify themselves as clerks, or during staff meetings when they have no intention of being involved in the politics of science or an institution administration. If these spheres of activity are not seen as core to someone's identity, then they participate in them without much personal involvement or zest. If new elements are internalized into an identity, however, and if someone accommodates to a new situation and becomes involved in their new roles, then boredom may not occur at all. If a staff meeting is perceived as core to someone's identity as a member of institution/community, and personally meaningful, then they will not become chronically bored with it and the occurrence of situational boredom may be lower than among those who do not internalize a role as, for instance, a committee member, as a core element of their vocational identity. Boredom is thus a signal that currently performed activity is distant from someone's core identity or in other words, the further activity is from the core identity, the more likely boredom is to emerge.

Boredom may be the emotional outcome of a transition between two positions/statuses, a characteristic of an accommodation period when old priorities and visions are in contradiction with currently performed activities. What used to be essential for satisfaction and flow is no longer possible (at all or in the way that it used to be performed). In some cases, this transitional, **anomic boredom** lasts only for a short period of time, but sometimes it results in the much longer-lasting state of chronic boredom. In both situations, boredom can be associated with a 'failure of expectations,' which, as Conrad (1997) points out, is one of possible causes of the feeling. If one expects something to happen or imagines something to have specific features and the reality does not measure up to the vision or interest then engagement may decrease and boredom appear. This reason for boredom may be seen at each career level at university.

Young scientists, to give the most apparent example, frequently have an inadequate vision of science and its practise because their undergraduate training is focused on 'fixed' problems created strictly for teaching purposes (Delamont and Atkinson, 2001). Their projections thus often collide with the realities of research work with its repetitiveness, boredom, and months of routine work conducted without visible (and measurable) achievements. Many people imagine following the steps of famous 'explorers of the truth,' but the majority of junior academics will be 'the artisans who do the commendable, but not earth-shaking, research which accumulates to form the foundation for future decisive advances' (Glaser, 1964, p. 1014). In the majority of cases, the dreams cannot be sustained, which may result in a feeling of disappointment, a kind of temporary or prolonged paralysis of creative powers and withdrawal of engagement (for instance, in a form of cynicism and an instrumental attitude, cf. Hermanowicz, 1998).

Some academics who enjoy great recognition in their field of expertise may become bored by it and modify their research field (e.g. because of a slowing down effect in their discipline) or choose to advance in their career in some other way (e.g. to become involved in research politics, or take an important administrative position). It is not uncommon to meet individuals who became tired of/bored with their daily activities as lower rank academics and entered the process of institutional career construction at the top of important institutions; administrative tasks are then not perceived as wasting time, and the goal is to 'have a career' rather than 'doing science.' The transition to a role as politician/administrator of science is not always desired by senior academics however, and there may be problems adapting.

> The transition requires thus an adaptation to a permanently new pattern of life, one which makes demands on the scientist's administrative and political abilities. It also requires a reorientation of values and aspirations. The scientist, raised in a tradition of science where the great discoverer is preeminent, does not find it easy to abandon his ego-ideal as an active researcher and is prone to internal conflicts in his new roles. The older eminent scientist, although filling some key position important to the development of science in his country, may yet not find his office deeply satisfying. Looking back upon former days of active investigation, he may view his present activities as a 'lesser task.' Thus the justifications of the non-research position may not even convince the person himself, let alone his colleagues. Some scientists, commenting on colleagues who have become saddled down with administrative

responsibilities, claim that these men 'asked for it,' that it is for them a 'socially accepted escape from freedom ... a decorous way of concealing that they are burned out.'

(Reif and Strauss, 1965, p. 309; cf. Glaser, 1964, p. 1012)

Such a 'scientific menopause' (Reif and Strauss, 1965, p. 309) is frequently connected to resigning from a previously held self-image and abandoning the long-cherished ideals of a profession. It may be associated with many kinds of career shifts before someone is used to their new roles and can transform their identity, and this can be seen in many occupations where a change of status is connected to changes in the character of a job that are incongruent with the core vocational identity. There are many examples indicating the presence of dissatisfaction and boredom among scientists who are at the top of their careers, as heads of their research group, unit, or institution, for instance. The schedule of such scientists (perceived as a successful person by their colleagues) is usually composed of staff meetings, typical group management tasks, money raising activities (preparing grant proposals for large groups, reports etc.), interviews (hiring new persons), selections (being members of various committees), evaluations (of the work of others, e.g. writing reviews), keynote speeches, mentoring PhD students, and also taking care of infrastructure, if the field necessitates expensive equipment (Zuckerman, 1967; Wagner, 2011a). Several of these activities do not directly affect an individual's advance in science – such scientists frequently call themselves 'managers of science' as they have no more time to actually undertake research.

Comparative failure

Boredom that emerges from the incongruence between previous expectations and existing realities can in many ways be perceived as one of many particularities of academic culture. Barney Glaser (1964) analysed the phenomenon of comparative failure, the negative feelings experienced by some researchers who perceive themselves as not 'good enough' when not achieving major recognition in their fields in comparison to other more recognized colleagues and/or scientific idols (famous scientists of the past). Joseph Hermanowicz (1998) studied physics specialists and showed how this phenomenon is dependent on the institution from which a scientist obtained their PhD – and thus, on the place of professional socialization. Immersion into an elite scientific environment significantly increases expectations about levels of achievement. Yet, it is extremely difficult to fulfil expectations during a career, especially if working in non-elite institutions requiring more teaching and bureaucracy, and providing worse working conditions in terms of equipment, space quality and/or scientific environment. This is a frequent reason why so many scientists educated in the top institutions and/

or holding high career aspirations, may experience a sense of comparative failure. This phenomenon can contribute to chronic boredom and long-term demotivation, and decreased involvement in a job. Such boredom can be prompted by abandoning life goals and replacing them with another, less desirable ones (see Bargdill, 2014). As one of the respondents conceded:

> Oh, yes, I get bored, all my life is boring, I have this impression. I once dreamed that I would be a geologist, a paleoanthropologist, and become someone like Indiana Jones, instead I became someone between Indiana Jones and Al Bundy, so all my life is somewhat boring.
> (Teacher, interview_25, male, PhD, humanities)

At the University of Warsaw, as at many similar institutions suspended between high aspirations and limited potential and opportunities, ambitious aspirations can often be only partially fulfilled, if at all. At some point a person has to abandon some ideals and accommodate to an everyday workplace experience. Boredom, therefore, is one of the possible outcomes of an incongruence between aspirations and self-image and the opportunities provided by a system/an institution.

An example of this process may be transnational researchers who, thanks to prestigious research grants/scholarships have an opportunity to work at the best Western institutions, and some of whom feel depressed and chronically bored after their return to Poland (Wagner, 2011a, p. 154). They began to feel comparative failure, as they had worked at the highest international level and now collided with a set of both personal and institutional constraints that made it impossible to maintain their expected level of research performance. Some even expressed direct regret about having ever returned.

Boredom and career dynamics

Boredom, its causes and perceptions, can vary according to one's career stage. Of course, there are also many differences between disciplines (or even subdisciplines), countries and cultures or organizational practices, nevertheless, some characteristics of boredom can be observed at specific career stages. At the very beginning of a scientific career, reasons for boredom, or the withdrawal of engagement due to a sense of meaninglessness, are mainly associated with a lack of belonging to the institution, due to precarious employment (no future prospects), a flawed recruitment system (not being an integral part of an institution) and a low position in the highly hierarchical structure of a university (being delegated to do dirty work, for example, teaching introductory courses or simply classes not of one's choice). This last issue means that junior staff are more frequently bored owing to 'dirty work' which is delegated to them, the menial, frequently tedious tasks such as washing glass in laboratories, being a unit's secretary, writing grant proposals for the unit or doing interview transcriptions for older colleagues. They more frequently feel stress because of employment uncertainty, the high pressure of applying for grants, publishing in international journals, and/or achieving habilitation in due time. Some also have problems with academic identity which they feel involves research, and are then greatly shocked by their multi-job overload – especially high teaching loads, with courses frequently out of one's field of direct expertise. Junior academics are thus much more affected by the current academic system, in which they are simultaneously in the lowest position on the food chain but also the main pillars of the system – the resemblance to wage-workers, or semi-slaves is thus evident. Such circumstances may create trajectorial potential in one. As generalized concept of trajectory specified, trajectory constitutes an experience associated with

> ... social processes structured by conditional chains of events that one cannot avoid without high costs, constant breaks of expectations, and a growing and irritating sense of loss of control over one's life circumstances. One feels that one is driven, that one can only react to "outer forces" that one does not understand any more.
> (Riemann and Schütze, 1991, p. 337)

The original concept (Strauss and Glaser, 1970) emerged from research into terminally ill patients, whose dying was quintessentially an unstructured anomic experience of losing control over their lives. Later, the notion was found applicable for many kinds of life-experiences connected to an extremely limiting sense of agency (e.g. migration). In the life of some young PhDs, an 'institutional expectation patterns' (normative principle of biography) overwhelms 'biographical action schemes' (intentional principle) disturbing 'existing structures of social order in biographies' (Riemann and Schütze, 1991, p. 339). An individual's expectations, ideals, and visions of their biography clash with institutional requirements and the realities of the research-teaching university position, which may result in a sense of losing control over life. An overload of duties that are often not compatible with one's interests and exceed one's expectations may create high trajectorial potential.

Senior, tenured staff live in a different, yet not necessarily boredom-free, reality. Such academics may be bored due to hierarchical obstacles limiting their agency, but they are not subject to precarious employment schemes and their sense of belonging to the institution is much higher. They can suffer burnout symptoms as a result of previous excessive effort to obtain a permanent position, but they may still be subjected to the overload of multi-job. An interesting observation in my research is that each category of academics cherishes some hope that they will have more time for core-identity activities (especially for doing research) in the next, higher position. PhDs overloaded with organizational and teaching duties expect that after obtaining habilitation they will quicken their research, but when it happens it turns out that their new duties, such as obligatory participation in staff meetings, being members of degree committees and/or reviewing the work of others (e.g. habilitation books or PhD theses) and exercising administrational functions (e.g. as deans, directors, chief of units) efficiently prevents many from major scientific advances. For instance, one respondent conceded that he would have never published his results without a major collaboration with his PhD student, thanks to which they were able to analyse data the professor had gathered 15 years ago before he was granted some important administrative positions at the institution.

Boredom among senior staff can also be a consequence of one's scientific success in obtaining symbolic capital (recognition) in one's field. As Joseph Hermanowicz (1998) noted, if one was once called an expert, it is difficult in some (sub)disciplines to change this. Such academics are frequently expected to continue highly-level research in a particular subject despite being bored or simply tired of it, but changing a field of expertise would require additional work and time to make a name in the new field and a high risk of failure to achieve comparable recognition to that gained in the previous field. As a result, some academics remain in the same research area despite a lack of major cognitive challenges and needs in that field, which may result, among other things, in boredom.

Notes

1. That is not to say that before the introduction of New Public Management to universities all academics were free from bureaucracy, administrative duties, evaluation, frustration, boredom, etc., but that there is a visible tendency for governments to impose more managerial control and philosophy that strongly affect the conditions in which academics operate, and to which they are socialized.
2. In Polish academia, there is a set of subsequent research-teaching positions in the hierarchical order of the institution through which each academic has to pass through: (1) assistant, (2) adjunct, (3) associate professor, and (4) full professor. I generally treat first two positions as junior staff and the last two as senior staff in this study. The Polish academic system, as some other European, non-Anglo-Saxon systems, has an institution of habilitation, i.e. another scientific degree after PhD, the achievement of which is usually equal to becoming an independent academic. It is noteworthy, however, that the division between junior and senior staff is not always congruent with the distinction between an academic with habilitation or without one, as on many occasions obtaining habilitation is not equal to advancing to the associate professor position (cf. Rodzik, 2016). For instance, at the University of Warsaw at the time of conducting present study, there were about 700 habilitation holders employed on the positions of adjunct (Godlewicz-Adamiec, Łuczyńska-Hołdys, and Opalińska, 2019).

3 University Study-Oriented System is the software system supporting information management in most Polish universities. It is used by students to enrol for classes/exams, monitor grades, and fill out application forms, and by teachers to monitor course participants and grade them.
4 The term 'underemployment' can also denote situations in which an institution employs workers who are not fully occupied. Alternative terms include 'disguised unemployment,' 'overstaffing,' or 'hidden unemployment.'
5 The situation seems to be gradually improving, but the introduction of the new neoliberal academic order was evidently not supported by an adequate administrative staff increase in terms of either quantity or quality (specialization).
6 As one respondent shared: 'Administrative duties take an awful lot of time, ... there I have drawers with scientific work, which I have not looked at for a few months, because there is no time, which is also sad' (Teacher, interview_55, female, hab., natural sciences).
7 'Some "superiors" in chairs or units push dirty, administrative work onto assistants, who often face a dilemma: whether to finish a buried article, or to fill in administrative shit given to them by a superior ... or conduct classes that then go to that superior's "account"', J, commentary to Zawisławska, 2017).
8 In the original (Polish): 'Moja wszystkim jest porada –/ Do szuflady pisma składać./ Gdy co ważne – sobie myślę –/ Wróci do nas drugim pismem' (translated by Anna Krutulska-Finkielsztein).
9 For example, meticulous repetitions of subsequent actions in the experiments, time-consuming cross-checking to confirm previously obtained data or pursuing strict codes of procedures required by ethical as well as safety protocols.
10 As the research of Jerry Jacobs (2004) showed, based on data drawn from the US' 1998 National Study of Postsecondary Faculty (NSOPF), the average weekly work hours of academic staff amounted to 54.8 for men and 52.8 for women and that 38.1% of men and 32.5% of women declared to work even over 60 hours per week.
11 The number of PhD students enrolled in PhD programmes at the Polish higher education institutions increased from 2,695 in the academic year 1990/91 to 41,318 in 2017/18 (GUS, 2005, 2018).

Chapter 5

Academic boredom in practice

The current chapter scrutinizes the situational boredom of consecutive academic activities performed by academics as an inherent part of their job. The exact order in which the content will be presented, is derived from the results of the tendency analysis displayed in Tables 5.1 and 5.2, showing how many respondents admitted to experiencing boredom in a given activity. Boredom was most commonly reported in scientific conferences, slightly less in staff meetings (especially faculty meetings), then teaching and research-related activities. Bureaucratic duties, which are significant time- and attention-consuming activities, were rarely directly connected with boredom and were analysed in the previous chapter.

The above tables are a succinct illustration of the outcomes of tendency analysis based on qualitative data, and are not to be analysed statistically in any way. The qualitative sample cannot be seen as representative, and conclusions concerning tendencies are tentative if not corroborated by observation or other data. The main focus of the chapter is to understand the dynamics of boredom in various areas of academic work. The above data does require a short commentary and explanation, however. There is an observable and known fact that age is a negative predictor of boredom, and so it is not surprising that professors tend to feel less bored during teaching and conferences as well as in private, but it can also be hypothesized that professors are less likely to admit to boredom, and are probably also much better boredom preventers and copers. For example, the main reason that professors are found not to be bored at conferences is because many of the respondent professors reported rarely or never attending conferences in the first place. Faculty meetings tend to be less boring for habilitation holders and more boring for PhDs – it can be hypothesized that freshly habilitated members of council perceived them as more interesting due to their novelty, and PhDs as less involving due to their lack of agency (they do not have a right to vote) and not being steady council members (they are temporary representatives of 'dependent' employees).

Table 5.1 Frequencies of respondents' boredom according to activities and disciplines

Do you ever feel bored during/at …		Disciplines			Frequencies	
		Social	Humanities	Natural	N	%
Conferences	Yes	16	16	11	43	59.72
Staff meetings	Yes	10	10	8	28	60.87*
(faculty meetings)	NA**	11	8	7	26	
Teaching	Yes	6	12	7	25	34.72
Research-related	Yes	5	6	6	17	23.61
Outside university job	Yes	8	13	7	28	38.89
Total number of participants		25	24	23	72	100

* 26 participants were not regular or periodic members of faculty boards – this percentage is calculated only for those who was obliged to partake in them.
** Not applicable.

Scientific conferences

> The turgid/self-aggrandizing keynotes and coma-inducing panels, followed by people (usually men) asking 'questions' that are really comments, and usually not on topic. The chairs who abdicate responsibility and let all the speakers over-run, so that the only genuinely productive bit of the day (networking at coffee breaks and lunch) gets squeezed. I end up dozing off, or furiously scribbling abuse in my notebook as a form of therapy, and hoping my neighbours can't see what I'm writing. I probably look a bit unhinged.
> (Green, 2016)

Boredom was most commonly mentioned in the context of scientific conferences – about 60% of my respondents admitted to at least occasional feelings of boredom during such gatherings, which is corroborated by many informal statements from various disciplines. For instance, social psychologist,

Table 5.2 Frequencies of respondents' boredom according to activities and degree

Do you ever feel bored during/at …		Degree			
		MA	PhD	Hab.	Prof.
Conferences	Yes	8 (66%)	13 (56.5%)	14 (70%)	8 (44%)
Staff meetings (faculty meetings)	Yes	0	9 (81.8%)	8 (44.4%)	11 (61%)
	NA	12	12	2	0
Teaching	Yes	6 (50%)	8 (34.8%)	9 (45%)	2 (11%)
Research-related	Yes	4 (33%)	6 (26.1%)	4 (20%)	3 (16%)
Outside university job	Yes	9 (75%)	12 (52.2%)	3 (15%)	4 (22%)
Total number of participants		12	23	20	18

Mihaly Csikszentmihalyi, referring to professor Heinz Maier-Leibnitz, the ascendant of famous philosopher and mathematician, called 'having to sit through endless, often boring conferences' a kind of 'occupational handicap common to academicians' (cf. Barley, 1989). As Duncan Green (2016) confessed: 'With the occasional exception, my mood in conferences usually swings between boredom, despair and rage.' 'Conference presentations – as Patrick Gamsby (2012, p. 11) noted – can serve as an example of the proliferation of boredom masked only by the absence of it being verbalized.' As an example of this statement, he cited Slovenian philosopher and psychoanalyst, Slavoj Žižek (2006) who suggested that the most polite way to imply that a presentation was boring is to say that it was 'interesting.' Some of my respondents claimed that 'the vast majority of scientific conferences are deadly boring' (Teacher, interview_21, male, hab., humanities), others that boredom is quite a rare guest at such events. Interestingly, the least bored definitely seem to be representatives of the natural sciences (especially biology), and the most bored are from humanities and the social sciences. According to some life science respondents, conferences are a good springboard from their usual work in laboratories. Conferences in such disciplines also seem to more frequently serve as job markets, and conference networking is a way to search for a prospective employee, or to look for another project/position.

The most frequently mentioned symptoms of boredom in conferences are (1) general inattention/disengagement ('of course, I sometimes disconnect on a particularly unsuccessful paper, but it is such a disconnection that I draw something and don't listen to a person,' Teacher, interview_10, male, hab., social sciences), (2) sleepiness ('I often zone out at conferences, this is not good, and I see that a lot of people have the same problem, I see people fighting simply with sleep, fighting for life,' Teacher, interview_21, male, hab., humanities), and (3) external preoccupations/secondary activities performed during the sessions.

Organizers commonly give three official purposes for scientific conferences: (1) presenting and discussing research outcomes (possibly research plans as well), (2) popularizing science in general or a specific discipline/subject in particular, and (3) integrating of the scientific milieu and establishing personal connections. All of these suggest exchange, interaction, and communication. Here boredom is to be analysed as an outcome and/or one of the crucial causes of not fulfilling some of these functions insofar as it is an emotion basically hindering communication, ceasing interaction, and making any sort of exchange ineffective, superficial, or banal. The main causes of ineffective conference communication are: (1) a format of conference presentations, (2) quantitative (to lesser extent also qualitative) overload, (3) the opportunism or cynicism of some participants, which may increase, and (4) a lack of actual integration, making the conference an empty ritual.

Format and content of presentation

The lion's share of conference time is spent on presentation sessions, which overall quality is considerably dependent on the form and content of individual papers. Those respondents who reported occasional feeling of boredom at conferences ascribed it above all to the tediousness of presentations. Listening to tedious papers evoked a deep sense of time-wasting, which many actively counteract with various kinds of coping strategies. For others, however, such a situation constitutes a vital issue for consideration because they believe leaving the room and/or looking inattentive is against the basic rules of propriety. Respondents noted that 'some papers are very boring, you can see that someone is neither a good speaker nor has anything special to say, so one is bored' (Teacher, interview_25, male, PhD, humanities), and that many present 'in such a narcissistic manner, he preaches what he has to say, not particularly considering whether it is interesting or not for the public, a significant proportion of people have no talent for presenting at conferences and do it in a way that is not very interesting' (Teacher, interview_46, male, hab., humanities). The main qualities of presenters that contribute to a feeling of boredom were described by respondents as: a lack of presenting skills/predispositions, chaotic, poorly-prepared, overloaded presentations, excessive pace[1] or extreme slowness and/or monotony of speaking, lack of charisma/engagement/visible desire to share, excessive self-preoccupation, lack of communicative skills/intentions, i.e. speaking to themselves or to no one, characterized by a lack of eye contact with the audience (speaking to screen, to the presentation on the wall, to some spot beyond the audience, to the moderator only, to a piece of paper with the text of the presentation, to the floor or sitting and hiding behind a computer monitor), and by rambling under the breath, speaking too quietly, appearing bored by/uninterested in their own presentation. Nonetheless, as tedious as papers might be, some respondents noted that many such presentations may have their merits: one can at least note some useful keywords, gain some minor understanding of the subject/field or they can constitute the basis for very good articles afterwards; nevertheless, the majority find such presentations misplaced, as they would prefer read them rather than be compelled to listen to them.

A crucial issue raised by many participants was reading out conference papers, which also includes 'terrible powerpoints crammed with too many words and illegible graphics' (Green, 2016).

> I switch off the most if it is a reading paper and yet read so monotonously and I catch myself when I stop grasping the meaning, I'm listening to the language as a sound, I start to completely turn off understanding in favour of that it's going like a melody, and if it is monotonous, it still puts me to sleep.
> (Teacher, interview_54, female, MA, natural sciences)

> The people who read from the sheet [of paper] drive me crazy ... then it's really hard for me to concentrate, such text read out loud, though, is completely different to absorb/ingest and these are the moments in which I'm bored.
> (Teacher, interview_60, female, PhD, social sciences)[2]

According to those respondents, reading presentations is a negation of the will to communicate anything. Many of such readers lose, at least partially, their connection with the audience to such an extent that it is sometimes difficult for the moderator to inform them of the approaching time limit – several times during my observations at conferences I witnessed situations where presenters were not able to see the card with time left, held by the moderator, for a long while.

The decline in engagement can be mutual. 'Spoken language is different than written language, has a different syntax and if we hear the second one, instead of the first one, then we switch off automatically, I think that's not only me [*laughs*]' (Teacher, interview_45, female, PhD, social sciences). By all means, there are different kinds of reading: performative reading that imitates spoken language, includes changes in intonation and in general suggests a higher level of preparedness, as far as the readers should have prepared not only the text itself but also themselves to read it competently. The majority of such presentations do not reach these standards, however, being merely more or less monotonously-read. This is equally true for reading presentation from the slides.

> It is unpleasant for the listener ... when people are reading their papers, because I also know that ... [sometimes] the text is prepared simply for reading, but such a text is completely differently prepared, and when someone reads it from slides and has entire slides of text, it's simply terribly painful for the listener.
> (Teacher, interview_20, female, MA, humanities)

To make things worse, some presenters do not read papers prepared for reading aloud, but rather articles that are to be published or even have already been published (see Kulczycki, 2012), which raises justified questions about the purpose of such presentations and takes us back to the reservation that some respondents had, that published articles are a far more effective and meaningful way of communicating science.

One of the participants noted that 'not everyone is aware that reading a fifteen-page paper in a monotonous voice puts to sleep [even] the most avid' (Teacher, interview_4, female, PhD, social sciences)? I dare to doubt that. I believe it to be a deliberate decision based on a simple pros and cons analysis (game theory would be probably applicable here). There are plethora of possible reasons for reading at conferences. First of all, it may be employed as an effective strategy to significantly reduce the amount of time needed to prepare for publication. One writes a text for a conference, and simultaneously saves time by not preparing any kind of presentation, and has a draft of a paper for the conference proceedings, monograph, or journal. Second, it can evoke a sense of control over one's presentation and its duration, insofar as one of the most frequently employed excuses for reading is to maintain 'time discipline,' which, *nota bene*, at times turns out to be completely misplaced, as presenters prepare texts that are too long, begin with lengthy spoken introductions or interrupt their reading with various kinds of (both on- and off-topic) interjections. Third, a major reason for reading may be a lack of self-confidence with language, and/or a low level of language skills, which is especially likely in big, international conferences that are also perceived as the most boring by many respondents. Unsurprisingly, the problem is most relevant for non-native speakers of English, as the majority of international conferences are held in this language. Some researchers are not competent enough to present confidently in English, which, according to my observations, is primarily the case for older researchers who have begun to learn the language late in their life, and/or grew up when English was not yet so vital a tool for communicating science. Such presenters frequently read texts heavily modified by proofreaders or simply translated *in toto* from their mother tongues. In extreme cases they may barely understand the meaning of the read words. The accent of some presenters can also be an obstacle to becoming engrossed in a presentation, and hinder its understanding.

> Frequently I understand nothing of what people are saying, because ... they just read and it seems to them that if they read in some way, they don't have to bother about how it should be said, because it is already written and if it's written correctly, so they will read it and it's okay, but it's not like that.
> (Teacher, interview_67, male, hab., humanities)

In some cases reading may be a preferable strategy within the framework of the current management culture ruling over the academic world, which places much emphasis on high scientific productivity, harsh competition and meticulous evaluation procedures (Halffman and Radder, 2015). In that kind of culture, reading articles that are already published or even advanced versions of finished texts may appear to some academics a highly reasonable strategy preventing the theft of ideas by other academics attending conferences in hope of gaining 'inspiration' (cf. Wagner, 2011a). Without negating the likelihood of such practices (I have been told about such practices several times), this reason for reading seems quite weak to me, as one might mention their published paper in the spoken presentation with the same effect of deterrence (from 'stealing'). The reason behind this practice is probably slightly different, namely, it is another strategy to save time preparing conference papers, which is very reasonable in a system where gaining credits is the ultimate aim of scientific activity (regardless of the form and quality of conference presentations, all attendees receive the same credit for participation).

Conference culture (and socialization within it) may also encourage reading as a form of presentation. It came as a surprise to me that there are some disciplinary cultures where reading conference papers is an accepted and even expected practice, testifying to scientific maturity and professionalism. There seem to be two contradictory approaches claiming reading conference papers as either a lack of professionalism or as proof of it. From my observations and according to my respondents, the culture of reading seems to be most common in Polish philology and less extensive in linguistics and educational studies. I have seen many presenters from these fields and the vast majority actually read their presentations. Some of my respondents (from both inside and outside these disciplines) who have attended conferences from these fields also observed this tendency. For these disciplines, or some groups within these disciplinary environments, reading papers seems to be such a common social practice that it has become a core part of disciplinary socialization.

Representatives of such fields often explicitly or implicitly criticize the very idea of 'performative' forms of conference papers as less professional and scientific. They are perfectly right in that many PowerPoint or other kinds of presentations are often poorly prepared, and do not include much concrete scientific content, being simply implausible displays of some barely-reflected hypotheses. There is a whole genre of 'performative' conference papers, excessively focused on the visual side of the presentation with a loss in the quality of the content, which according to many do not fit with the idea of a scientific meeting. In terms of boredom, we can say that listeners are caught between the devil and the deep blue sea, i.e. either bored by monotonous reading (see the first kind of boredom in Heidegger, 1995) or bored due to appealing and interactive presentations which afterwards are recognized as empty platitudes (see the second kind of boredom in Heidegger, 1995). A third option is possible – intense socialization to reading presentations over time means that its boring sting becomes blunt and the people embedded in such environments get used to it even to the extent of immunization.

The reading adherents argue that the quality of scientific content can be improved by saving time in preparing presentations, however, to my way of thinking, this argument is not sufficient, as the mere fact that the text of the presentation is written does not necessarily reflect its scientific quality, because the time-saving principle is often considered superior to all others; where there are constant shortages of time some academics save time both on preparing the content and the presentation itself. To some extent, this point may be corroborated by the fact that many presenters are still working on, or even hectically finishing, their presentations at the last minute before their due time. In the majority of cases, it is not the praiseworthy practice of perfectionism (polishing the presentation) but rather stems from spending too little time on preparing it before the conference. It may also testify to the relatively low status of conference presentations, especially in comparison to scientific papers.

To my mind, the ultimate, though unspoken, reason for reading a presentation is the assumption that it is exemplary scientific, which corresponds to a deeply inscribed vision of scientists/scholars and science in some disciplines, or at least in some of their representatives. A scientist/scholar should be serious, deliberate, precise, intellectually disciplined, led by reason – in short, be scientific. In this regard, though, written, formal language appears far more scientific than spoken language in a presentation. To be scientific, therefore, one should present boringly, use disciplinary jargon, be as concrete and intellectualized as possible, regardless of losses to communication. As Baghdadchi (2005) suggested, scientific language was not invented to be entertaining or interesting but to 'withstand attack' by 'the construction of rigorous arguments' and '[i]f an audience finds a rigorously argued piece of scholarship boring, that is their problem, since they cannot expect that it was written for their enjoyment' (p. 322). One of the aims of the conference presentation is therefore to prove one's ability to produce such arguments in that language. I would even hypothesize that boredom is sometimes recognized as the basic quality of being scientific: unless you are able to be perfectly boring on demand, you cannot be recognized as a scientist/scholar. No one openly says it, but if we were asked to compare two presentations, one of which was vivid, 'performative' and limited in its use of jargon, and another turgid, jargon-ridden and boring, assuming that their content was at the same scientific level (and if one was able to objectively assess and compare it), the majority would identify the second as more 'scientific,' because the more incomprehensive a presentation seems, the more credit it may obtain (this is especially relevant in presentations outside one's specialty). Reading may thus be a strategy to create and maintain one's (self-)image as a highly competent, professional, and well-socialized member of the scientific/scholarly milieu. As a result, some conferences might be boring, or dull 'by normal standards' (Barley, 1983), as boredom is virtually a prerequisite of being competent (not by itself but because many qualities of 'scientific quality' are intimately associated with the concept).

Another reason for conference boredom mentioned by the respondents was predictability, or the repetitiveness of presentations, which is epitomized by rediscovering well-established knowledge, repeating one's presentation at numerous conferences, speaking on the same subject all the time or a low quality of presentation in terms of its originality and depth of analysis. As one of the respondents noted:

> If there is a paper from my field and I see that it is boring or poor, then usually this boredom will be accompanied by frustration, because I see someone mess up scientific work, or [a paper] is boring in terms of 'come on, you should read this [the literature in a field] instead of discovering America here, 10 years ago people wrote about it, do your lesson.'
> (Teacher, interview_19, male, MA, social sciences)

Boredom may, thus, be positively correlated with one's knowledge of a particular field. If one specializes in the subject they may find many presentations 'not very revealing' (Teacher, interview_36, female, MA, humanities), because they repeat concepts that are well-known within the domain, reproduce platitudes and clichés or describe widely-used methodology that is presented as a revelation but is perceived as patency in other disciplines. As one of the respondents said about one of the conferences he used to attend:

> ... at some point I felt that nothing new was going on ... it is either constantly discovering the same [thing], because, for example, people who don't have pedagogical and teaching competences discover things that have already been known for a long time in pedagogy, such as how to conduct classes with adults, in turn, ... other people who represent the humanities, social milieus, 'discover' technical tools that have long been known and have been used for a long time.
> (Teacher, interview_22, male, PhD, social sciences)

Another problem may be attending conferences in which the same people participate all the time, especially when one may know their work from written publications. As one of the respondents pointed out:

> In the case of scientific conferences, it seems to me that contact between us today, thanks to new media, thanks to books, thanks to the circulation of papers, is very tight, it's nice to meet these people, but when I meet them for the tenth time and hear how for the tenth time they say more or less the same [things], they talk about the same research ....
> (Teacher, interview_21, male, hab., humanities)

All these things may contribute to the feeling of boredom insofar as it does not engage participants on an optimal level. The whole formula of the scientific conference itself limits opportunities to engage in a meaningful, productive, and cognitively rewarding way, unless opportunities are provided by the presentation, which, in addition to the hotness and stuffiness that characterizes many conference rooms, may result in sleepiness and/or boredom.

Some respondents noted that scientific conferences do not provide them with enough novelty and cognitive added value. As one of the respondents claimed:

> I have come to the conclusion for a while that I don't gain anything at scientific conferences, if I'm already going this is because someone has a request in this matter. I don't learn anything anymore, I don't have any intellectual needs that would be satisfied.
> (Teacher, interview_50, female, prof., humanities)

Boredom might be also prompted by a lack of interest in the subject of a particular presentation or session. The least boring conferences are perceived those with one major subject and not too many participants (middle-sized thematic conferences), which seem to hold relatively high levels of interest in the content of presentations, simultaneously avoiding the problem of anonymity. Lack of interest may constitute major problem at the big conference with many simultaneous sessions on different subjects or disciplinary conferences with high level of variety and intricacy of content. One may wrongly choose sessions that do not meet their expectations, may be not interested in each subject presented and unless the presenter does manage to arouse their audience interest, boredom might constitute a prompt answer.

> there are definitely such papers on which I sit and I think about them to end, but not because they are bad, simply because I'm not interested at all, and people don't have that ability to grip the listener.
> (Teacher, interview_20, female, MA, humanities)

The problem might also be too broadly defined thematic scope of the conference – there are plenty of '**ragbag conferences**,' as I would be inclined to call them, with titles such as 'Human and Society,' 'Challenges of Modern Life,' etc. that hope to attract as many participants as possible simply to make profit and/or produce academic credits for their organizers. Ragbag conferences and the big, international ones cover the whole variety of subjects and it is perfectly understandable that not everything is to be found equally interesting for everyone.

> [O]ur field is quite narrow, but on the other hand there are different branches, and I admit that not all branches are fascinating for me, so for example, I don't know, I cannot remember that I was at a conference that was very general, because it seems to me that with such, it can be boring, when there ... basically everyone is talking about everything.'
> (Teacher, interview_20, female, MA, humanities)

Another consequence of interdisciplinary or broader disciplinary conferences not consolidated by concrete subject may be boredom due to lack of content understanding. One not having sufficient knowledge in the subject of a presentation is not able to attentively follow the content and, as a result, may withdraw their engagement altogether. This situation, though perfectly possible in any discipline, seems to be more common in those where the processes of specialization are highly prolific and usage of technical, very advanced and distinct language especially indispensable to adequately communicate the subject. This is specific for example, for mathematics, where lack of understanding appears to be quite widespread irrespectively of scientific experience. Below two excerpts derived from young and senior academic illustrate the point.

> Mathematics is such an area that if you don't have something, the basics then you don't know what is going on, and it doesn't sometimes make sense to follow the conference, what is happening, because if you don't know at all, so it doesn't matter if you understand the transition from A to B, because you still don't know what the whole presentation is about, so at conferences, I often get bored, because I simply don't know what's going on.
> (Teacher, interview_34, female, MA, natural sciences)

> The presentation ... may be incomprehensible for various reasons, due to the lack of preparation of the listener, even though I have already seen, read, listened to many things, sometimes I'm unprepared ... the fact that one sits at the lecture and doesn't understand nothing or almost nothing from it, it is not an exception, it is close to the norm, it's really very common ... in my field it is quite typical and difficult to avoid that jargon is used, without this you cannot communicate the information.
> (Teacher, interview_69, male, prof., natural sciences)

At times, when a presentation is outside one's field of expertise, minor lapse of attention (due to exhaustion, for example) may result in getting lost and a deterioration in understanding. There may also be difficulties with understanding the language of the presentation due to poor accent and/or the language skills of a presenter, or lack of sufficient language competency on the part of a listener. Come conferences in the field of linguistics are a radical example of the latter, where, especially at the international level, presentations are frequently held in more than one language. Within one session there might thus be papers delivered in two or three languages.

> Due to the fact that I deal with linguistics, translation, sometimes I go to presentations that are in a language I don't know, if the conference

is international and, for example, it is a programme arranged in such a way that there is a given time, for example, two [papers] in German and two in Russian, I don't know these languages, so if I want to go anywhere, or not go out of the room for these 20 minutes, then I sit and I don't understand, so then I get bored.
(Teacher, interview_36, female, MA, humanities)

In general, therefore, boredom may be induced by anything in the form or content of a presentation that baffles communication, make the content useless, or meaningless or discourages attentive participation.

Overload of conference assembly line

Another major factor contributing to conference boredom noted by my respondents was overload in many different meanings. The sole idea of a conference meeting involves many hours a day spent sitting and listening to various presentations. It is difficult to maintain interest and a high level of attention throughout the entire conference day. From that perspective boredom may be a natural defensive mechanism against content overload.

It is impossible to always be active for an hour, especially so receptively, so maybe boredom is such a defence of the organism, the brain ... because if I have to absorb content that I don't need, and I have quite a lot of absorbed content on a regular basis, somehow disordered, ill-conceived, not sleeping on it, so maybe it's simply a defensive reaction, I think, you cannot be on the high gear all the time, I think boredom is needed sometimes, although you can feel it as something unpleasant because I'm bored, why do I sit here, I'm wasting my time [*laughs*].
(Teacher, interview_62, female, PhD, social sciences)

This kind of overload may involve a general satiety with conference participation that over time may prompt a substantial decrease in engagement.

When you are at the first conference, you absorb everything, listen to it, because even when there are topics distant/unknown for me, you listen because "I'm at the conference" and then when you have a few conferences each year it's a little bit like overeating. Well, the first ice-cream always tastes good, but when you eat five ice-creams every day, it tastes a little less well.
(Teacher, interview_2, male, hab., humanities)

The most devastating problem is therefore quantitative overload. There are more and more conferences organized each year and, importantly, the majority of their programmes are crowded with too many presentations to the level of nausea. Many respondents claimed such conferences as increasingly widespread standard which puts the very idea of a conference meeting to question, because listening attentively to a dozen or more presentations per day is near to impossible (approximately 15 to 20 15- or 20-minute presentations per day seems to be common practice).

Many respondents shared a reluctance to attend big, international congresses gathering great numbers of academics – these are also claimed to be the most boring.

> Sometimes there are big congresses, where there are a lot of short presentations, simultaneous sessions, but these are conferences you don't want to attend, sometimes you attend for social reasons, to meet someone with whom, instead of going to these presentations, you sit somewhere in the corner and work, but ... I don't like [them], and I'm not alone.
> (Teacher, interview_59, male, PhD, natural sciences)

> Whereas the most boring conferences are those large, big conferences, where the absolute scientific top arrives, etc., where the entry fee costs a huge amount of money, and sometimes it is just boredom, boredom, boredom and boredom again. They are often ill-conceived, chaotic, with mega far-fetched sessions there.
> (Teacher, interview_25, male, PhD, humanities)

Irrespective of their size, many conferences currently resemble industrial assembly lines. One presenter goes after another, and another, and another, then after one session there is another session and so on for two, three, four, even five days. Sessions take place in some cases from 8–9 a.m. even to 9 p.m., breaks become shorter and shorter because the organization of the conferences is more and more frequently ruled by the logic of capitalistic production. The more participants can be squeezed into the programme, the more money will be raised and the more profit/less loss will be created for the organizing institution and/or the more prestige will be credited to the organizers. I saw many conferences with simultaneous sessions when the only audience at each was the presenters – thanks to that more participants could be accepted. In some cases, organizers accept (almost) all received abstracts only to have audience at all, because no institution refunds passive attendance – one is paid only when they deliver a paper. This begets situation of casual participation: attendance motivated simply by a general interest in the subject without having any real content to present.

The conference assembly line may result in producing fatigue and sleepiness in some participants, and thus, be a cause of conference boredom. By all means, those states might have been prompted by other factors such as intensive social activities the previous evening, minor indispositions or exhaustion accumulated before the event, but an excess of (even valuable) presentations in a particular unit of time can be perfectly sufficient to trigger this effect.

Another consequence of the Fordisation of scientific conferences may be limited time for discussion, especially during sessions, but sometimes also outside them.

> There is not always time to ask questions, because sometimes these conferences are so overloaded with presenters that there is no time even for discussion. There is no time even to stand somewhere and talk.
> (Teacher, interview_4, female, PhD, social sciences)

> For me, conferences are associated with deadly boredom and what hurts me the most is the lack of a real exchange of information, a genuine dialogue during such conferences.
> (Teacher, interview_46, male, hab., humanities)

Moderators are often unsuccessful in keeping 'time discipline' which may result in limiting time for discussion. Sometimes the thematic scope is so broad or participants so exhausted that there are no questions at all. Another issue involves a culture of criticizing instead of debating. Some respondents observed that sometimes people taking the floor during the time scheduled for discussion simply comment or criticize the presentation or presenters themselves. Some suggest that it is a strategy (even if only unconscious) to show off, a form of 'narcissism in bad taste' (Teacher, interview_46, male, hab., humanities), to make an impression of being well-informed and better, and thus to undertake personal marketing, gaining symbolic capital, and elevating themselves by 'trampling/intimidating' a presenter and only a few people actually want to find out anything at all. A boring presentation is often followed by a poor discussion, which may be boring in itself (some respondents also observed the opposite phenomenon – interesting discussion after tedious presentation) – either because there is no discussion at all or there is no actual exchange of thoughts that could stimulate participants. Much depends on the particular conference, particular session, moderator, discipline and participants, and discussions are the only redeeming feature at many events.

Opportunism

A substantial factor in conference boredom may involve the opportunism of some participants, encouraged by the current system of academic management and evaluation. The system requires as many credits/points/achievements to be obtained as possible, which is especially relevant for academics on short-time contracts working in precarious conditions. Here is how one of the respondents explained his participation in a conference.

> The programme of this conference itself is terribly boring, terribly horrible, but you have to go, say your piece, do 'achiev,' i.e. publications,

conferences, attendances etc., 'achiev' is a language cancer [derived] from an administrative language, the funniest thing is that there are people who have to have achiev and there are people who don't have to have it and people who simply have done nothing for years, nothing completely, they have nothing to show off ... and the rest has to do achiev in order to spin it around somehow, the so-called pecking order.
(Teacher, interview_25, male, PhD, social sciences)

As emphasized above, not all academics are equally compelled to perform 'achiev' (Polish *wykon*, a neologism, probably abbreviation from some form of the verb *wykonywać*, 'to perform,' 'to execute' – in the form of a noun meaning an measurable outcome of one's performance) and in fact many senior academics that I spoke with were often surprised hearing about it and its importance for some younger academics, arguing that it is not important in academic assessment. It certainly has its meaning, however, as many Polish academics before obtaining habilitation are employed on short-time contracts and after each contract there is an open employment competition that involves the 'objective' assessment of one's achievements. It goes without saying, therefore, that when a harsh competition system is introduced some might attempt to maximize their 'score' by all means available, endeavouring to reach system requirements by ethically dubious means and/or without much genuine engagement. The one possible result of this may be participating in conferences only for the certification of attendance, and thus for the points needed for scholarship/grant applications, institutional assessment, or simply advancing a scientific CV.[3] Such opportunist presenters have one agenda – to gain proof of performance that may serve for assessment purposes, and be accepted as a valid document of achievement. The consequence of this may be superficial, ectypal, meaningless, boring presentations of low quality that make a conference hollow, empty ritual.

Some such presentations that you don't know why they were created, you don't know what these people are doing here, you don't know why it's spoken, it doesn't make any sense and is such a production to gain points in the academy.
(Teacher, interview_10, male, hab., social sciences)

In extreme cases, even presenters themselves may not be interested in their presentation, the cause of which might be (1) presenting on a subject adjusted to the conference thematic scope not to one's interests, (2) conviction that the quality of the presentation does not matter at all as long as one obtains a certificate (as yet nobody has dared to annul a certificate because of poor performance), or (3) presenting the same paper/reading the same text for the umpteenth time, which is called 'presentation recycling.'

The latter is mostly characteristic of local/regional conferences, preferably those covering a very broad spectrum of subjects (ragbag conferences). In some disciplines/environments this practice is perfectly visible, as shown on one of the conference organizers webpages:

> Individuals attending various conferences and delivering the same or only a slightly changed paper will not be accepted .... we declare that we will not accept people who send an abstract of a speech, of which we know from somewhere else that it has already been presented in the same or in a very similar form.
>
> (Konferencyjny savoir-vivre, n.d.)[4]

Increasing demand for opportunities to easily gain achieves have resulted in organizing more and more scientific conferences of dubious quality. The culmination of this system is entrepreneurs organizing online conferences (usually 1–3 hours of chatting about the sessions' subjects) or even offering certificates of attendance simply for paying a conference fee (a certificate along with conference materials is sent by post). As long as evaluation does not take into account the actual quality of conference performance (obviously hard to assess) and is preoccupied only with their technical qualities – the market for such art for art's sake will maintain steady. By technical qualities I mean, for instance, the number of participants from abroad in international conferences or calling the conference international when in fact all or almost all participants are Poles, which creates the paradoxical situation that in the centre of Poland, a Polish institution organizes a conference in which all participants are Poles, attempting to give their presentations and hold discussions in English merely because international conferences are valued more highly in the evaluation system (see also Kulczycki, 2011).

All above-described phenomena strongly resemble Gambetta and Origgi's (2013) theory of LL game, which constitutes the implementation of game theory into the analysis of academic practices. In their terms, the phenomena described above would be called 'the culture of Lness,' where L stands for low quality of performance. They analysed different kinds of exchanges, specifying that the most problematic are those in which participants provide mismatched levels of performance. In scientific conferences this can be, for instance, a situation where a high-level presentation is delivered at a conference that are led by low standards. The H doer would feel cheated because they put a great deal of effort into preparing an original and well-presented paper which turned out to be misplaced, and the L doers would feel baffled because the H presentation debunks their low quality performance, which is even more obvious against the background of the high quality presentation. It also brings to the surface the fact of their Lness which they had silently agreed on. In such L conferences the most common exchanges are those of LL. Nobody expects high quality, ground-breaking analyses or discussions, some people recycle their papers, read poorly-written texts in monotonous voices and bore one another for a while. It seems to be the realm of a smoothly functioning 'mutually assured boredom pact,' as Baghdadchi called it (2005, p. 322). Being boring indeed might be a perfectly functional defensive strategy that is capable of discouraging even many H doers from asking questions, especially difficult ones for casual, opportunistic attendees, and may still prove to be effective even at more challenging conferences. Baghdadchi encapsulated it: 'I get up and bore you, you get up and bore me, and, at the end of the day, we are all left standing' (2005, p. 322).

Another kind of opportunism that may induce the feeling of boredom is conference tourism (Høyer and Naess, 2001), i.e. attending a conference with the aim of sightseeing, relaxing, and limiting conference participation to the indispensable minimum.

> People attend conferences, first of all, to bore and then to eat dinner and explore the city. I'm not kidding.
> (Teacher, interview_25, male, PhD, humanities)

> When I look at people, people often treat it more as an opportunity to ... well, for example, to go somewhere, if the conference is in a nice place ... because if the university pays for the ticket, why should I not go to Lisbon, to the conference, where I will deliver a 15-minute paper, someone will ask me two questions and for the rest of the time ... I will be walking around a nice city.
> (Teacher, interview_67, male, hab., humanities)

For some academics, even those very prominent in their disciplines (I have observed several such key figures, important committee members), this kind of behaviour is a tempting opportunity to take a few days holiday on taxpayers' money (at least in some part). Sometimes they also travelled with their families and attended the conference only as much as they had to (i.e. when they had presentation of their own, chaired a session(s) or had obligatory meetings of some sort). Paradoxically as it might sound, this could also be a kind of deliberate prevention strategy against being exposed to conference boredom that they predict will exist (they probably have vast experience both in producing and experiencing conference boredom and attend the conference with a different agenda in mind). It might thus be a strategy to mitigate the otherwise high opportunity cost of attendance (loss of benefits from alternative activities that may be performed in the same time instead). Another cause of such an attitude may be general work overload of many academics, who are constantly very active and in a hurry with many simultaneous projects. In this view, such conference tourism can be seen to have compensatory function, constituting an opportunity to rest in a tourist location.

Disturbances in integration

In terms of cognitive benefits, many conferences are perceived as wasting time but the prime aim for many respondents was networking, meeting other scientists interested in similar issues in order to discuss things, get to know each other, establish contact or for collaboration, which for some also functions as a factor distinguishing good conferences from bad ones.

> It seems to me that there is rarely such a chemistry at conferences, what's most interesting in conferences is happening in the lobby and all these speeches, well, I'm afraid that this is something that needs to be served.
> (Teacher, interview_21, male, hab., humanities)

> It is certainly, in a sense, largely wasted time, but conferences also serve for meetings, so there is always value, even if the conference is poor, in meeting people, getting to know people. On the one hand, people get to know me, but I also meet people, I know what they do, I make contacts, people come and talk ... meeting with people is always valuable.
> (Teacher, interview_70, female, prof., social sciences)

> ... we're meeting, talking, inventing new things, we come up where we could, for example, cooperate with each other ... we exchange information about 'hey, listen, I have this equipment, you have that equipment, this is what mine can do,' because in another place, especially in an international environment, there is no time to meet, [and] a conference is a good excuse for this type of meeting.
> (Teacher, interview_41, male, prof., humanities)

For some academics conferences serve a function as places to meet acquaintances, which at times even partially supersedes other aims of the conference (i.e. presentation sessions). Some respondents admitted that in many conferences only a fraction of participants actively participate in sessions while the rest is usually sitting outside and talking. I observed such situations on numerous occasions, which seemed to be more characteristic of massive international conferences. If this is actually such a crucial and common way of spending time for many participants during conferences perhaps '[w]e need to get better at shaping the format to fit the precise purpose of the conference' (Green, 2016). The current format of the majority of conferences does not seem to match the aim of interaction, due to imposing many hours of presentation sessions. It might be also a justifiable hypothesis that in some cases sessions seem more boring because attendees partake in the conferences with the clear aim of networking, waiting for the opportunity to do so, thus, for coffee/lunch breaks and the end of the day, which usually culminates in social meetings.

More relevant to boredom are, however, all these situations when real networking and integration failed to happen at a particular conference.

This seems to be a crucial point, especially for ragbag conferences, where thematic scope can be extremely broad. In those circumstances, it is very difficult to put the attractive principle of intense networking into practice, because the participants represent such a varied disciplinary composition that they usually have little idea of what others present. In my experience, collaboration as a result of such a conference is extremely rare. In extreme cases, participants have nothing in common and hold conversations on extra-scientific subjects, such as the hardships of academic life. I myself was extremely bored at such conferences, both during the sessions (due to causes mentioned in previous sections of this chapter), and during breaks when I had nothing to talk about with anyone among the participants. Neither was I interested in their subjects (frequently boringly presented in sessions) nor did I see any kind of possible future collaboration with them.

Another obstacle to actual integration is the practice of some participants, who attend only the sessions with their presentations and leave the venue as soon as they obtain their certificate. This may be (1) an example of pure opportunism (strategy 'pick up and run'), (2) an effect of lack of time due to other, more pressing, obligations (parenting, job outside the academia, deadline for journal article or grant proposal, etc.), and/or (3) evidence of the low status of a particular conference or conferences in general as a genre of academic activity. In extreme cases, therefore, tax payers simply finance a quick trip for a piece of paper called a certificate of attendance. The indirect proof that attendees behaviours described above might not be incidental in some environments can provide the point from regulations of one of many conferences stating that '... people arriving only at their presentation and then not participating in the conference do not receive certificates of participation' (Konferencyjny savoir-vivre, n.d.). Seeing this from another angle, one can come to the conclusion that it constitutes a distant, less wealthy cousin of conference tourism – and thus, that it is not limited to young researchers but maybe also apply to senior researchers as well, insofar as they sometimes seem to feel compelled to participate in some conferences only because someone with their status should attend a particular conference.

> In my situation, sometimes it's like this that at a conference, I say rudely, you should be, somebody invites me to some organisational committee ... and this conference is such that if I, let's say, attend what I was interested in, I would be at the conference for two hours, but sometimes there are three days, well then it's clear that in these three days I feel that I have wasted time.
> (Teacher, interview_53, male, prof., social sciences)

As some respondents suggested, a conference may be a form of self-reproduction of scientific society, a kind of social ritual. For young researchers it may be a passage ritual, as they are socialized to the academic culture, observe senior academics in action and take the first steps on the same track. For others, it may be a form of maintaining contact with other members of society who are busily occupied on an everyday basis with their own research, frequently in a different part of the country or globe. It may be a kind of counterpart of the phatic function of language that serves merely to sustain communication without much engagement. Through participation people signal and corroborate their membership in the milieu, which may constitute the ultimate reason for attending the event.

Sometimes participation can be motivated by directly sustaining mutual contact between the organizing institution and that of the participants. As one of the respondents noted:

> Right now on Sunday I am going to a conference abroad and the programme of this conference is so boring, so horribly boring, but it's hard, I'm going there, first of all, I have my own presentation, etc., but it is important because the organisers are also our partners in the Erasmus programme, so it's more like sustaining and creating some kind of contact, supporting the ritual, yes, but besides, you have to keep in touch with them.
> (Teacher, interview_25, male, PhD, social sciences)

Prevention and coping techniques

Not all academics actively suffer from boredom during scientific conferences, however, thanks to their vast employment of various prevention and coping techniques. Even if many respondents do not associate them with boredom but rather with avoiding/minimizing time wastage, I claim they serve as sometimes indeliberate strategies against boredom, as a means of time management.

The most basic and effective strategy is not attending conferences at all. Some respondents have strong reluctance to the very idea of a scientific conference, do not find its currently employed formula meaningful and/or efficient or simply believe it to be a waste of their time that can be spent in more valuable way. I would imply that in many cases boredom may be one of deterring factors. Some academics are highly sceptical whether it is the most efficient way of doing and communicating science, and perceive it rather as semi-leisure activity.

> In my opinion, scientific work is primarily done in the laboratory and publishing results in journals available to the whole community that is interested in the subject matter, is the basis of scientific activity, and conferences are such a social occupation, but this is an isolated opinion, rarely anyone thinks so, all my colleagues rush to all these conferences, they go somewhere, but whether they really do science or make liaisons? I think that in most cases, it's simply a semi-holiday journey.
> (Teacher, interview_26, male, prof., natural sciences)

This strategy is essentially available for academics with a strong institutional position and permanent contract, as younger researchers are not usually in the position to avoid this kind of activity even if they dislike or underestimate it. Those who are not fond of conference tourism, and flourishing social contacts, if possible, attempt to distance themselves from the conferences and send their younger colleagues as representatives of an institution/unit, etc. Some participate only if they are invited as keynote speakers, others carefully choose even among those invitations or attend only when asked by their acquaintances.

The rest, less privileged, and impelled to at least occasional attendance, apply less extreme strategies to avoid time wasting, for example, by 'minimising the risk of slip-up' (Teacher, interview_27, female, hab., humanities), i.e. careful selection of conferences and/or the panels they participate in. Based on their experience, they intentionally try to choose conferences that they envisage as being interesting in terms of subject/discipline coverage and/or having a sufficiently substantive level, which they determine according to the inter alia organizing institution (choosing a conference, e.g. at Queen's College of London instead of one at a provincial community college). The careful planning of conference time itself, picking the conference sessions they intend to attend, is both a matter of conference experience and part of the preparation for it.

> A scientific conference, this is a meeting where you usually have to plan your time very carefully because a person is unable to absorb eight or twelve hours of presentations, which are on constantly all day long, so the key issue here is to make a selection of material and decide on it… it means deciding the part in which one wants to actively participate. Also here it's a matter of one's own work, to make use of this time well and not to feel bored.
> (Teacher, interview_12, male, PhD, natural sciences)

> You just don't go for things that you predict will be useless, be good for nothing, or at least at some point you stop going to things that seem to be useless, you go to what you are interested in and even if the presenter speaks boringly, they still say things that we're waiting for.
> (Teacher, interview_52, female, hab., social sciences)

Some academics check presenters and/or the chairs of the sessions before the event, others know them already from previous meetings and are able to make more adequate decisions about attending particular sessions.

> When I already know some presenters and I know that they are boring, I don't attend their presentations, I look at posters, I meet people, I

know who will be speaking the same thing fifth year [in a row], so I have already heard it, so then I manage my time somehow differently.

(Teacher, interview_51, female, hab., natural sciences)

Some respondents admitted to leaving some sessions when uninterested or when bored or potentially bored with a particular panel, leaving the room in the course of the session and/or undertaking alternative activities instead (having coffee, prolonging lunch, conversing, leaving the conference venue altogether for sightseeing or other activity).

When I don't make use of someone else's presentation as I would like, simply because the organisers of the conference allowed, for some reason, someone to stand at the blackboard or those slides, and to say some not particularly interesting things on a shallow/anodyne topic, reasonably obvious, reasonably boring, he [the presenter] needed it, because he had to write some work, do some doctorate or settle a grant and now he's simply talking bullshit about something, but then you can tap a friend with whom you have a joint project on the shoulder and say, 'come on, let's talk about something more interesting,' you know, boredom is such a simple, common description of what... what could have happened if I gave in to this process, but I don't want to give up, I say to myself 'no! I'm the master of what is happening to me, not the situation.'

(Teacher, interview_63, male, prof., natural sciences)

Some respondents to prevent or to cope with unsatisfactory situation at a session switch it for another one, i.e. migrate between simultaneous sessions if available. Others believe that abandoning a session is a kind of rudeness, impropriety or arrogance, or are too embarrassed to stand up and leave, and so they employ coping strategies inside the conference room. Some zone out, daydream, switch off, or simply wait for the end, others employ more active techniques, such as thinking about other things.

I'm planning something, I don't know, the next conference I will go to …. [I can] think about various things, make up some things concerning, let's assume, scientific work, or think about things such as "oh, what will I do tomorrow?," and whether I go to the cinema on Saturday or not, think about something that awaits me, and [what] I'm planning.

(Teacher, interview_2, male, hab., humanities)

I deal with some issues of mine that I can do without using a computer, notebook and other things, that is, for example, I plan a semester of classes, how I will conduct [them], I wonder what I will say sequentially the day after tomorrow when I'm in class, or any work plan, well, I try to do something with time so that it won't be disruptive and very visible, I mean so that it would not be very visible that I don't listen to it [a presentation].

(Teacher, interview_36, female, MA, humanities)

For some participants this response is so automatic that they do not perceive the presence of boredom at all and refuse to contemplate even the slightest adequacy of the term (see the issue of boredom as a 'conveyor belt'), for others it is the first line of deliberate or semi-deliberate defence against the feeling. The most common activities employed to alleviate the sense of time wasting are scrutinizing the programme of the conference, ticking presentations in which one is interested, using a sheet of paper to write something down, talking with neighbour(s), drawing, doodling, or going over/working on one's presentation. Other techniques aimed at optimizing time in a conference are taking actions associated with relaxing, communication, or administrative/scientific work. I believe the quotes below are an adequate illustration of such activities, performed in the hope of distracting one from a sense of time wasting, and not being bored.

> I recall instantly the things that I have had to do for a long time and for which I haven't have time and in fact it is a great opportunity to use these 20 minutes to write a provisional budget, or to prepare some diagram or a template for something in manuscript.
> (Teacher, interview_39, female, MA, social sciences)

> I always have a computer with me and I absolutely don't hide myself, this is, I'm simply, Facebooking, replying to e-mails, running a remote office, etc.
> (Teacher, interview_60, female, PhD, social sciences)

> I also take some materials there, I don't know, a master's thesis, which I read, correct, and then after the conference I give it back to the student, these kinds of things, those ... that result from some administrative procedures, not so much from the need for scientific development.
> (Teacher, interview_53, male, prof., social sciences)

> Someone is talking and I simply zone out and think about my things, well, mathematics is convenient, that only a sheet of paper and a pen are needed and you can create something there, I mean I don't deal with some very difficult problems, but when I have some counter-example to calculate, some idea, so I try not to get bored.
> (Teacher, interview_34, female, MA, natural sciences)

The intensity of employing boredom coping strategies may depend on (1) the level of boredom experienced or general individual threshold of boredom (boredom proneness), (2) the overall workload at the time (how many tasks/much work one has to do at the time surrounding the event), (3) the level of one's divisibility of attention (the higher it is, the more one is capable of being simultaneously engaged in following the session and performing secondary activities), and (4) the strength of conviction that it is not proper to be distracted from the main course of a session, which, as a few of my respondents suggested, could be positively correlated with experience in attending conferences (the more experienced an academic is in conference participation, the more advanced and automatic their coping reaction might be). When someone observes themselves or colleagues that they meet regularly at conferences, they might see a gradual erosion of the initial assumption of propriety and imperative of full participation. Ideals clash with conference realities and one begins to fight against all conference's shallows. Some even respond to the argument of a lack of respect for a presenter, that it is the presenter who lacks respect for the audience, by offering a non-engaging, boring, and mediocre paper.

Staff meetings

An analysis of boredom at university staff meetings, mostly faculty meetings, due to its very nature, is to some extent, analogous to an analysis of conference boredom. This is an area of academic activity that elicits various reactions and boredom is one of them. Similarly as in scientific conferences, many participants are willing to admit to an occasional occurrence of the feeling, whereas others emphasize different aspects of the phenomenon.

Faculty councils are a crucial part of university democracy with a wide range of competencies. Their prerogatives include deciding on the financial, developmental, organizational, and personal matters of the faculty. They form advising committees to the dean, give an opinion of appointments, accept degree advancements, and discuss pressing issues on strategies of faculty development or curricula of degree courses. Participation is limited to independent, tenured scholars (or a selection of them), that is academics with habilitation, and representatives of the other categories of academics (PhDs, PhD students, and students), and they usually take place once a month.

I have not found anyone who was passionate about such meetings, compared to, for example, research which was frequently the object of great interest and passion. The majority narrative seemed to be that of duty, working for a common cause, being responsible for the quality of the academic life of the unit – a kind of obligation on which depends the lives of very real people, even if it is not always a pure pleasure. The quote below vividly illustrates this point.

> We go [to the meeting] to have a quorum to vote. If we don't vote on something, we, as a community, will fall behind, or someone personally won't get a promotion, they won't be granted an academic title, we won't open the [employment] competition, there will be no quorum, because the faculty council didn't concern us personally. No, the faculty

meeting always applies to us, personally, we are members of a group and even if it's just our votes that are needed, it is our duty.
(Teacher, interview_33, male, hab., natural sciences)

The duty of attending faculty meetings provokes many various reactions. For some it is an interesting experience, being cognitively beneficial, for others it is associated with frustration, a sense of wasted time and/or boredom. Those who feel that they benefit from such meetings noted that they were opportunities to find out about the life of the faculty, providing participants with the feeling of being up to date which increase the sense of belonging to the community/institution. This attitude may more frequently apply to new members of the council: those who have recently obtained habilitation and gained privilege of participation.

Faculty meetings are surprisingly interesting, this is, of course not every issue discussed on the faculty council is equally interesting to me, but it seems to me that the interaction of a large group of quite colourful people makes it so. I haven't been particularly bored at the faculty meetings up to now, perhaps people with longer experience feel some fatigue, find the material repetitive, but the issues raised at the faculty meetings concern, for example, PhD students or the habilitation dissertations considered at our faculty, therefore even to hear briefly about who deals with what, it seems to me quite interesting.
(Teacher, interview_57, male, hab., natural sciences)

Some respondents, however, perceived these meetings more in terms of frustration, and irritation, a kind of discontent, because, depending on faculty and dean, and their office politics, some meetings took a form of open criticism of their members, and were a forum for complaining about faculty problems, such as not fulfilling top-down demands.

There is nothing new substantively, but it is often more annoying, because we learn about the situation of the university, and what threatens us, what the punishments will be if we won't do something. This is frequently very punitive, not very inspiring or not very encouraging. [It's] more what will happen to us if we won't accomplish certain things, we won't do them, we won't pass them on, we won't apply for something.
(Teacher, interview_68, female, hab., social sciences)

There is no boredom, there is simply nervousness at the faculty meetings ... We are always striving for something, we never praise the employees, we don't praise ourselves, we don't praise the faculty, there is always an element of reprimand, or we have too few points or too little money, or too little internationalisation, or too few classes, or too few students. We always have some pain and around this pain further

> faculty meetings are created, therefore when we go to the faculty council we wonder which pain we will be considering this time.
> (Teacher, interview_52, female, hab., social sciences)

This situation seems to be rare, only arising in some units, under some deans, and not all members of such meetings feel similarly; some participants in the same meetings find it absurd or boring. Highly technocratic directives imposed by the government or rector's office, or issues raised at the council that are banal and/or trivial in comparison with the dignity of members that deal with them, may seem absurd.

> But usually, I would say, these meetings are so ridiculous and absurd sometimes, because there are, I don't know, 20 professors, sitting and wondering how to set up chairs, or what time to open the doors to classrooms. Well, this is absurd, a bit. I rather enjoy myself too.
> (Teacher, interview_14, female, PhD, humanities)

Boringness of the meetings

> The dominant feeling – recalls Professor Leszek Szczepański – that accompanied me during my first attendances at the Faculty Meetings, was boredom and a sense of loss of time. [It was] only rarely that something interesting happened. The caregivers of doctoral and habilitation conduct and the chairpersons of faculty commissions read multi-page descriptions of candidates. A few people are probably listening, many have casual conversations with their neighbours. I either don't hear, because there is noise or I don't listen, because I'm not interested in it, and usually both. Most of the attendees leave before the end of the meeting.
> (Tokarczyk, 2009, p. 31)

It has been a long time since the boredom of formal academic rituals such as various university staff meetings became the object of anecdotal content. Many academics more or less openly admitted to an occasional feeling of boredom at faculty meetings. Although about one third of my respondents did not participate in these meetings (never or not on a regular basis), it was the second most common response, to my general question about boredom during any academic activity.

The most frequently mentioned possible cause of boredom at such meetings was dragging time, the feeling of longueur, that 'these things could probably be settled faster by some other channels' (Teacher, interview_21, male, hab., humanities).

> I get bored at meetings. Well, like at any such meeting, there are thrilling, important matters that engage attention and raise adrenaline, and

there are things that one would like to sleep on or fast-forward to get out of here faster.

(Teacher, interview_62, female, PhD, social sciences)

Some respondents noted that some meetings, instead of being 'essential' and as concise as possible, are to some extent verbose, and that some members treat meetings as an opportunity to chat, to exchange minor personal comments or as 'collective psychotherapy sessions' (Teacher, interview_27, female, hab., humanities) that are, as a few respondents wryly suggested, a kind of compensation for the lack of opportunity to converse outside the council ('to be honest I have the impression that they missed conversations at home,' Teacher, interview_27, female, hab., humanities).

Some people just like to talk, they maybe don't have a different life, they are hardly decisive and we often belabour topics that could be finished in three minutes. I get tired of it, but that's how it happens.

(Teacher, interview_46, male, hab., humanities)

Protracting issues beyond the standard amount of time needed to raise the point and expound on it is conceived boring. Similarly is viewed 'arguing about commas and Latin phrases, or ... what should be better or more elegantly done, not about the meritum [the essence of an issue]' (Teacher, interview_56, female, hab., social sciences). One of the respondents suggested that boredom in staff meetings may be prompted by their excessive ceremoniousness.

In the case of councils [boredom stems] from the ceremoniousness, from the fact that things that could really be done in five minutes are extended up to one and a half hours to show that they are important, that we care about them, that we treat them seriously, so some pathos, a certain ceremoniousness, which may have been fascinating and very interesting the first or second time, then begins to be tiring.

(Teacher, interview_21, male, hab., humanities)

Some recollected the elongated reading of reports from works of commissions, or descriptions of candidates and their achievements, that in many trigger a reaction of impatience and wish that the meeting would end faster (counting the schedule points that remains). The feeling is amplified, similarly to scientific conferences, by opportunity cost. Some respondents had a strong sense of wasting time and that the time spent in the meeting could be shortened and used more efficiently, leaving more time for other necessary and valuable activities.

Each of us is a human being, and now who is taking part in such, let's say, ceremonial situations, they won't get to kindergarten on

time, or they won't go for a walk, or write an article, or they won't read an article, they will take part in something they might equally well not take part in.
(Teacher, interview_53, male, prof., social sciences)

All this is even more apparent due to the general feeling of overload shared by many academics (Jacobs, 2004). Some even suggested that this feeling is more evident after obtaining habilitation, when an academic begins to be obliged to attend more and more meetings and is expected to be part of more and more commissions and committees,[5] which significantly affects their time budgets, and faculty meetings, even if are usually held only once a month, add to that battery of staff meetings.

What prompts boredom in some respondents was also the fact that many issues raised at the meetings were of routine, predictable character. Meetings seem to become more and more 'voting machines' (Teacher, interview_26, male, prof., natural sciences) and the majority of issues are quite obvious, thus, the voting is simply a formality enforced by regulations.

> For example, we have to approve a lot of doctorates in various fields that are of little interest to us, the regulations say that they must be approved by the faculty council, usually it is automatic, usually there is no doubt, we trust each other that if the commission proposes approving a doctorate, apparently they know what they are doing, but it takes a lot of time ... The vast majority of these matters are obvious, so the results of the voting is predictable, but they must take place.
> (Teacher, interview_69, male, prof., natural sciences)

> Some habilitation, everyone votes in favour, everyone is delighted – such a ground for discussion when everyone agrees [*laughs*], if there are some voices saying that you have to think about it, then you are focused.
> (Teacher, interview_48, male, prof., natural sciences)

At many units the situation is partially addressed through the use of electronic voting pilots, which quickens the process (the computer automatically counts the votes and gives the results), but traditional paper voting is still used in some units. Voting can comprise some 80% of some meetings, which makes it a substantial issue.

Another issue constitutes the fact that not all subjects raised in meetings are equally relevant and interesting for all participants. This is mainly due to the federal character of the majority of faculties – they consist of many, sometimes very distant, institutions (institutes/chairs) all of which have their own issues, interests, and priorities. Not all issues raised during these meetings, therefore, are equally compelling to all members, especially when they do not concern them directly, and they do not have an opinion, or knowledge of them, which makes them abstract and non-engaging.

> If, for example, I have to vote and I have to undersign the list that I voted at the faculty meeting that we are announcing a competition for the position of assistant in the chair, which is somewhere in the second wing, so, from my point of view, if there is such a need for that chair, if the faculty has money for it, [then] let a competition be, but why should I, from another organisational unit, vote and undersign the list that I voted in a matter that concerns a completely different issue, which I have no knowledge of and no competence whether this assistant will be needed or will not be needed there. If the formal requirements are met, the person is suitable, there is a teaching need, why do I, from a completely different hallway, have to speak up in those matters?
> (Teacher, interview_53, male, prof., social sciences)

As another trigger for boredom was mentioned habilitation quolloquia,[6] i.e. the public presentations by people obtaining their habilitation, followed by a series of questions from the members of the habilitation commission and/or council, a discussion of the candidate's answers and achievements and, if the decision is positive, a lecture by the newly appointed independent scholar. As one of the respondents recollected:

> It took the entire meeting, in which, incidentally, you can sometimes be bored deadly. I remember when X [academic discipline] was also in my faculty, which over time became disaffiliated, so we listened to, for example, habilitation colloquia in fields A, B, C, D [specialisations within discipline X], in other words, from fields that we had nothing to do with. As for me – I'm not a literary expert, so if there was a habilitation concerning, for example, some kind of linguistic complexity, then we were literally sitting there feeling that we were losing time a little bit.
> (Teacher, interview_8, male, prof., humanities)

Some points raised at the meetings may also be difficult to understand for those lacking expertise in them, such as issues associated with a faculty's finances or legal issues. Such subjects require time and attention to become familiar with them, which many academics are neither interested in, nor willing to do.

Prevention and coping techniques

Above-presented issues may result in the whole variety of prevention and coping techniques, very similar to those employed during scientific conferences. The first possible method of preventing the feeling of boredom is to find something to be mentally or physically occupied with. Some respondents make notes, volunteer to be responsible for protocols, or take some functional position (a dean's advisor, a member of a commission, etc.), try to somehow induce interest in the subject of the council, which are especially useful strategies in a situation of high visibility, such as when a faculty, and thus its meetings, is relatively small, and the list of acceptable alternatives might be shortened. Some respondents denied ever being bored during meetings because they nap or, conversely, are constantly preoccupied with their thoughts.

> You cannot get bored, well, even if the subject that is discussed doesn't interest me, I always have something in my head that interests me and I simply switch off from what is happening. I think about things there, and I'm not bored.
> (Teacher, interview_32, female, hab., humanities)

As we can see in the above statement, some council members admit that there are issues that might be boring for them, but that they do not feel boredom due to prompt semi-automatic mobilization of cognitive coping mechanisms aimed at providing them with additional stimulation (see the Menton Theory of boredom by Davies and Fortney, 2012). Some council members therefore participate in the session while simultaneously employing strategies calculated to increase stimuli. The important thing is having a highly developed ability to divide the attention, which decides whether side activities can be engaged in during the meeting at all, and if so, the extent to which someone would do that and how complex those activities are.

From my observations, corroborated by many respondents, certain members of some meetings give the impression, sometimes equal to certainty, of being preoccupied for some/most of the time, not directly with boredom but rather with various passive or active means of alleviating/averting the feeling. The least complex ones include relaxing using smart devices[7] or being active on social media (simply browsing content, communicating with other users, or even publishing their own content[8]). Slightly more advanced copers read newspapers ('not very scientific things, because it's impossible to divide the attention so much' (Teacher, interview_9, female, PhD, humanities), skim or read books, sort through their lecture/class notes/slides, plan future classes with students, think up future lectures, prepare teaching materials (e.g. exercises for students), examine student assignments/essays/bachelor's or master's theses, review articles/habilitations, read and/or respond to e-mail messages, write or complete administrative documents, proofread their own articles (sometimes those of others as well) before or after peer review, and some are even capable of thinking about their research problems or reading/writing scientific papers. In other words, they optimize time usage and increase a density of the proceedings by performing secondary activities/external preoccupations. In doing so, they strongly resemble their own students, practicing similar strategies during university classes (Finkielsztein, 2013).

Some members evidently prepare careful plans of activities they intend to perform during the council. Some attempt to sit in the same places in the room in each meeting – of which those at the edges are the most desirable (i.e. places furthest from the person(s) chairing the session).

> At almost every faculty meeting, and it's not just me, a large part of my colleagues before the faculty meetings wondered what to take to the faculty meeting, so as not to be too bored.
> (Teacher, interview_53, male, prof., social sciences)

This can be interpreted as a reasonable strategy to cope with the general overload of activities that all academics are obliged to perform.

> You know, within our mode of work sometimes there is a situation where one has to do something, and they have to be on the council, because it is a matter of a quorum, so they use every moment.
> (Teacher, interview_41, male, prof., humanities)

At the majority of faculty meetings this practice seems to be a perfectly acceptable and tolerable, at least to some extent, however, its prevalence may vary significantly depending on the number of members, the institutional culture, the politics of the dean, and their office or social capital.

> Everyone accepts it [performing side activities], because everyone is doing it, so if someone started to break down, the whole structure would collapse ... It's a system that has achieved a balance, everyone accepts each other and they only wake up for their relevant 15 minutes, and then again they go into their hibernation, so it's ok, it's such a developed mechanism, nobody forces anyone to anything, it's better not to interfere with this compromise.
> (Teacher, interview_25, male, PhD, humanities)

The fact that meetings are recurrent and held with a regular group of people is the main distinctive quality of such meetings, in comparison to scientific conferences, and simultaneously encourages particular preventive/coping strategies, of which the most visible (or to be exact audible), serving an essential but non-official function of faculty meetings, are conversations between council members. It came as a total surprise to me when I participated in these meetings as a representative of PhD students that the room was often full of talk, even when the chair or a commission secretary was speaking, and that nobody intervenes unless the noise becomes too loud, when the dean or somebody from their office asked for silence. Frequent intense talk, despite others speaking publicly, may have been peculiar to the council I observed, but some of my respondents also noted talking with each other as an activity present during the staff meetings. As one of the participants observed:

> Among practices of this type, here very frequent is reserving places for each other, that is, 'oh if you will be at the council, reserve me a seat, so we will talk, discuss issues, oh, ok, listen, maybe we will talk it through at the council, because now I have to take care of children, I won't be able to be earlier, but we will talk it through at the council,' some paper that we're writing together, or some issues related to a grant or something, current issues, so from such practices it is this reserving places, sitting in groups which are also like social circles, and simply some minor gossiping, or some issues more to talk through, for which there is no other time.
> (Teacher, interview_29, female, MA, humanities)

My own observations fully corroborate the above. Council members converse on a variety of subjects, from private to scientific matters, catching up on social life, discussing the latest books/papers in the field/written by mutual colleagues, sharing the latest information about common acquaintances, intensively networking. When spatial circumstances allowed some migrate from colleague to colleague, settling various issues. At the council, the most common form of social morphology (Mauss, 2004) seemed to be the dyad (two people, a pair), which is probably the more efficient spatial distribution for intense conversation (this is only applicable to big rooms with definitely more chairs than people obliged to occupy them – which was exactly the case in the council I observed, with more than 80 people on the attendance list and never more than 50 or 60 actually participating, which took place in a room able to hold slightly more than a hundred).

It seems to be a justified conclusion that faculty meetings constitute a special kind of staff meeting, at which in some institutions there are silent but enforced imprimatur for a variety of activities not acceptable elsewhere, such as (1) engaging in external preoccupations without hiding under the table, (2) occasional verbal interactions outside the main course of the event, and even (3) leaving the room before time or being frequently late, which can be interpreted as a preventive technique. I have even heard of some participants who leave their voting pilots with colleagues staying to the end of the meeting, so they can vote for them in their absence. In this way they are officially doing their duty, i.e. contributing to the quorum, officially voting on the issues, yet not spending much time at the meeting. These are not equally common to other kinds of staff meetings (institute meetings, university senate meetings, etc.). Evidence, therefore, seems to suggest that the level of boredom is highest in faculty meetings, and is significantly less common in different kinds of staff meetings.

Teaching

The most frequently mentioned cause/factor of a teacher's boredom during classes is a lack of student engagement (cf. Alvesson, Gabriel, and Paulsen, 2017, pp. 37–38). One of the respondents admitted being bored in her own lecture when only four out of the 20 students enrolled showed up. For a teacher the most demotivating, frustrating, and boring situation is one when students do not interact with them.

> It's frustratingly boring for me when I see that I'm standing in front of the classroom, and – I call it banging my head against the wall – I'm talking to the wall. This is the most frustrating for me, demotivating when there is no reaction.[9]
> (Teacher, interview_16, female, MA, humanities)

> In classes where no one has read the text and everyone is sitting and looking at the ceiling or the floor and trying to avoid my eyesight, one can be bored to death. Really, one just looks at their watch, wondering how long they will be talking to themselves about matters of only their interest, which is absolutely tragic.
> (K3, cited in Kowzan et al., 2015, p. 36)

Student disengagement may significantly affect a teacher's attitude to such a group, lecture or, when recurrent, teaching in general.

> Here we are also dealing with such feedback, because the lecturers who have to deal with such passive student mass are subject themselves to such an erosion, because they become also overtaken by a kind of apathy. Well, how to work here? This is the proverbial tillage of the fallow field then. This job doesn't go forward as it should.
> (Teacher, interview_8, male, prof., humanities)

> I'm always bored when I see a lack of engagement from the other side. Because I see that someone buggers it and in this moment I also feel like buggering it, leaving, sleeping or doing something else.
> (Teacher, interview_1, female, hab., social sciences)

Some teachers perceive such situations as frustrating rather than boring, but even they acknowledge that, when prolonged, it may prompt feelings of disengagement and boredom in the teacher. Teaching passive, unmotivated, disinterested students who wait lethargically for the end hoping to 'serve the classes' (like a prison sentence) makes the teaching process hollow, superficial, and meaningless. As a result, teachers may enter a trajectory of burn out – moving from engagement, through frustration, then resignation, demotivation, boredom, to cynicism, and perceiving teaching as a bitter duty performed at a minimal cost. It may also be aggravated by the massification of higher education in Poland,[10] which results in the anonymization of the teaching process by increasing the student-staff ratio.[11]

Teachers may be bored when their expectations about student engagement are not met – it is boring for some to talk to themselves during seminars or other conversational classes.

> During the classes I sometimes get bored when the group doesn't talk to me, I have to pull out everything myself and talk to myself, the things I prepared at home, and if I don't see a reaction, then sometimes I get bored, because there is nothing new, only what I have prepared and possibly deliver ... We have [something] shown on the board and I ask this group what they think about it, how they like it, [and] when they sit, smile, so I answer myself, how I like it, then there is no reaction again, so then it's a bit boring when its only me talking to myself.
> (Teacher, interview_36, female, MA, humanities)

Boredom in that kind of situation may be the result of a lack of challenge – for some teachers it is extremely important that classes are a sort of inter-action, inspiration, and actual exchange of ideas – when this element is absent, boredom may constitute a prompt answer. Situations such as that described by one of the participants may be also be demotivating, and thus, boring.

> At the moment, when I come to classes and I propose students the traditional, in parenthesis, boring, way of conducting classes, and they [classes] take place in a boring way. There is some reaction. And then I come to class and give them, in my opinion, something above the standard and the reaction is the same.
> (Teacher, interview_16, female, MA, humanities)

When additional engagement, or a time-consuming effort put into preparing new materials/texts/exercises/educational games, and so on, does not beget reaction, there is no appreciation (for instance, through intensified student engagement) – it affects teacher's attitude enormously. It may at times work as a vicious circle – students get used to cynical and unengaged (but nevertheless totally correct) teachers, and teachers resign from their initial enthusiasm to serving their teaching duty without much readiness for major improvements and additional engagement. Both parties work out a mutual point of equilibrium, a silent non-aggression pact. Teachers after an early *sturm und drang* period (frequently just after being employed), characterized by high motivation and involvement, turbulent emotions, or at least stress, when they have to put much effort into preparing classes (many of which are often completely new for them in terms of the subject), begin to get used to it, they domesticate/tame the situation of teaching, and, depending on experiences with students, may decrease their engagement with teaching.

> I know that I have such a tendency to care, to be curious ... and if it doesn't work, then it's terribly exhausting and I'm slowly learning how to

> let it go, 'okay, no is no,' when I see after a while that it cannot be so with this group, I simply can't do it with them, I don't have more tools ... well, it will be a bit boring and calmer on my part, because I don't have the strength for more.
> (Teacher, interview_56, female, hab., social sciences)

Teachers soak into the system, accommodate to the situation of teaching students and readdress their initial engagement in teaching to a point they can maintain in the long run.

Many teachers denied being bored during teaching because they are active (which, from their perspective is somehow contradictory to being bored, see Chapter 1) but the situation described below by one of the respondents may also be perfectly possible.

> I'm also a little bored, because I see their boredom and I operate in two ways, one track is active and tries to conduct classes, but they don't go as I want and as I would expect it, and I'm bored in one half of myself in such a situation. I think so, I get tired, I'm bored.
> (Teacher, interview_62, female, PhD, social sciences)

Another factor contributing to decreasing engagement during classes may be fatigue, both physical or psychological, which is strictly connected to a frequently given reason for boredom in teaching – repetitiveness/sameness. Many teachers admit that they are fatigued and/or bored with cyclical, repetitive, and for the most part, basic and mandatory, classes they are obliged to conduct each year.

> It used to be more, especially at the beginning, when one was excited about these classes and courses that you conducted, they were new to me, in that I had a fresh mind, but slowly with the passage of time conducting the same classes raising the same theorems, they are becoming more and more schematic. I don't see anything new, and every definition is perfect. And I'm getting bored with this topic. I'm trying to lecture about things in some other way, or to see it from another side, but unfortunately some subjects are already so schematic and belong to the core curriculum, that they cannot be overcome.
> (Teacher, interview_7, male, hab., natural sciences)

> Sometimes I feel this burnout, but I don't know if it's a result of the fact that for some years, some classes are very similar to each other, and even X [name of the course] for first-year students, well, I don't have much space for manoeuvring because I have to tell them all these basics every year and I don't know how I would do it differently. I have to do these basics, so I'm really repeating myself, and what I'm doing, let's say, for ten years, so I'm bored with these basics.
> (Teacher, interview_2, male, hab., humanities)

Some academic teachers may become exhausted with teaching duty after several years or more, they may also experience more general or simply a periodic state of teaching burn out, work out a teaching routine that is hard to change that make them feel stagnant in that field of activity. As Josif Brodsky (1995) famously claimed, 'repetition is boredom's mother' and many teachers experience it as a sterilizing experience that causes some changes in their attitude to teaching, from liking it to wariness or even reluctance. This is why many teachers try to avoid teaching the same course for more than a few years in a row – as one of Wagner's respondents in her study of transnational scientists said: 'I don't like doing the same classes for a fourth or fifth year, because I'm bored' (2011a, pp. 179–80). The cause of such boredom is the rigidity of the academic system and lack of agency on the part of many teachers. It especially affects junior staff, who are less likely to have much control over the courses they teach (mandatory introductory courses or elective courses of their own making – it depends greatly, however, on institution culture and the relations in a particular unit).

> Very often it happens to me [to be bored], especially with courses that are cyclical, obligatory and have a rigid programme, and where every year you have to repeat the same thing. It's terribly boring, and the worst is when you have two groups, one, for example, on one day, the second on another day, and you repeat exactly the same thing, and it's really boring. But this is simply a programme of studies, compulsory subjects that must be taught. There is a syllabus, some rigid form, and so it must be so, then it's actually boring, but with such more original courses I'm rather not bored.
> (Teacher, interview_25, male, PhD, humanities)

Limited opportunities to be creative may prompt boredom, especially when one cannot change the course curriculum because all students are obliged to pass an exam prepared by someone else according to material discussed during classes. Some introductory courses are obligatory for students and essential for discipline, thus, someone has to teach them. Such courses frequently are perceived as boring, unchallenging, and sterile, and are delegated to junior employees who occupy the lowest positions and have no or little clout. A disproportion number of lectures and more interactive forms of classes may also be boring – as one of the respondents put it: 'too many lectures – boredom, too many seminars – boredom, some reasonable proportions' (Teacher, interview_12, male, PhD, natural sciences).

Teaching overload

Discussion of a lack of agency and repetitiveness introduces the issue of systemic causes of teaching boredom. This needs, however, a short introduction. According to Polish law (Ustawa z Dn. 20 Lipca 2018 r. Prawo o

Szkolnictwie Wyższym i Nauce, 114) an academic worker can be employed in one of three kinds of positions: (1) research-teaching, (2) research, or (3) teaching. Here, I am focusing on the first, because the vast majority of Polish academic teachers work in such positions, and as a result, they comprise the majority of my sample. The term for this position itself suggests the dual character of such employment, which is not anything unusual by itself, yet it makes the whole system a bit schizophrenic. This is because, according to the law (Ustawa z Dn. 20 Lipca 2018 r., 127,2) the annual requirement for teaching duty amount to a maximum of 240 teaching hours (one teaching hour equals 45 minutes). To put the issue to further extremity, however, the above act specifies that 'in special cases, justified by the necessity of the realization of the education programme, an academic teacher may be required to conduct teaching classes for oversize hours,' which cannot exceed a quarter of the workload of the research-teaching position (Ustawa z Dn. 20 Lipca 2018 r., 127,6). An academic teacher is thus compelled to accept up to 60 additional teaching hours per academic year, which amounts to a maximum of 300 hours. The law enables university governors to require even more teaching hours 'in an amount not exceeding twice the annual teaching workload' (i.e. up to additional 540 teaching hours annually[12]) with the consent of an academic teacher (Ustawa z Dn. 20 Lipca 2018 r., 127,7) – and many are not in a position to refuse such a proposition. Allegedly, the act of 2005 (Ustawa z Dn. 27 Lipca 2005 r. Prawo o Szkolnictwie Wyższym, 130,4) gave the rector authority to lower teaching duty in special circumstances (e.g. substantial engagement in research projects), but in practice it constituted a rare phenomenon, and in the bill from 2018 this paragraph disappeared. This creates the situation in which

> on the one hand, it's required that the research staff are of a high [scientific] level, and on the other hand, they [staff] are swamped with such an amount of teaching that it's simply impossible and it's exploitation, it's intellectual exploitation.
> (Teacher, interview_50, female, prof., humanities)

In everyday practice, this research-teaching position turns out to be either two separate and mutually hampering positions for a single salary or an almost purely teaching position due to a shortage of time for doing research. It clearly constitutes a strategy of university governance operating in a situation of limited resources – it is much cheaper to employ one employee with a teaching duty of 240 hours and to make them do research than employ two employees with a teaching duty of, for instance, 120 hours. In financial terms, it is the most economic strategy, but it causes many tensions and problems, such as between teaching and research, which is found to have a significant effect on scientific output (Kwiek, 2015), both in terms of quantity (number of published works) and quality (e.g. partaking in anonymous national conferences frequently being the assembly lines for producing scientific credits merely for the evaluation purposes). It creates the paradoxical situation that people are employed primarily to fulfil teaching duty and at the same time are obliged to reach 'scientific excellence.' The majority of academic teachers in my sample applied to university due to their scientific interests, with the intention of pursuing research (cf. Szwabowski, 2019, p. 95). Becoming an academic teacher is, in the majority of cases, the cost people have to pay for being a researcher at the university, which in Poland seems to have higher prestige than the Polish Academy of Science (Polska Akademia Nauk, PAN – a strictly scientific institution). In many ways, it is a high price, as for many academics the majority of their time in the academic year is occupied by teaching.[13]

Underestimation of teaching

To make things worse, teaching seems to be underestimated both by the reward system and, perhaps as a result, among academics themselves. On the one hand, teaching is treated 'zero one' in the periodic assessments of academic employees, the only thing that matters is whether teaching duty (workload) was achieved (in a strictly numeric manner) – teaching hours are correct and student evaluation are at least average. Such a system provides no motivation for any additional engagement on the part of the teacher. As Łukasz Marciniak indicates:

> … being a good, valued by students lecturer has no consequences for the teacher other than personal satisfaction. It does not bring any advance in position at university or recognition in the academic world. (2008, pp. 99–100)

In the majority of cases, it provides no additional rewards at all, neither symbolic, nor material. Except for one faculty, there have been virtually no symbolic rewards associated with excellence in teaching. I have also heard about only one initiative to regularly reward the best teachers financially. In that kind of system there is no difference, in terms of any kind of rewards, between engaged, enthusiastic, active, and highly-valued teachers and those who are not (cf. Wagner, 2011a). As 'the rewards are insensitive to the quality of performance (for example, the salary at the end of the month is the same), there is no point producing at an H [high] level of quality' (Gambetta and Origgi, 2013, p. 11). This encourages mediocrity in teaching because there is no rewarding difference between, using the terms proposed by Gambetta and Origgi, L (low-quality) doers and H (high-quality) doers. One respondent even suggested that a senior lecturer (*starszy wykładowca*, one of the legally specified positions at the university, associated solely with teaching duty – with an amount of up to 540 teaching hours yearly) had a lower salary than the parallel research-teaching position of adjunct. This information cannot be fully verified by the existing law,[14] but even if those salaries were be the same, the sole assumption that they are not is significant, which may show a more general perception of teaching positions as mediocre/menial in comparison to research ones. Such perceptions of teaching positions may also contribute to the fact that in many institutions a switch from a research-teaching to a teaching position is not only perceived as a demotion, but is employed as such (especially when someone fails to meet the requirements for a higher position in a given time, which is, as far as I know, applied only in obtaining habilitation). This corresponds to a colloquial view, shared by both some students and academic teachers, that people occupy teaching positions because they have failed scientifically. Being only a teacher is therefore sometimes perceived as a failure, which is probably prompted by the general pattern of becoming an academic teacher as a side-effect of being a researcher employed at a university.

Between teaching and researching – teaching disengagement

Teaching overload and its underestimation means that research is frequently done at the cost of private/leisure time – many respondents share the impression of working in two separate positions, one regular teaching position with some organizational work and a second extraordinary research position pursued nightly, during weekends and teaching-free periods (see also Jacobs, 2004; Wagner, 2011a; Kowzan and Zielińska, 2016). Some participants also complained that the authorities rarely agreed to any dispensations in teaching duty, even when an external research grant was obtained. Moreover, when such dispensations are eventually granted, they entail a proportional lowering of the basic salary, which is perceived as a kind of punishment for research activity. These problems are especially poignant for junior staff, PhDs trying to meet requirements for obtaining habilitation (eight years for a series of highly-valued journal articles and/or book on a subject different to the PhD thesis, Ustawa z Dn. 20 Lipca 2018 r.) and are rarely raised by senior staff. As authors of report *Nie zostaje mi czasu na pracę naukową* [*I don't have time for scientific work*] noted:

> The very fact that scientists in the context of teaching share their survival strategies rather than development plans is highly disturbing. The dilemma "either-or" (either teaching – or research) from the first years after the PhD, sometimes turns into a sad statement "neither-nor."
> (Kowzan et al., 2015, p. 63)

Many PhDs eventually realize they are unable to simultaneously pursue teaching and research at a high level.

> You cannot do everything, you simply cannot do everything physically, always one of these elements escapes, either teaching or research, usually people muck up teaching, because they don't want to muck up research, because they wanted to be researchers, so they won't muck up what they wanted, simply what they have to.
>
> (Teacher, interview_25, male, PhD, humanities)

This situation prompts the feeling of being in cul-de-sac in some academic teachers. When an academic has a preference for teaching, they are frustrated that many other things distract them, and take their time and that there is not enough time left to prepare classes to a personally satisfactory level – they have the impression that they could do it better, the feeling of being an artisan, labourer. If, however, an academic teacher has a preference for research (which is favoured in the current system introduced by neoliberal reforms), they are frustrated that teaching takes an excessive amount of time and perceive teaching as a burden, a bitter duty, which results in applying optimization techniques, i.e. lowering the quality of classes to average level, which is acceptable for the evaluation, minimizing their personal input of time, energy, and attention as much as possible (Marciniak, 2008; Pieniądz, 2017). This strategy is highly recommended from the career point of view as 'when you want to be a good teacher, you risk rotation' [in the meaning, being dismissed due to low scientific output] (Pauluk, 2016, p. 293, cited in Szwabowski, 2019, p. 95).

> According to some people teaching interferes …. From the point of view of your academic career, it's best to whip through teaching in a least-effort way. 'You devote little time, do not get involved, do it well enough not to be dismissed' … so some people told me that teaching is a trap … quite a few people told me not to be too engaged in teaching, because it distracts you.
>
> (Teacher, interview_19, male, MA, social sciences)

For some academic teachers, teaching constitutes a necessary evil, an addition to doing research. Some 'go teaching like to a beheading' (Teacher, interview_71, female, PhD, natural sciences), and either whip through teaching ('they conduct classes by reading from slides and repeating themselves every time, they don't execute knowledge, don't try to interest nor demonstrate the usefulness of what they're talking about,' student, cited in Izdebski et al., 2015, p. 92) or conduct classes mainly by setting student presentations, as one of Marciniak's respondents admitted:

> The assignation of projects was a good solution, it didn't take me extra time, and it occupied whole classes. The readings were also good at first, I know them anyway, and in the classes I only indicated who would discuss which chapter. (2008, p. 59)

Another strategy to save time and energy for conducting research is the repetition of the same classes from year to year (see Wagner, 2011a, p. 180). This is also one of the reasons why some senior staff have time to look into their old, not yet analysed, non-published, or only partly published data after years of intense teaching and organizational activity – they begin to spend less time on preparing classes, because they repeat them year after year and establish their teaching routine.

The system that maintains teaching duty on a high level and simultaneously places significant emphasis on scientific achievements (on the international level preferably) creates a situation in which even some engaged teachers, who are generally keen on teaching, are often reluctant to actually teach – as one of the respondents said: 'I like teaching students very much, but I don't like teaching' (Teacher, interview_27, female, hab., humanities). Teaching is something that distracts from other, more valuable things from the career point of view, or simply more imminent duties that have to be done in the same time. It becomes, on many occasions, rather an interlude between them, such as in the case of some researchers working in the laboratories.

> This is also the problem, that hardly anyone deals with teaching so full-time, it's known that for most people it's something that is done between their own experiments ... Sometimes they have fun, sometimes not, but generally it's often something that breaks their day more, and even when they want to conduct it well, there are so many distractions that, in effect, a lot of teaching in the department is frequently done quite amateurishly.
> (Teacher, interview_43, male, PhD, natural sciences)

Many systemic factors may contribute to decreasing teacher engagement in teaching. In the current system, teaching is rather an excessive baggage, or an albatross around one's neck, slowing scientific progress, and in consequence, career advancement. Academic teachers, therefore, may be prone to experience a kind of teaching burn out. They begin with enthusiasm, a calling, a sense of mission and end up with cynicism, disengagement, and boredom, treating teaching as a chore. Although burn out seems to be a relatively rare phenomenon – in my sample only two or three respondents can be described using this term – boredom as an effect of the academic system is less uncommon. The majority treat teaching in terms of duty, and only a small minority of my respondents were passionate purely about classes with students. As Aneta Pieniądz, active academic teacher and member of *The Citizens of Science* movement (*Obywatele Nauki*), indicates:

> Teaching hinders the increase of this [scientific] performance – it is difficult to measure, does not count significantly in the assessment of individual achievements, is associated with 'wasting time' on working

with random students who are often perceived as too weak, lazy and ill-prepared. It is also not worth investing in improving teaching skills, especially since short-term employment does not give a chance to see the effects of one's own work.

(Pieniądz, 2017, p. 308)

These seem to be perfect conditions for boredom to emerge, as far as a sense of futility, meaninglessness, and opportunity cost is likely in that kind of system. Many teachers, especially junior staff, have little or no stability of employment (short-term contracts on less than three years), which makes it harder to engage with both the institution and teaching, as far as their future depends on their scientific performance, not on quality of their teaching. The high opportunity cost of teaching, its underestimation in employee assessment, low student engagement, repetition of courses (especially introductory ones) for many years – all these factors may affect teacher involvement, and thus contribute to a periodic feeling of boredom, exhaustion with teaching duty or to more severe state of didactic burn out.

Boring didactic tasks

The previous section dealt with factors/causes of boredom on more general level, but what concrete situations most commonly prompt boredom among academic teachers? One may be student presentations during classes. Once or more students are obliged to read a given text and recount its content to other students and a teacher. The aim of this didactic form is to provide the teacher with some support (they do not need to present everything themselves), to release students from a reading second or third text in the same classes and to teach/improve a student's skills in presenting. Some respondents admit this form as occasionally boring for them, because of the quality of some student presentations. Others, conversely, claim that they have never been bored on such an occasion, because they had to actively listen to the presentation in order to intervene if the presentation was not precise enough, incorrect, or not sufficiently comprehensible. As one of the respondents admitted:

> I would be bored terribly during [student] presentations, if not for the fact that I have to listen to them and watch over the course of the narrative ... The more boring they are [presentations], the more I cannot get bored, because if the paper is damn boring, nobody listens to it ... so the more boring the presentation is, the more I have to listen carefully to catch the important content and repeat it again.
> (Teacher, interview_62, female, PhD, social sciences)

Another situation that some of respondents recalled as occasionally boring involved unassisted student work. This contains all tasks set by the teacher which students pursue without the teacher's active assistance. All the teachers do is wait for the students to end the task (e.g. calculations or an exercise).

> Sometimes when I'm sitting in the seminars, I get bored, because the students solve the task too slowly, but I think it cannot be avoided .... Well, when they solve a task and they still don't know, or they count for long time and it can be seen, we know what it will be, but you have to count it to the end, so sometimes I get bored, but without exaggeration, there are some short periods.
> (Teacher, interview_34, female, MA, natural sciences)

Some respondents find it boring to grade students. This includes all activities associated with student evaluations, i.e. checking tests, exams, etc. and watching students during the written exams. Examples of such boredom are given below.

> It is boring to check [student's] assignments ... the stack of works that needs to be checked for tomorrow, the day after tomorrow, recurring solutions; I grow more and more tired of it and it's more boring and I really don't like it, but it's a necessary element (Teacher, interview_59, male, PhD, natural sciences) .... later checking these tasks, well it's also repetitive, mistakes are also repeated, so it's difficult to call it something exciting.
> (Teacher, interview_57, male, hab., natural sciences)

> The tests were boring when I was sitting, because I had colloquia and I was sitting with them for ... four and a half hours and they were writing, it was monstrous, these last hours ... I thought I wouldn't make it and this is on the one hand a situation where you have to watch a little for them not to cheat, and on the other hand, if they don't cheat, there is simply nothing to do [*laughs*].
> (Teacher, interview_20, female, MA, humanities)

Both these activities are highly repetitive but at the same time require maintaining some level of attention – and thus may constitute a model boring experience, where one is not engaged in the current situation at a satisfactory level and simultaneously cannot pursue another, more subjectively valuable activity.

For a few respondents (from physics and mathematics) tedious calculations before or during classes were boring. The quotes below illustrate that case.

> [In my field] there are pieces that rely on calculations, where the starting point is interesting, the end point is interesting, and what is happening on the way may not be extremely fascinating, but on the other hand, the

completeness of the university education requires that students know what the transition looks like.

(Teacher, interview_6, male, PhD, natural sciences)

> Sometimes there is something to be recalculated, some task that we will do with students, I try to calculate it earlier as to some surprises won't come out and it's somewhat boring, because nothing interesting is happening there, I'm not concentrated substantively too much on it, only I simply have to calculate it, so it is also tedious.
>
> (Teacher, interview_34, female, MA, natural sciences)

In that situation, therefore, the tedious transition between a well-known starting point and well-known end point is boring, where everything is established but needs to be done merely to check it.

Two respondents found it occasionally boring to co-teach classes with another teacher.

> When you conduct [classes] with two teachers and somehow we share who is talking about what, when another person speaks, and it's known that the same seminars have been conducted with the same person many times, this boredom is sometimes a bit inevitable.
>
> (Teacher, interview_43, male, PhD, natural sciences)

Here, again, boredom is a matter of repetition, inactivity and waiting – an intermittent lack of engagement.

Prevention and coping techniques

For each potential cause of boredom there is a remedy that can be applied to alleviate the feeling. If the cause of particular boredom was a lack of student engagement, then student activity will be the best remedy. Some of the respondents indicate student activity as the main reason for not experiencing boredom during classes. Students ask questions, initiate discussions, force teachers to rethink issues, to reformulate their knowledge, or reconsider their plans for classes. Student involvement make classes unpredictable, non-boring, because 'there will always be students who will have different reactions to the material other than I assumed and other than I have ever seen' – as one of the respondents said (Teacher, interview_12, male, PhD, natural sciences). Some teachers actively stimulate themselves during classes by changing the plan or form of work on an ongoing basis, introducing new exercises, manipulating subjects/tasks, or changing their order so as to be constantly engaged during the classes. Others use physical movement (e.g. walking during lectures).

If teachers are periodically inactive during classes, for example, while waiting for students to accomplish a task or waiting for their part of the class (when co-teaching), they may use computers or phones to occupy themselves (two respondents gave such an answer).

Boredom due to repetition can be fought by constantly introducing change, either within classes (change of materials, texts, theories, approaches, methods, 'testing various types of non-standard forms of conducting classes' (Teacher, interview_12, male, PhD, natural sciences) or, if possible, by rotating courses. Some teachers are forced to prepare new courses on an annual basis due to changes in the general curriculum of studies or changes being a consequence of creating a new unit, specialization or degree programme, others choose to introduce some kind of class rotation to prevent emaciating. As one of the respondents described:

> Perhaps boredom is too big a word, but some material fatigue in connection with teaching occurs relatively quickly. I try never to conduct the same course more than three, or in individual cases four years in a row, because I have the impression that I'm a much worse teacher after this time. In the first year it's okay, in the second year is much better, it's sensational, but in the third year I have no further ideas for improvement, sometimes only single ones, but fatigue emerges, because if I had to read the same texts, told the same jokes and anecdotes and showed the same slides for three, five or 10 [years] ... then I'd cease to enjoy it as much and it seems to me that this enthusiasm I have in the first years of teaching is very important for these classes, that students somehow note it, understand it, and it infects them, so I try to rotate classes, and never run the same class longer than those three-four years in a row.
>
> (Teacher, interview_21, male, hab., humanities)

It seems justified to assume that this kind of course rotation may be interpreted as a semi-deliberate method to prevent boredom, disengagement and burn out, which would be a possible outcome of repeating one course for many years. Of course, personal characteristics, including individual boredom proneness, may play a significant role in whether an academic teacher feels bored or exhausted in this kind of situation, or constantly finds new stimulation to remain active and engaged in teaching the same course for several years or even decades. Some fulfil their need for change through small amendments each year, some need a less or more radical change of subject every few years, some seem to be immune to the corrosive effect of repetitiveness and always find a way to remain creative, to find something new in an old subject, and others feel bored if they have no or few opportunities to change courses they teach.

Research-related work

> Science is exciting. Science is cutting-edge. Science is fun. It is now time to come clean. This glittering depiction of the quest for knowledge is... well, perhaps not an outright lie, but certainly a highly edited version of the truth. Science is not a whirlwind dance of excitement, illuminated by the brilliant strobe light of insight. It is a long, plodding journey through a dim maze of dead ends. It is painstaking data collection followed by repetitious calculation. It is revision, confusion, frustration, bureaucracy and bad coffee. In a word, science can be boring.
>
> (Battersby, 2009, p. 58)

Science is frequently an object of veneration, and many scientists and philosophers of science still mythicize and portray it as a set of constant intellectual challenges or puzzle-solving (Fleck, 1979; Kuhn, 1996). This polished discursive strategy obscures the everyday work of researchers, however, with its frustrations, dissatisfactions, and boredoms, which are, even if significantly less visible and painful than in others areas of academic activity, still far from non-existent. Kevin Donnelly even suggests that boredom is such a pervasive element of scientific life that it 'cannot go unexamined' (2013, p. 503). In this section, I would like to respond to that claim and scrutinize the experience of boredom in the research-related work of academics. This part of the chapter will concentrate almost exclusively on the experiences of a small fraction of my sample – it is, therefore, far from providing a finite picture of academic boredom in that area, and is instead a selection of possible boredom-inducing research-related activities characteristic of academics in particular disciplines, employing particular methodologies, and working in particular places.

Tediousness

Some participants admitted that scientific work may at times be laborious/tedious, and that it occasionally prompts minor boredom due to repetitiveness, routine, monotony, predictability, and the failure of expectations. Some students might conceive of research as a constant process of making discoveries, but it frequently involves many invidious technical tasks that simply have to be done, but do not always provide imminent joy and satisfaction. Some researchers may experience moments of demotivation, tedium, and discouragement, for instance, when they are compelled to repeat the same activities many times when they fail to be successful, and the desired result is toilsome, arduous, and laborious to accomplish, at times becoming a kind of drudgery and chore. Yet, such activities are the condition *sine qua non* for any kind of positive outcomes. As studies on scientific work have shown, many breakthrough discoveries and advances were achieved 'at the cost of an enormous amount of tedious labor in the face of serious and very complex – but ultimately uninteresting – obstacles' (Traweek, 1992, p. 87). Repetitiveness may be a major cause of situational boredom during research activities. An example may be provided by some common activities in archaeological excavations.

> For example, washing the pottery sherds, you know, I also went through all the stages and at the beginning washing the sherds was interesting, for the simple reason that they are painted, relics, so every sherd was taken, cleaned, examined, but when you do it the hundredth or thousandth time and then you see these sherds again, you still draw [them], well it's boring as hell ... at the beginning it interests you, because you want to know what [it] is, then as you already know what's that when you see a dirty sherd and you already know that this is an amphora of such and such [kind], and this is a jug of such and such [kind], you know what to expect, you don't expect anything new, so it becomes like ironing the shirt, because the brain also switches off and you just clean [the shell] automatically.
> (Teacher, interview_41, male, prof., humanities)

This kind of boredom is thus a function of acquiring knowledge and can be successfully managed by the hierarchical order at the university as such tasks are frequently delegated to the least advanced researchers. When someone habituates to such an activity they usually already reach a position enabling to delegate it to someone with a lower position, for whom it is new and still challenging. This transition often takes many years, however, which results in boredom due to the repetitive performance of simple, no longer engaging tasks. In some cases, when the work is more individualized and grants are hard to obtain, even advanced researchers are compelled to do simple, routine activities on their own, but it still seems to be a problem specifically connected to lower positions in academia.

Another example of qualitative underload can be derived from the field of positional astronomy (the branch of astronomy popular in the nineteenth century, with the main aim of mapping the sky), which was described by Donnelly (2013) based on historical records. Thanks to technological advances in research methods, a large part of the work at the observatory 'was of a kind that almost any bright schoolboy could learn to do in a few weeks' (Newcomb, 1903, p. 129, cited in Donnelly, 2013, p. 487) and no longer required high skills. Such human 'computers,' doing repetitive, sedentary, and unchallenging work, were bored irrespective of the scientific significance of the final outcomes of their work, which advanced astronomy in a way unknown before. This situation is also relevant for some of my respondents, who are operating without any kind of support from technical staff, or without grant funds for PhD students to be hired to undertake such repetitive, simple tasks that nevertheless are essential for any kind of serious and successful scientific endeavour (Donnelly, 2013; Latour and Woolgar, 1986, p. 31).

Satiety/overload

Another cause of boredom may be satiety and general weariness with one's research. This is frequently associated with a kind of repetitiveness, although not necessarily with unchallenging tasks. This can be a consequence of (1) an overabundance of data, (2) prolonged work on a particular dissertation or book, a particular domain/subject, etc., or (3) the performance of a particular research task for a long time. The quotes below from respondents may serve as examples of these situations.

> It bored me at the level of analysis, when I overdid the data and now I have to introduce about a thousand questionnaires to Excel ... Well, at some point I feel bored ... and this is a moment of boredom and overflow and I do get bored at the analysis level, unfortunately.
> (Teacher, interview_60, female, PhD, social sciences)

> I don't know whether it was due to some external factors or my discouragement [with] what I was working on, but the issue of habilitation where you write about a specific subject for several years ... at some point it starts to get boring ... and at one point writing this habilitation was an unpleasant experience for me, precisely because of the necessity to limit my interests to a very selected field.
> (Teacher, interview_46, male, hab., humanities)

> In the case of the research, I had moments of boredom at the beginning, when there was a long study and I didn't have a break, and now it's the other way around, it rather research is something additional and I'm bored with reading or theoretical work.... Fatigue probably depends on how often I have to do a particular activity. When I did more research as part of the work it was research [that was] more tedious, and reading was relaxing, and texts were more absorbing, now when I have to supplement the theoretical stuff it's reading [that is] more boring, and the study is such an interlude.
> (Teacher, interview_19, male, MA, social sciences)

It is worth noting that all the above statements come from representatives of the social sciences and humanities which may be partially explained by the fact that researchers in the natural sciences more frequently work on a project basis. Projects are usually shorter, and there are more opportunities to pursue a few projects simultaneously and to work in groups, which to some extent can avert the feeling of boredom. It is also suggested, albeit in an anecdotal manner, that human sciences are not primarily based on the refutation of theories or solving issues but rather on 'growing tired' of

(Barrett, 1975, p. 551) or getting bored with them (Gordon Allport, cited in Bauman and Leoncini, 2018). Noteworthy, all quotes were from non-tenured researchers (or referred to the period before obtaining habilitation), which might be associated with more opportunities to delegate a surplus of tasks, establishing research groups and higher level of 'immunity' to boredom thanks to habituation.

The method of data gathering and analysis is also an important issue, and it differs between (sub)disciplines and may affect the degree, form, and severity of boredom experienced, and the disciplinary culture may make academics less or more open to including researcher's emotions as an integral part of the process and affect the likelihood of admitting boredom. Two of the most frequently mentioned areas of potential research boredom, which epitomize the qualities described above, will be presented below: field and lab work.

Field boredom

Many anthropologists in their publications, and some of my respondents, confessed that ethnographic/qualitative research fieldwork can be associated with both situational and chronic boredom (Lévi-Strauss, 1961; Rabinow, 1977; Barley, 1983, 1989; Malinowski, 1989) – although this does not mean that field research in the social sciences is a quintessentially boring method of investigation. For instance, Bronisław Malinowski (1989) experienced boredom in all possible understandings – he was idle, lazy, demotivated, bored with the research itself and his subjects, touched by existential spleen, and suffered from loneliness, isolation, repetitiveness, climate hardships, and lack of leisure opportunities (he was always waiting for new sets of books to be sent to him from Australia). The French anthropologist, Claude Lévi-Strauss, also seemed to suffer a clinical example of field boredom and he undertook field research only once in his long and fruitful scholarly life. One can only speculate whether boredom was one of the main reasons for this. In his famous book, *Tristes tropiques* (1961), he repeatedly complained about tedium, fatigue, forced idleness, frequent waiting and the repetitiveness of ethnographic endeavour, which he compared with military service (discipline and drudgery) and bureaucracy (cataloguing genealogies or other data). He noted that there is no place for adventure in the life of an anthropologist, because boredom effectively superseded it.

The primary cause of field boredom is waiting for respondents/informants to arrive or for something significant (or at all) to happen.

> There was terrible weather, then it was just really terrifying and windy, and X [a place of research] was in such a place that you had to get to it quite a lot and then there were few people and I sat there for six-seven

> hours, and really one, two people per hour came, and then I just had to sit for a few hours and doing not much.
> (Teacher, interview_20, female, MA, humanities, cf. Rabinow, 1977)

> These two months—although professionally revealing and at times exciting—were characterized by an all-encompassing feeling of boredom. In the beginning I would sit in the same chair, in the same corridor, for hours and hours, day after day, with nothing to do and seemingly very little to observe.
> (Bengtsson, 2012, p. 536)

This is a quintessentially boring/transitional situation, as a researcher has nothing/little to observe at the moment but ought to be prepared for action immediately when something happens. A researcher, thus, is not involved in the situation at hand, but cannot disengage entirely and begins a new, non-research-related activity instead. This seems to be an essential characteristic of some qualitative research methods, basically defined by their low density. Ethnographic research in general and participant observation specifically can be described as waiting for revealing moments, for events that may push research forward.

> It happens that it's boring, but on the other hand you are waiting for this breakthrough point .... one lives for these breakthrough points ... and then indeed there is a month of such intense agitation, then everything settles again into a traditional rhythm, something is happening there somehow, so yeah, of course research is often boring, but [it] is like an inherent element of this research process, to wait for this wonderful breakthrough moment.
> (Teacher, interview_25, male, PhD, humanities)

Some fields/methods are thus characterized by a low density of events and a high level of repetitiveness and monotony. Monotonous may all be: (1) the landscape, physical environment of a research unchanging for many days,[15] (2) everyday routines, sets of necessary activities performed day in and day out,[16] and/or (3) observed subject behaviours. On many occasions, therefore, a researcher is bored due to lack of challenge, and to predictability, as they share not constantly excited lives of their subjects. As John Van Maanen (1974) described in his research into police work:

> Certainly most of my time in the police world was spent in long conversations, looking for something to do, and attending to the routine, tedious, everyday tasks the police are everywhere required to do. Occasionally such mundane matters are interrupted by an exhilarating event, and in those moments I have found myself swept away by them. (p. 116)

Yet, it is these new events that are the rare and steady routine of everyday life that defines field work. Another issue may be that sometimes research merely confirms common knowledge that appears obvious, but nevertheless needs confirmation by research. In such situations, some researchers may feel bored as they do not acquire new knowledge but rather ground the one they previously have. The same situation may be a symptom of research saturation, when a researcher has already gained all knowledge relevant to their investigation and their scope of interests, and become habituated to their subjects' culture/social life to the extent of naturalness (cf. Barley, 2018).

> During research boredom occurs .... there were phenomena that I already recognised and of course I could verify what was happening, but there was nothing intriguing about it ... simply from time to time I had such moments that I just pulled a book out.
> (Teacher, interview_19, male, MA, social sciences)

Of course, such a lack of novelty is highly subjective and may be just a sensation of a researcher, but it definitely suggests that a researcher is tired with their field and has lost, to some extent, interest in it – thus, boredom may serve as a vital sign of the excessive internalization of the field, as the actions of actors appear obvious, normal and predictable to a researcher. As a result, a researcher distances themselves from their role and lessens their engagement in the field, epitomized by reading a book during field observations, as noted by the participant above. These moments in which a researcher doubts the meaning or sense of their presence in the field can all be described as field boredom, both in the short or long term, and for instance, due to exhaustion, a sensation of wasted time, or lack of significant data acquisition. Boredom, nevertheless, may also constitute a key component in such a method, as it can be valuable data, a feature that defines the lives of one's subjects (see Bengtsson, 2012). It is natural to neglect these moments of boredom, however, and focus attention on meaningful events: rituals, active interactions, conversations, and so on, and not on the empty time between them.

Another situation in which boredom may occasionally be present during qualitative fieldwork is when interviewing. It is very rare for a researcher to be bored during a conversation because it would spoil the interview and more experienced researchers have learnt not to let themselves be bored, and how to maintain the necessary level of involvement even in boring moments, moments when the content of an interviewee's talk is repetitive, predictable, not relevant to the research subject, or not significant from the researcher's point of view. There is always the possibility that a participant will turn out to be a bore, which is, an interpretative category but may correspond to a sense of meaninglessness in a particular interview or a subject's disengagement from the situation of the conversation (e.g. long, off-topic stories couched in an incomprehensive manner).

Some respondents admitted also that making transcriptions: writing down the content of interview from the audio recording, may at times be extremely boring. On the one hand, the activity itself is tedious and arduous and the content predictable if the interviewer and transcriber is the same person, on the other hand but, it can include moments of revelations, a valuable time to recollect the content of conversation and reflect on it.

It is also worth noting that boredom may serve a positive role as a creativity booster and research facilitator. Field boredom may trigger the creative process and make it easier to make sense of observed phenomena. On the other side, a subject's boredom may make them more willing to talk to a researcher as a way to mitigate the feeling. On numerous occasions, it is thanks to boredom that prospect respondents are eager to interact with a researcher. In this sense, it can serve as a gate-keeping feature. An ethnographer can serve as a curiosity and an inexhaustible source of conversation topics – as a boredom breaker (Rabinow, 1977; Barley, 1983; O'Neill, 2017).

Laboratory boredom

Another area of potential research-related boredom is laboratory work. On the one hand, many researchers deny being bored in the lab, possibly due to boredom habituation, a strong internalization of the passion narrative, and treating the lab reality as something natural beyond the realm of reflexivity (Campbell, 2003), or because of a prevalence of frustration and weariness rather than boredom. Many of my respondents highlighted the constant threat of frustration as closely connected to lab work: (a) frustration because an experiment or some procedure was unsuccessful and had to be repeated over and over again without positive outcomes that may be strengthened by the failure of expectations; reality-shock associated with the fact 'that failure is a normal outcome of routine work' (Delamont and Atkinson, 2001, p. 88; cf. Firestein, 2015); (b) frustration because some other scientists may overtake one, may publish the positive results of their research on the same problem faster; or (c) frustration because of consecutive grant rejection and the resulting instability of funding that can have a tremendous impact on research process (Wagner, 2011a). Despite passion and frustration narrations, however, some respondents found 'boredom' to be a relevant label for some experiences of lab work. The occurrence of boredom in respondent narratives depends strongly on individual attitudes, personal characteristics, work environment (e.g. co-workers), and position in the project (being supervisor or 'wet job hands'), but participants seem to be in agreement that potential boredom-inducing factors may be (1) quantitative underload (e.g. waiting), (2) qualitative underload (routine, repetitiveness), (3) poor work organization, and/or (4) social isolation.

Lab boredom, according to some respondents, may be prompted by the necessity to wait for something to happen; for instance, an experiment or procedure to end. This potential boredom is often not realized, as scientists successfully and meaningfully occupy their waiting time by gossiping, socializing, eating, reading scientific publications, doing paper/bureaucratic work (ordering agents and lab equipment, or preparing documentation, etc., as the majority of Polish laboratories lack lab managers), or relaxing/resting. These options are not always possible, however, or people are too fatigued to perform such activities in a meaningful way, and begins to simply kill time – for instance, because an experiment failed and it has to be repeated, and one is compelled to stay late in the lab waiting for the results, but not fully capable of doing job-related activities. This leaves an amount of time empty, when it is not possible to be engaged in lab work due to weariness, and people resort to killing time, for example, by surfing the internet or watching videos.

> Sometimes it's like this that you feel a kind of fatigue or such discouragement, resulting from fatigue, and simply a little bit anaemic, ... sometimes you would like not to be here anymore, but you have to sit here, because you have to finish something, or, I don't know, turn off some equipment or wait for something and you're only sitting. You would not want to be here, but you know that you have to finish something there because it's somehow your, maybe not so much a duty that somebody will examine you, but you know that if you don't do something, something will be wasted, or you'll be back in time with further research and you sit here and would like not to be here.
> (Teacher, interview_44, male, PhD, natural sciences)

Work organization may result in a similar situation. As many Polish laboratories lack steady lab managers, much technical and bureaucratic work associated with the lab's everyday functioning has to be done by the scientists themselves. Such activities detach researchers from their scientific projects and may disrupt the day, leading to the situation described by one respondent that 'it's still early enough that I won't leave the laboratory, and already so late that I won't do what I planned for this day and then very often boredom appears' (Teacher, interview_43, male, PhD, natural sciences).

Another potentially boredom-inducing situation are all those moments between two actions in an experimental chain (strictly written in the protocol) when a machine is working and a scientist is forced to wait for the results to do the next manipulation. These periods of time (from 10 minutes to several hours – if we consider the time for pipetting) do not require a high level of concentration or vigilance – some tasks are done quasi-mechanically, or thoroughly by the machines. Some experiments require regular and frequent activity, for instance, once in 10 minutes. Such short breaks are not sufficient to perform the majority of activities listed above that make a meaningful use of time, and may prompt occasional boredom, as one is unable to engage fully in anything due to the necessity of being alert to, for instance, changing a buffer once every 10 minutes. Time in general plays a highly significant role in the lab research process, and organizing it in a meaningful way is a matter of training, socialization, growing experience. Boredom may occur under poor work organization (see Delamont and Atkinson, 2001; van der Heijden, Schepers, and Nijssen, 2012), and this is especially likely for beginners – MA students or first year PhD students. The ability to manage time is basic and a crucial competence in laboratory work. If the time necessary to finish an experiment or procedure is not correctly estimated, then one may be unprepared to spend waiting time in an engaging way.

The second major potential cause of lab boredom highlighted by my respondents was routine and repetitiveness. Laboratory work is based on repetitive activities that must be performed routinely in a strictly defined order as the essential method of achieving meaningful results. Such activities may occasionally induce boredom and stress, because if one makes a mistake it may result in the failure of a whole procedure, making it necessary to repeat it from scratch. One frequently performs such repetitive procedures semi-automatically without much cognitive involvement but enough attention has to be maintained so as not to make a mistake. Some respondents noted that unlike their counterparts from better-funded academic systems in Polish laboratories, there are few or no technical staff, and thus all researchers have to perform many simple activities that in prestigious labs are usually done by technical staff (see e.g. Wycisk et al., 2018, p. 15). As one of respondents noted:

> You do the same things many times, especially since these are simple manual activities that you must do and you don't need to have a scientific education, there is some simple algorithm, you could teach it to a child who would not have to know what they were doing, but could be set a certain number of activities. If you have to do such things often and they don't end with success, it can be something that generally arouses some boredom or discouragement, because it isn't something that is intellectually stimulating, nor is it a type of movement that is stimulating for you.
> (Teacher, interview_44, male, PhD, natural sciences)

Another possible reason for boredom is lab bureaucracy, which is also frequently included in the duties of scientists, such as stocktaking for control purposes

> ... where every cupboard, every refrigerator, everything must be labelled and you need to dig out some apparatus for electrophoresis, long broken, which everyone has already forgotten, but it's in papers that it is there, so it must be, because if control comes and there is no apparatus,

there will be a row ... The lady in the secretary's has a huge pile of tables, which is unearthed whenever there is an inventory and control, actually it take so much time that one gets an impression that it's one after another ... and then there is boredom on one hand and irritation on the other, because you would like to focus on your experiments and it's not always possible.
(Teacher, interview_43, male, PhD, natural sciences)

The last potential cause of lab boredom noted by respondents is performing experiments without belief in their success. As one of the respondents indicated, at times an experiment had been planned, but in the meantime a scientist had lost the conviction that it would work. In such a situation 'by the power of inertia and tenacity one pushes it forward, at the same time having the sense of wasting time and boredom anyway' (Teacher, interview_43, male, PhD, natural sciences).

Lab boredom can be also caused by social isolation, when a person is without a team, and works alone, and is separated from animated scientific exchange with professional colleagues. This is also precisely the case of 'visionary' scientists who are ahead of their time, who cannot find another person to converse with and feel lonely. The lack of scientific interaction could be also a source of boredom, because of the impossibility of performing science at an expected level due to the expectations of a research partner or collaborator that are not fulfilled (cf. Gambetta and Origgi, 2013; see Wagner, 2011a).

Communicating science

Many academics admitted that communicating their results in the form of books, theses, scientific papers, and so on was a frequently disliked, procrastinated and at times boring activity (cf. Maeland and Brunstad, 2009, p. 8; Svendsen, 2005, p. 34). Many also noted that they definitely preferred researching as cognitively much more rewarding than simply writing and then editing their publications. As one of the respondents explained:

We have an interesting study, but you already know everything, you have already counted and been in the field and illustrated it, and now you still have to sit down and describe it all, and everybody thinks so, that you would actually go to the next project and another intellectual challenge and not necessarily now being involved in writing, arranging it in a report, or even a book .... The great mathematician Banach is probably the most famous example, whose colleagues wrote his PhD with his scattered notes, because he never dealt with something that he had already solved.
(Teacher, interview_56, female, hab., social sciences)

If we assume, following sociologists and philosophers of science, that science essentially comprises a series of puzzle-solving that are meant to satisfy one's cognitive curiosity, then writing a disciplined report of the findings would constitute a form of obstruction, a delay until the next fulfilling research experience. In fact, it is sometimes perceived as such, for instance, when one is obliged to demonstrate a number of publications in a grant report. Of course, publications, as a basic way of sharing one's scientific knowledge and paying back the debt to tax-payers, are also vital measures of one's career progress, end points of some stages and an essential way to be visible in the academic world, but the process of their production, with long editing and reviewing phases, may at times be conceived as drudgery and a tiresome nuisance.

> When I'm about to sit down and do something, I'm looking for a million different things so as to, God forbid, not deal with writing papers. Processing research results, doing something in the laboratory – it's ok, but when I sit down and I'm to produce this paper, something twists inside me somewhere, and this is the last thing I will get into .... All these editing issues, amendments, conversations with the publishing house, it also takes so much time ... there is no proper comma here, switch the dots here, this is not a proper formula here, here the lower case letters, then big letters again, and here something has not gone through, and transform the picture here into some other software, and hours are spent on such a work, which is neither research nor teaching, simply such a boring work, which is also a bit frustrating that you have to change it five times.
> (Teacher, interview_71, female, prof., natural sciences)

As some respondents noted, scientific work is characterized by delayed gratification, because it may take years from the moment of the initial idea to its final outcome in the form of publication (cf. Wagner, 2011a). This may result in a temporary decrease in motivation and satisfaction from work.

Writing academic texts

The next issue involves the sensation described by a few respondents that some parts of scientific production are simply art for art's sake, and that formal schemes are common in the realm of scientific publications. This applies to degree theses that, as some respondents suggest, are expected in some disciplines by tradition, to be long, jargon-ridden and boring in order to satisfy the tastes of conservative reviewers. 'A boring PhD thesis is a good PhD thesis' (Teacher, interview_62, female, PhD, social sciences) because, as mentioned earlier, it seems to be a rule of a thumb in some disciplines or groups that boringness is equated with scientific quality and serves as a final proof of the high quality of a researcher's scientific competence. As Malamud (2016) noted: '[t]his is academia's dirty secret: if your work is too straightforwardly interesting, there's something wrong with you; we celebrate dullness and obscurity as brilliance' (cf. Becker, 2007). Jargon serves as secret language, as sorcerers' spells (Andreski, 1972; Zijderveld, 1979) whose aim is to distinguish insiders from strangers (dilettantes). Cioran compared jargon to a drug which produces the illusion of depth which is meant to ravish and intimidate outsiders. He observed that 'the philosophical text, translated into a common language, somehow strangely loses importance' (1999, p. 175). Wright Mills drew a similar conclusion in his famous *The Sociological Imagination* (2000), where he translated the work of the famous American sociologist, Talcott Parson, into regular English, revealing its apparent sophistication as a set of platitudes, unverified assumptions and theses on the level of introductory course of academic sociology. It is interesting that the tendency for using jargon seems to be more common among young researchers who, as a few of the respondents suggested, want to gain credits thanks to using obscure and strangely overformal language in their texts. The other side of the coin is that, for instance, some PhD advisors and senior academics require such language as the inevitable element of a good scientific text. In that capacity, however, much depends on national/academic/institutional culture, as well as the personal idiosyncrasies of some academics.

In general, two kinds of activities performed by academics can be distinguished; those perceived by them as being of a creative nature and those that are uncreative. The latter may frequently be found boring, as they provide little or no space for one's invention/creative freedom, being imitative and schematic. An example of such an activity may be writing a standard journal article with a very strict and predefined structure, leaving little room for creative work. One is required to reproduce a well-known scheme, which some respondents found boring and overly restrictive.

Reading scientific publications

This schematism and the use of jargon may lead to the boredom of some academics when reading such scientific texts. As Kaj Sand-Jensen (2007) noted, insisted excitement and adventurousness of research is rarely reflected in scientific publications which are 'consistently boring' (his ironic article consists of recommendations about how to write such a boring text). As Baghdadchi (2005) explained, academic publications are not produced to be interesting but to present 'rigorous arguments that can withstand attack' (p. 322). This transition from meaning to pure functionality epitomizes the inner logic of boringness. It can also be an efficient strategy with which to defend one's argumentation, as a critical reader may: (1) not understand the argumentation at all, (2) not be sure whether they have reconstructed it correctly, and thus, not be too critical in case they reveal their incompetence, or (3) become bored with it to the extent of being unwilling to go deeper in the nuances of the reasoning.

Many academic texts are found boring because of their limited creative input and/or explanatory value (fragmentation and gap-spotting), methodological and/or theoretical stiffness or formulaic, impersonal and frequently incomprehensive language. Alvesson, Gabriel, and Paulsen (2017) diagnose 'a proliferation of meaningless research of no value to society and of only modest value to its authors' (p. 4) that not contribute much to the existing corpus of knowledge and are published primarily for instrumental reasons (competition for employments, promotions, or financial benefits) and not out of intrinsic quest for knowledge. They call such text 'yawn-papers,' which suggest the boredom reaction while reading them.

Yet, this is not to say that all boring texts are irrelevant for science. Quite the opposite: many crucial publications in various disciplines are generally perceived for some reason as extremely boring, but are still taught to students. They are generally called 'classics' which are proverbially defined as publications that everybody has heard of or knows about, but (almost) nobody has ever read them. As one of the participants confessed:

> I get bored, for example, when I'm preparing a major review of literature, which may sound paradoxical, because these are very interesting things described [*laughs*], but I sometimes fall asleep over the texts and force myself to learn what is written there.
> (Teacher, interview_45, female, PhD, social sciences)

Reviewing texts of others

A similar problem was noted by some respondents reviewing PhD theses, journal articles and/or habilitation and professor's books.[17] As one respondent complained, many promotional books are produced 'by weight': they are excessively long in comparison with their original contribution.

> When I read such books, 500 pages, a professor's book [books that are advanced in the process of obtaining a university professor position] but actually material for a 40-page-long study, that's when I get bored and think to myself, 'God, why do I have to read, I don't know, some information I find, everyone would find on Wikipedia,' so I'm bored with it.
> (Teacher, interview_28, female, prof., humanities)

Such a verbosity means that the duty of reviewing such works occasionally turns out to be boring, and in a situation of overload can constitute an obstacle to performing scientific work. The same respondent even joked that she should publish 'collected reviews instead of a scientific book' (Teacher, interview_28, female, prof., humanities), which may result in some kind of frustration. The reviewing process can be boring due to predictability, repetitiveness, lack of originality, or the low level of the reviewed text, but a reviewer is obliged to read papers carefully from desk to desk, and at times this duty may induce boredom during the process.

Prevention

For most types of boredom described in above sections, the only remedy is habituation and socialization. The only potential cause of boredom that is vigorously dealt with by my respondents is waiting, being stuck between projects and tasks. Pursuing many open projects at the same time constituted frequent preventive technique. As one of participants noted:

> Fortunately, I have so many projects open that even if there is stagnation in one, we are waiting for measurements, or sample preparation, or the arrival of a reagent, I have several other projects in which something is happening all the time.
> (Teacher, interview_38, male, PhD, natural sciences)

Yet, even if someone has only one project it usually has many strands, and thereby it is perfectly possible to rotate the activities in the way that prevents satiation and a feeling of boredom. It can often be connected to job experience: the time one has to accumulate the knowledge and/or contacts needed to be able to have many projects open simultaneously, which would prevent stagnation. Mathematics may be an example. As one of respondents noted:

> Around 10 years after a PhD thesis one has only just got a sufficiently large resource of ideas that one works on at the same time. It grows, things that didn't work out are put aside and it starts to roll like a snowball, when an idea, when one thing doesn't proceed, as one accumulates experience, one begins to find the keys to those other problems that were put aside. I hope that it works like that, at the moment I have a feeling that mathematics starts working out for me again.
> (Teacher, interview_59, male, PhD, natural sciences)

For the same reason, some respondents praise the multidimensionality of academic work, including such diverse activities as teaching, bureaucracy and research, which, when stirred in the right proportions, may keep stagnation and satiety at bay – boredom as well. Moreover, many academics seem to be sensation seekers in a very specific sense – they are addicted to novelty and challenge of a specific, intellectual kind. Many respondents, especially junior ones, admitted to a strong reluctance to work constantly on one subject for a long time – over time their cognitive curiosity becomes satisfied and they begin, quite involuntarily, to search for a new field of interest as they grow tired of the previous one. Some continue their old projects while simultaneously starting a new ones, preparing a book on one subject performing desk research on the next one, and so on. They are foxes, according to Isaiah Berlin's (1953) distinction, who need regular change and challenge, diversifying their fields of expertise, even if only slightly, and energetically fighting boredom before it manages to emerge. The opposite type, hedgehogs, who concentrate on one main idea and pursue one big project for a long time, would probably be much more liable to boredom, but at the same time, they have higher boredom threshold and may rarely reach their limit of personal meaninglessness.

Another preventing or coping strategies are employed against the many moments of monotony in the lab. A radio is always the privileged partner of long laboratory days. The bench and experimental work space are usually prepared for several people – so discussions are frequent; the main topics are jokes, politics, movies, cuisine, and Facebook stories; rarely personal confidences. Laboratory problems only occasionally become the subject of conversation, and usually the dynamics of discussions are adjusted to accompany the main task of pipetting, so all subjects that require more attention or animated discussions are avoided. Those discussions are supposed to make tasks be less repetitive and less boring (cf. Wagner, 2011a, 2014b).

Notes

1 Interestingly, many boring qualities are not entirely inherent to presenters but stem from the inaccurate preparation of papers, including too much content that is impossible to cram into 15 or 20 minutes of time for the presentation. As a result of the shortage of time and too much information to share, some speakers begin to speak faster, to omit slides or threads to the extent that it becomes incomprehensible. Thus, many problematic qualities of presentations stem from a tendency to include too much information in the presentation – the pace increases, narrative breaks makich speech chaotic and the aim of communication is superseded by the aim of fitting the information into the time limit (which is often not met anyway).
2 Cf. 'come to The Conference Presentation not as trained public speakers, but as sheets of white paper densely packed with lines of Courier-New, which we intone nasally while modulating with amazing rapidity from a mind-numbing drone to an ear-piercing shriek. We stand before our sleepy audience – regardless of time of day, they're understandably drowsy between the shrieks – and dutifully waste 20 minutes of their time' (Castronova, 2013, p. 66).
3 This might to some extent be specifically Polish, as when I organized international conferences only Polish prospective participants used to ask how many points the conference provides for active participation.
4 Cf. Kulczycki (2011): 'The bane of Polish conferences are 'regulars.' Appearing at various conferences, you can meet the same people. At first, it seems to be an ordinary case, however, after some time it turns out that we still hear

the same paper! The title (always matched to the conference title) and the main 'variable' of the text change. Once there was a presentation about the role of women in culture, and the second time (almost the same paper) about the dilemmas of modern man. It is also symptomatic that such 'regulars' do not give their texts to post-conference volumes. And what if someone noticed something.'

5 'Unfortunately, I guess [that] after habilitation, there is a point when one is exploited on various sides, if, God forbid, one leans into the corridor, 'oh, there you are, you will do this and this, and this [*laughs*]' (Teacher, interview_55, female, hab., natural sciences).

6 It was abolished by the novelization of the law introduced in 2011 (Ustawa z dn. 18 marca 2011 r. o zmianie ustawy – Prawo o szkolnictwie wyższym), however, it has been restored for humanities, social, and theological sciences according to the law brought in 2018 (Ustawa z Dn. 20 Lipca 2018 r. Prawo o Szkolnictwie Wyższym i Nauce, 221, 9).

7 'Now I have such a nice game on the phone and recently my approach to faculty meetings has changed because of this game, because it's a time when I can uninterruptedly play on the phone, pressing the button during voting' (Teacher, interview_46, male, hab., humanities).

8 'They are actually sitting on Facebook or on Twitter, which can also be deduced later based on the hours in which they post something' (Teacher, interview_21, male, hab., humanities).

9 This situation was certainly amplified during Covid-19 pandemic when many educational institutions shifted to online learning on a regular basis. Usually many students do not show their faces and/or use their microphones to talk to the teacher. In such circumstances, a teacher frequently has an irresistible impression of 'talking to the wall' in the form of a computer screen, which can be a highly alienating experience.

10 The number of students increased from 390,409 in the academic year 1990/91 to 1,841,251 in 2010/11 (GUS, 2005, 2011). During the academic year 2017/18 1,291,870 students were registered in all Polish higher education institutions (GUS, 2018).

11 From about 9 in the academic year 1990/91 to 18.4 in 2010/11. SSR in the academic year 2017/18 amounted to 13.6 (14 for University of Warsaw, GUS 2005, 2011, 2018).

12 Interestingly, the 2005 bill was less specific on this point, specifying only that employees can obtain additional teaching hours, and leaving the rules and mode of entrusting academics up to the university senate (Ustawa z Dn. 27 Lipca 2005 r. Prawo o Szkolnictwie Wyższym, 131,2).

13 Especially for junior staff, which differentiates Poland from some Western European academic systems, where younger scientists are primarily focused on doing research with a minimal teaching load (Kwiek, 2015, p. 448). Among countries included in the research, in comparison to Poland, the teaching load was significantly lower in Germany, Norway, Switzerland, and Great Britain, slightly lower in Austria, Finland, and the Netherlands and similar in Portugal, Italy, and Ireland (Kwiek, 2015, pp. 453–4).

14 Viz. Rozporządzenie Ministra Nauki i Szkolnictwa Wyższego z Dn. 2 Grudnia 2016 o w Sprawie Warunków Wynagradzania Za Pracę i Przyznawania Innych Świadczeń Związanych z Pracą Dla Pracowników Zatrudnionych w Uczelni Publicznej, appendix 1), which determines the minimal salaries of these two positions at the same level. It is, nevertheless, possible that different universities or faculties fixed different pay rates for adjunct and senior lecturer.

15 Cf. 'Boredom got the upper hand of adventure. For weeks on end the same austere savannah would unroll before me – a land so dry that living plants could scarcely be distinguished from the dead stumps that marked the place where someone had lately struck camp' (Lévi-Strauss, 1961, p. 313).
16 Cf. 'Every day was spent in exactly the same way: setting up camp, slinging our hammocks, with their mosquito-nets, putting our baggage and pack-saddles out of reach of the termites, seeing to our animals, and making ready for the same procedures, in reverse, the next morning. ... Should an Indian band come in sight, we put another routine into action, making a census, taking note of the names given to the various parts of the body and to certain family relationships, drawing up genealogies, and making an inventory of the natives' possessions. If this was 'escape,' I was one of escape's bureaucrats' (Lévi-Strauss, 1961, pp. 313–4).
17 In the Polish academic system, in order to advance in an institutional hierarchy one is compelled to advance a book (currently it can also be a set of interconnected journal articles) for reviewing. This applies to a PhD holder being promoted habilitation and to habilitation holders advancing to university professor (the latter is practiced only in some universities).

Conclusions

Science, as irresistible pursuit of knowledge, emerged from boredom. Some say that out of curiosity, but it is a difference comparable to that which occurs between a glass half empty and a glass half full. Science answers the questions of what, how, and why – these are fundamental questions arising not in the moment of active involvement in the course of affairs, but as a result of reflection, observation, standing aside. These questions are born out of unquenchable thirst for meaning, a state of cognitive void. Thereby, science is initiated and motivated by the mechanism of moving from a wish (question) to its satisfaction (answer) – each subsequent answer raises new questions and pushes the researcher towards a new challenges. No wonder then that at some point the reflection on boredom was initiated. This is how boredology, as I would dare to name the field of boredom studies, has been created, and this is how and why this book has been written. Out of curiosity, to fill the cognitive void but primarily out of boredom – because of boredom and thanks to boredom. Boredom is a main mechanism of human's search for meaning, valuable incentive to intellectual endeavour and simultaneously an emotion that may constitute a curse, result in inhibition of intellectual process in the conclusive direction, be a sign of barrenness and well-being dysfunction associated with extreme exhaustion, demotivation, hopelessness, and dejection. The current book forms an outcome of boredom in both presented meanings (cf. the case of melancholy being the mixture of creative trances and depressive downtimes). The pleasures of absorbing new knowledge was intertwined with reading some banal, boring, jargon-ridden academic papers; the thrill of analysis and constructing meanings was disturbed by a drudgery of technical tasks of transcribing, editing, referencing, or managing proofreading; the joys of academic work were at times shadowed by dispiritedness and discouragement caused by its sorrows such as sense of uncertainty, lack of future, lack of belonging, and alienation. This book, therefore, is not only a result of desk and field research, but is deeply rooted in my own biographical experience of situational and chronic boredom. In that capacity, this book is not merely the description and analysis of various facets of boredom from the theoretical standpoint but may be read also as my personal interpretation of it. I was not only an external observer and a reviewer, I was a participant of my research with all pros and cons of such a standing.

When I declare boredom as my research subject the most frequent reaction is that of disbelief in two interconnected meanings: (a) 'does the university really allow for researching such a minor subject'? and (b) 'It sounds appalling but you must be kidding.' Boredom seems to be still underestimated and many people still take it for granted, many scholars and scientists included. Yet, from all what have been written in this book, it should be highly apparent that the claim of the significance/seriousness of boredom is all but exaggeration and that it is worth closer sociological attention, which still is relatively scarce in comparison to other disciplines and to the social prevalence and consequences of the feeling. This book was meant to be an exemplification of the statement that 'the familiar is not necessarily the known' (Hegel, cited in Gardiner, 2000, p. 1), which fits it into the tradition of reflection on everydayness.

The present study aimed to bridge the gaps in the literature on boredom in several interconnected dimensions by

1. analysing the common perception of boredom basing on both utterances of the respondents (academics) as well as dictionaries and some scientific literature (triangulations of perspectives and fields) and pointing the main methodological problems in researching boredom that may constitute a useful methodological point of reference for future boredom researchers, mainly but not only for sociologists employing qualitative methods of investigation (Chapter 1);
2. providing close scrutiny of existing approaches to defining boredom in various academic disciplines and detailed presentation and systematization of their perspectives on boredom (Chapter 2);
3. providing thorough definitional reflection on boredom and the proposition of sociological, interactional conceptualization of it, which highly exceeds the attention drawn to that matter by the vast majority of boredom researchers – thereby, it constitutes an attempt to bring boredom into the domain of sociology by interpreting it within the context of sociological theory and in sociological terms (Chapter 3);
4. conducting the qualitative sociological investigation on boredom in the work of academics (scholars and scientists employed at the universities), which is presented as an example of work-related boredom in the milieu that has never been research in the context of boredom (Chapters 4 and 5).

The book employs the interactional approach towards boredom. In this theoretical approach, the human being is perceived as an active actor of social life who is not merely a passive receiver of external stimuli but a

Conclusions 189

creator and interpreter of meaning. The central category in this perspective constitutes meaning that arising in the process of interaction between people. Boredom occurs when the interaction is interpreted as bereft of meaning and is expressed in disengagement from active participation in social relations (a 'role distance'). The conceptualization of the phenomenon proposed in the current book is based on these essential premises and constitutes their amplification being an outcome of thorough reflection on both theoretical perspectives derived from literature and empirical data generated in the process of research on the subject that I have been conducting since 2011.

The original definition of situational boredom offered in this book was formulated as follows:

> Boredom is a transient, negatively perceived, transitional emotion or feeling of listless and restless inattention to and engagement withdrawal from interacting with one's social and/or physical environment caused distinctively by an atrophy of personally-valued meaning, the frustrated need for meaning.

Situational boredom is an emotion, if unconscious, or a feeling, if conscious, that is not negative *per se*, while it is axiologically neutral, but it is only negatively perceived. It emerges in the process of interaction between an individual and their social and/or physical (when alone) environment. Thereby, it is a strictly relational as it always emerges in the context of some interplay between one's personal attitude, perception, characteristics, etc. and something external (activity, object, one's social position, institutional ambient, one's life from which one is alienated, etc.). Every manifestation of boredom somehow breaks or ends an interaction, each case of boredom implies its negligence and constitutes withdrawal of engagement and attention (which are interpreted here as virtual synonyms). Boredom is also a state of suspension between engagements – one involvement ceased but another is not yet to begin, it constitutes a kind of stuckness in-between and is characteristic of any on-going transitions that inhibits the process of becoming; a bored person is imprisoned in a kind of limbo, stuck between activities, statuses, experiences, engagements and, in this sense, it is a transitional state. Boredom is a state characterised simultaneously by both listlessness and restlessness, which are oppositely directed – to be bored is to experience listlessness and restlessness at the same time, from which the former is directed towards the situation at hand and the latter is focused on a prospective activity, thus, on escaping from the anaesthetising experience. Another distinctive feature of boredom is its causal relation with a sense of meaninglessness, and to be more specific, personally-perceived lack of meaning in a concrete situation. Chronic boredom in this book has been conceptualized as analogous in its characteristics to situational boredom differing from it in longevity and scope – being a mood that results from the accumulation of situational boredoms within one sphere of life. Such a definition of both situational and chronic boredom is, for all I know, quite novel and constitutes an original proposition of microsociological conceptualization of boredom that yet might be useful for all kinds of further research on the subject.

The main, empirical part of the thesis shows that academics employed at the university occasionally experience work-related situational boredom and that (Polish) academic system and working conditions may contribute to creating a favourable environment for periodic occurrences of a chronic variant of an affliction as well. If 'invention' and 'creativity' are frequently conceived as the keywords describing academic work, the empirical part of this thesis has added a complementary and, to some extent contrary, perspective on this work environment. Boredom was shown to be a social construct, an emotional state emerging in the relationship between the individual and institutional/organisational/social circumstances of one's workplace. It constitutes the role distance response to all these situations that lack real communication, exchange, and interaction, in which meaning is superseded with mere functionality, and an attitude of fiery interest with disengagement. Boredom is an inevitable fact of the current rationalised, bureaucratised, secularised, and commodified academic work, which constitutes nothing else but a kind of knowledge job. The feeling, therefore, needs to be domesticated in the academic discourse not as a synonym for 'idleness,' but as an inevitable part of a job of some aetiological complexity. An acceptance of boredom is an essential part of being an adult and managing, rather than escaping or neglecting it, is a crucial quality of being an academic. A capacity for the adaptation and continuation of work, and surviving boring situations is necessary in the job of a researcher and academic teacher, and young academics should be socialised to the job not only through the discourse of passion but also by laborious artisanry, at times marked by boredom. They should not be raised in a boredom-free illusion, but learn how to endure, effectively cope or even use boredom for their own benefit, trigger its creative potential so as not to lose interest and engagement in their work.

The most frequently respondents feel/declare/connote boredom with academic conferences and faculty meetings, less prevalently with teaching and research. The major factors contributing to the feeling are quantitative and/or qualitative underload, i.e. having too little to do in terms of the amount of tasks (e.g. at classes with disengaged students, during boring conference presentations or while waiting for the results of some research procedures) or having to perform activities of relatively low level of difficulty that underutilise their competences (e.g. due to being outside their field of expertise like in the case of some administrative duties that make them feel less researchers or teachers and more clerks, 'clerk academics'). Overload of duties: having to perform excessive number of tasks may be another boredom-inducing factor. In such situation tasks lose their personal meaning, which is transform into a mere functionality – as in the case of opportunism and assembly line of scientific conferences (excess of conferences and its overload that hinders serving their proper functions such as exchange of knowledge and networking). Another systemic contributor to boredom may constitute lack of belonging prompted by precarious employment, non-inclusive recruitment system, hierarchical order of the university (lack of agency), and lack of closer connection to university spaces and colleagues (university as a non-place). An identity disturbance, i.e. being in the situation of changing position and/or unclear status as well as performing tasks distant to one's primary work identity may be seen as another potential cause of boredom. Thereby, boredom may emerge when one is stuck between positions/statuses and/or when performed duties are loosely associated with one's core identity (this is, for most academics, a researcher identity). Boredom was also found a function of one's position in the hierarchical order as those of higher status usually have more means of protecting themselves from the feeling than those occupying lower positions. The majority of boredom risk factors are more prevalent for younger academics as dirty work is delegated to them, they have usually less agency and control over their work, they are less habituated to the work conditions and feel less belonged to the institution as they are employed on short-term contracts.

Table C.1 below summarises all systemic contributors to the work-related boredom of academics that were described and analysed in Chapter 4. I claimed all of them as the main factors of situational boredom in all areas of academic work (scientific conferences, staff meetings, bureaucracy, didactics, and science). Some, when recurrent, may also contribute to chronic boredom and burn out, but this relationship still needs to be established and researched.

Table C.1 Systemic contributors to work-related boredom of academics

(Post)modernisation	Secularisation	Knowledge job
	Rationalisation	McDonaldisation
		The Supersedure of Meaning by Function
	Bureaucratisation	Instrumental attitude
		Dirty Work
	Individualisation	No community
Lack of Belonging	Precarity	No future, lack of prospects
	Recruitment system	Flawed inclusion
	Non-place	Unsettlement
	Hierarchy	Lack of agency
Identity Disturbance	Role distance	Failure of expectations
		Roles non-core for identity
Workload	Underload	Underemployment
	Overload	Burnout

There is also one more point worth mentioning, the opposite of boredom – passion, drive momentum or flow,[1] all of which, despite some differences between them, share the main characteristic of being states of total engagement married with a sense of meaningfulness, a 'combination of motivation, engagement, high energy, optimism, enthusiasm, perseverance' (Wagner, 2011a, p. 82). All boredom-inducing factors that were mentioned in this book, are basically obstacles to experiencing these states, to feeling scientific/teaching passion (is an academic passionate about clerical work imaginable at all?). Boredom is an outcome of disillusionment and disenchantment with academic work, which is not warmly welcomed in the working paradigm led by the principles of achievement society. Passion, constituting an essential driving force of academic work, is exploited (cynically or not) by various scientific entrepreneurs. Prospective scientists who are encouraged to devote their careers to research, are socialised via the narrative of passion without real prospects and security that would enable to cherish it. It can be hypothesised that this constitutes a kind of exploitation strategy. In this view, research is by definition conceived to be a 'labour of love' (Freidson, 1990) and researchers to be quintessentially passionate individuals. Yet, passion is being capitalised in a system of scarcity. Managers and politicians of science expect high academic ethos, passion, and devotion, at least discursively, but provide insufficient conditions to feed these things. Passion is expected to compensate for low salaries, poor work conditions, high employment insecurity, and the general overload of duties – for real exploitation in Marxian understanding with surplus value appropriated by politicians. Passion is a key component of the whole academic system, and constitutes its driving wheel, especially in the natural sciences where market opportunities are usually much higher (Figure C.1).

Boredom, frustration, and burnout are negative emotions associated with academic work; a risky base, the quicksand in which many academics at times settle. The immediate response involves a variety of preventing and/

Figure C.1 Passion triangle.

or coping techniques of different efficiencies, which are essentially (1) avoidance (e.g. task delegation or procrastination, careful activity selection), (2) multiplication and/or rotation (of projects, activities, interests, milieus), (3) reengagement of various kinds (e.g. institutional politics, personal fights/competitions, administration, etc.), or (4) habituation (domesticating the feeling to the extent of immunization). The real *spiritus movens* of academic work, however, is passion and all preventive and coping strategies are calculated to defend its inner territory from demolition – they are means of protecting a calling, core identity. Some academics are capable of managing negative factors of academic work and cherish passion in it, others, to some extent, fail in this project, settling at the basic level, scrabbling between boredom, frustration, and/or burnout, and immediate preventing/coping techniques. Passion is the driving force of an academic world, a quality that enables academics to advance despite the heavy systemic burden put on academic work, and contributing, inter alia, to boredom – job disengagement and distancing oneself from one's social role(s). Yet, along with such a boredom the hope follows as 'the more bored one is, the more self-conscious' (Cioran, 1995, p. 88) – and the more creative – someone may add. Thereby, boredom is a double-sided coin and it is up to each individual which side they choose and focus their attention on, the stultifying, numbing, and anaesthetising or the creative, revealing, and energizing (or even rebellious) one. I hope this book will contribute to awakening the latter.

Note

1 Some authors claim flow to be a direct antithesis of boredom (Bruss, 2012, Chapman, 2013, Mann, 2016), others indicate its absence to be a primary cause of the feeling (Fisher, 1998; Winokur, 2005; Misztal, 2016; Raffaelli, 2017). Yet, as Andreas Elpidorou (2017a) noted, boredom is not the only possible opposite of flow and neither its absence constitutes a defining feature of it – however in the conceptualization presented in this book that highlights disengagement as an essential characteristic of the phenomenon, the notion of flow, being the state of total engagement associated with unanimous sense of meaningfulness, may serve as the closest possible antithesis of boredom. Thereby, I am of opinion that flow is the main opposite of boredom, but boredom only one of many antitheses of flow.

Bibliography

Acee, T. W. *et al.* (2010) 'Academic Boredom in Under- and Over-Challenging Situations', *Contemporary Educational Psychology*, 35(1), pp. 17–27. doi: 10.1016/j.cedpsych.2009.08.002.

Adler, A. (1917) *The Neurotic Constitution: Outlines of a Comparative Individualistic Psychology and Psychotherapy*. New York, NY: Muffat, Yard and Company. Available at: https://archive.org/details/neuroticconstitu00adle/page/n3 (Accessed: 28 January 2021).

Adler, P. (1981) *Momentum. A Theory of Social Action*. Beverly Hills, London: SAGE Publications.

Adorno, T. (2001) '*Free Time*', in The Culture Industry. *Selected Essays on Mass Culture*. London and New York: Routledge, pp. 187–197.

Aho, K. (2007) 'Simmel on Acceleration, Boredom, and Extreme Aesthesia', *Journal for the Theory of Social Behaviour*, 37(4), pp. 447–462. doi: 10.1111/j.1468-5914.2007.00345.x.

Alvesson, M., Gabriel, Y., and Paulsen, R. (2017) *Return to Meaning. A Social Science With Something to Say*. Oxford: Oxford University Press.

Anderson, B. (2004) 'Time-Stilled Space-Slowed: How Boredom Matters', *Geoforum*, 35(6), pp. 739–754. doi: 10.1016/j.geoforum.2004.02.005.

Anderson, L. (2006) 'Analytic Autoethnography', *Journal of Contemporary Ethnography*, 35(4), pp. 373–395. doi: 10.1177/0891241605280449.

Andrade, J. (2010) 'What Does Doodling Do?', *Applied Cognitive Psychology*, 24, pp. 100–106. doi: 10.1002/acp.

Andreski, S. (1972) *Social Sciences as Sorcery*. London: Andre Deutsch.

Asimov, I. (1964) *Visit to the World's Fair of 2014, The New York Times*. Available at: https://archive.nytimes.com/www.nytimes.com/books/97/03/23/lifetimes/asi-v-fair.html (Accessed: 28 January 2021).

Augé, M. (1995) *Non-Places. Introduction to an Anthropology of Supermodernity*. London and New York, NY: Verso Press.

Avramenko, R. (2004) 'Bedeviled by Boredom: A Voegelinian Reading of Dostoevsky's Possessed', *Humanitas*, 17(1–2), pp. 108–139.

Baghdadchi, A. (2005) 'On Academic Boredom', *Arts and Humanities in Higher Education: An International Journal of Theory, Research and Practice*, 4(3), pp. 319–324. doi: 10.1177/1474022205056175.

Baker, R. *et al.* (2010) 'Better to Be Frustrated than Bored: The Incidence, Persistence, and Impact of learners' Cognitive-Affective States During Interactions With Three

Different Computer-Based Learning Environments', *International Journal of Human Computer Studies*, 68(4), pp. 223–241. doi: 10.1016/j.ijhcs.2009.12.003.

Bańko, M. (ed.) (2000) *Inny Słownik Języka Polskiego, T. 1 A...Ó [Different Dictionary of the Polish Language]*. Warszawa: PWN.

Bańkowski, A. (2000) *Etymologiczny Słownik Języka Polskiego, T. 2 L-P [Etymological Dictionary of the Polish Language]*. Warszawa: PWN.

Baratta, P. (2014) *The "Noonday Demon", Weariness, Inattention, or All of the Above? Refining the Definition and Measurement of State Boredom*. The University of Guelph, Ontario, Canada. Available at: https://atrium.lib.uoguelph.ca/xmlui/bitstream/handle/10214/8365/baratta_patricia_201408_MA.pdf?sequence=1&isAllowed=y (Accessed: 29 January 2021).

Barbalet, J. (1999) 'Boredom and Social Meaning', *The British Journal of Sociology*, 50(4), pp. 631–46. doi: 10.1080/000713199358572.

Bargdill, R. (2000a) 'A Phenomenological Investigation of Being Bored With Life', *Psychological reports*, 86(2), pp. 493–494. doi: 10.2466/pr0.2000.86.2.493.

Bargdill, R. (2000b) 'The Study of Life Boredom', *Journal of Phenomenological Psychology*, 31(2), pp. 188–219.

Bargdill, R. (2014) 'Toward a Theory of Habitual Boredom', *Janus Head*, 13(2), pp. 93–111.

Bargdill, R. (2016) 'Habitual Boredom and Depression: Some Qualitative Differences', *Journal of Humanistic Psychology*, 59(2), pp. 294–312. doi: 10.1177/0022167816637948.

Barley, N. (1983) *The Innocent Anthropologist: Notes From a Mud Hut*. Long Grove, IL: Waveland Press.

Barley, N. (1989) *Not a Hazardous Sport*. New York, NY: Henry Holt.

Barley, N. (2018) *A Plague of Caterpillars: A Return to the African Bush*. London: Eland Publishing.

Barnack, J. (1939) 'A Definition of Boredom: A Reply to Mr. Berman', *The American Journal of Psychology*, 52(3), pp. 467–471.

Barrett, W. (1975) 'Leibnitz's Garden: Some Philosophical Observations on Boredom', *Social Research*, 42(3), pp. 551–555.

Barry, J., Berg, E., and Chandler, J. (2006) 'Academic Shape Shifting: Gender, Management and Identities in Sweden and England', *Organization*, 13(2), pp. 275–298.

Battersby, S. (2009) 'Now that's What I Call Boring', *New Scientist*, 204(2739), pp. 58–61. doi: 10.1016/S0262-4079(09)63329-7.

Baudrillard, J. (2007) *Fragments: Cool Memories III, 1990–1995*. London: Verso Press.

Bauman, Z. (2000) *Liquid Modernity*. Cambridge: Polity Press.

Bauman, Z. (2007) *Consuming Life*. Cambridge: Polity Press.

Bauman, Z., and Leoncini, T. (2018) *'Evil Has Been Trivialized': A Final Conversation with Zygmunt Bauman'*. The New York Review of Books. Available at: https://www.nybooks.com/daily/2018/12/06/evil-has-been-trivialized-a-final-conversation-with-zymunt-bauman/?fbclid=IwAR142eELqk3S9hnuNgJliDM9y9f_QPMw66PF8eI_TNrTSvgLdDFGzgDFrVw (Accessed: 28 January 2021).

Beckelman, L. (1995) *Boredom*. Parsippany, NJ: Crestwood House.

Becker, H. (2007) *Writing for Social Scientists: How to Start and Finish Your Thesis, Book, or Article*. Chicago, IL and London: The Chicago University Press.

Bellow, S. (2007) *Dangling Man*. London: Penguin.

Bench, S., and Lench, H. (2013) 'On the Function of Boredom', *Behavioral Sciences*, 3(3), pp. 459–472. doi: 10.3390/bs3030459.

Bengtsson, T. (2012) 'Boredom and Action – Experiences from Youth Confinement', *Journal of Contemporary Ethnography*, 41(5), pp. 526–553. doi: 10.1177/0891241612449356.

Benjamin, W. (2002) *The Arcades Project*. Translated by H. Eiland and K. McLaughlin. Cambridge, MA, and London, England: The Belknap Press of Harvard University Press.

Benjamin, W. (2007) 'The Storyteller', in *Illuminations. Essays and Reflections on the Works of Nikolai Leskov*. New York, NY: Schocken Books, pp. 83–109.

Beres, D. (2017) *Does Boredom Really Exist?*, *Big Think*. Available at: http://bigthink.com/21st-century-spirituality/does-boredom-exist (Accessed: 28 January 2021).

Berger, P., and Luckmann, T. (1991) *The Social Construction of Reality*. London: Penguin Books. Available at: http://perflensburg.se/Berger social-construction-of-reality.pdf (Accessed: 28 January 2021).

Bergler, E. (1945) 'On the Disease-Entity Boredom ("alysosis") and Its Psychopathology', *Psychiatric Quarterly*, 19(1), pp. 38–51.

Berlin, I. (1953) *The Hedgehog and the Fox. An Essay on Tolstoy's View of History*. London: Weidenfeld & Nicolson.

Berlyne, D. E. (1960) *Conflict, Arousal and Curiosity*. New York, NY: McGraw-Hill.

Bernstein, H. (1975) 'Boredom and the Ready-Made Life', *Social Research*, 42(3), pp. 512–537.

Berra, L. (2019) 'Existential Depression: A Nonpathological and Philsophical-Existential Approach', *Journal of Humanistic Psychology*, pp. 1–9. doi: 10.1177/0022167819834747.

Bibring, E. (1953) 'The Mechanisms of Depression', in Greenacre, P. (ed.), *Affective Disorders*. New York, NY: International Universities Press, pp. 13–48.

Biceaga, V. (2006) 'Temporality and Boredom', *Continental Philosophy Review*, 39(2), pp. 135–153. doi: 10.1007/s11007-006-9015-4.

Bizior-Dombrowska, M. (2016) *Romantyczna nuda. Wielka Nostalgia Za Niczym [Romantic Boredom. Great Nostalgia for Nothing]*. Toruń: Wydawnictwo Naukowe Uniwersytetu Mikołaja Kopernika.

Blumer, H. (1986) *Symbolic Interactionism: Perspective and Method*. Berkeley, LA, London: University of California Press.

Boltanski, L., and Chiapello, E. (2007). *The New Spirit of Capitalism*. London and New York: Verso.

Borelli, G. (2021) 'Digging Around Heidegger, Benjamin and Lefebvre. Prolegomena to the Philosophical Oriented Social Research on Boredom', *European Journal of Social Theory* [in press].

Boryś, W. (2005) *Słownik Etymologiczny Języka Polskiego [Etymological Dictionary of the Polish Language]*. Kraków: Wydanictwo Literackie.

Bourdieu, P. (1984) *Homo Academicus*. Stanford, CA: Stanford University Press.

Boyns, D., and Appelrouth, S. (2011) 'Studies in the Suspension of the "flow" of Social Life', *Sociological Spectrum*, 31(2), pp. 193–223. doi: 10.1080/02732173.2011.541342.

Breidenstein, G. (2007) 'The Meaning of Boredom in School Lessons. Participant Observation in the Seventh and Eighth Form', *Ethnography and Education*, 2(1), pp. 93–108. doi: 10.1080/17457820601159133.

Brisset, D., and Snow, R. (1993) 'Boredom: Where the Future Isn't', *Symbolic Interaction*, 16(3), pp. 237–256.

Brodsky, J. (1995) 'In Praise of Boredom', in *On Grief and Reason*. New York, NY: Farrar Straus Giroux, pp. 104–113.

Brückner, A. (1989) *Słownik Etymologiczny Języka Polskiego [Etymological Dictionary of Polish Language]*. Warszawa: Wiedza Powszechna.

Bruss, K. (2012) 'Searching for Boredom in Ancient Greek Rhetoric: Clues in Isocrates', *Philosophy and Rhetoric*, 45(3), pp. 312–334. doi: 10.1353/par.2013.0005.

Burn, C. (2017) 'Bestial Boredom: a Biological Perspective on Animal Boredom and Suggestions for Its Scientific Investigation', *Animal Behaviour*, 130, pp. 141–151. doi: 10.1016/j.anbehav.2017.06.006.

Caldwell, L. *et al.* (1999) '"Why Are You Bored?": An Examination of Psychological and Social Control Causes of Boredom Among Adolescents', *Journal of Leisure Research*, 31(2), pp. 103–121.

Campagne, D. (2012) 'When Therapists Run Out of Steam: Professional Boredom or Burnout?', *Revista de Psicopatologia y Psicologia Clinica*, 17(1), pp. 75–85.

Campbell, R. (2003) 'Preparing the Next Generation of Scientists: The Social Process of Managing Students', *Social Studies of Science*, 33(6), pp. 897–927. doi: 10.1177/0306312703336004.

Carroll, B., Parker, P., and Inkson, K. (2010) 'Evasion of Boredom: An Unexpected Spur to Leadership?', *Human Relations*, 63(7), pp. 1031–1049. doi: 10.1177/0018726709349864.

Castronova, E. (2013) 'Down With Dullness: Gaming the Academic Conference', *The Information Society*, 29(2), pp. 66–70. doi: 10.1080/01972243.2012.757262.

Centre National de Ressources Textuelles et Lexicales (n.d.) *Ennui*. Available at: http://www.cnrtl.fr/definition/ennui (Accessed: 28 January 2021).

Chan, C. *et al.* (2018) 'Situational Meaninglessness and State Boredom: Cross-Sectional and Experience-Sampling Findings', *Motivation and Emotion*, 42(4), pp. 555–565. doi: 10.1007/s11031-018-9693-3.

Chapman, K. (2013) *Boredom in the German Foreign Language Classroom*. University of Wisconsin-Madison.

Chapoulie, J.-M. (2001) *La Tradition Sociologique De Chicago, 1892–1961*. Paris: Seuil.

de Chenne, T. (1998) 'Boredom as a Clinical Issue', *Psychotherapy: Theory, Research, Practice, Training*, 25(1), pp. 71–81. doi: 10.1037/h0085325.

Chin, A. *et al.* (2017) 'Emotion Bored in the USA: Experience Sampling and Boredom in Everyday Life', *Emotion*, 17(2), pp. 359–368. doi: 10.1037/emo0000232.

Cioran, E. (1995) *Tears and Saints*. Chicago, IL and London: The University of Chicago Press.

Cioran, E. (1999) *Rozmowy Z Cioranem [Conversations With Cioran]*. Warszawa: Wydawnictwo KR.

Clark, B. (2002) 'University Transformation: Primary Pathways to University Autonomy and Achievement', in Brint, S. (ed.), *The Future of the City of Intellect: The Changing American University*. Stanford, CA: Stanford University Press, pp. 322–341.

Collins, R. (2004) *Interaction Ritual Chains*. Princeton, NJ: Princeton University Press.

Concise Oxford Dictionary. (1990). Oxford: Clarendon Press.

Conrad, P. (1997) 'It's Boring: Notes on the Meanings of Boredom in Everyday Life.', *Qualitative sociology as everyday life*, 20(4), pp. 123–133. doi: 10.1023/A:1024747820595.

Costas, J., and Kärreman, D. (2016) 'The Bored Self in Knowledge Work', *Human Relations*, 69(1), pp. 61–83. doi: 10.1177/0018726715579736.

Couldry, N. (2011) 'Post-Neoliberal Academic Values: Notes from the UK Higher Education Sector', in Zelizer, B. (ed.), *Making the University Matter. Shaping Inquiry in Culture, Communication and Media Studies*. Abingdon: Routledge, pp. 135–143.

Csikszentmihalyi, M. (1997) *Finding Flow. The Psychology of Engagement With Everyday Life*. New York, NY: Basic Books.

Csikszentmihalyi, M. (2000a) *Beyond Boredom and Anxiety* (25th ed.). San Francisco, CA: Jossey-Bass Publishers.

Csikszentmihalyi, M. (2000b) 'Boredom', in Kazdin, A. (ed.), *Encyclopedia of Psychology*. Oxford, New York, NY: Oxford University Press, pp. 442–444.

Cummings, M., Gao, F., and Thornburg, K. (2015) 'Boredom in the Workplace: A New look at an Old Problem', *The Journal of the Human Factors and Ergonomics Society*, pp. 1–30.

D'Abate, C. (2005) 'Working Hard or Hardly Working: A Study of Individuals Engaging in Personal Business on the Job', *Human Relations*, 58(8), pp. 1009–1032. doi: 10.1177/0018726705058501.

D'Hoest, F., and Lewis, T. (2015) 'Exhausting the Fatigue University: In Search of a Biopolitics of Research', *Ethics and Education*, 10(1), pp. 49–60. doi: 10.1080/17449642.2014.998023.

Dąbrowski, M. (2012) 'Chory uniwersytet' [Sick university], *Antropos*, 18–19. Available at: http://www.anthropos.us.edu.pl/anthropos10/texty/dabrowski.htm (Accessed: 29 January 2021).

Dalle Pezze, B., and Salzani, C. (eds.)2009a) *Essays on Boredom and Modernity*. Amsterdam, New York, NY: Rodopi.

Dalle Pezze, B., and Salzani, C. (2009b) 'Introduction: The Delicate Monster: Modernity and Boredom', in Dalle Pezze, B., and Salzani, C. (eds.), *Essays on Boredom and Modernity*. Amsterdam, New York, NY: Rodopi, pp. 5–34.

Damasio, A. (1999) *The Feeling of What Happens: Body and Emotion in the Making of Consciousness*. New York, NY, San Diego, CA, London: Houghton Mifflin Harcourt.

Damrad-Frye, R., and Laird, J. (1989) 'The Experience of Boredom: The Role of the Self-Perception of Attention', *Journal of Personality and Social Psychology*, 57(2), pp. 315–320. doi: 10.1037/0022-3514.57.2.315.

Danckert, J. *et al.* (2018) 'Boredom: Under-Aroused and Restless', *Consciousness and Cognition*, 61, pp. 24–37. doi: https://doi.org/10.1016/j.concog.2018.03.014.

Darden, D., and Marks, A. (1999) 'Boredom: a Socially Disvalued Emotion', *Sociological Spectrum*, 19(1), pp. 13–37.

Daschmann, E., Goetz, T., and Stupnisky, R. (2011) 'Testing the Predictors of Boredom at School: Development and Validation of the Precursors to Boredom Scales', *The British Journal of Educational Psychology*, 81(3), pp. 421–40. doi: 10.1348/000709910X526038.

Davies, D. R., Shackleton, V. J., and Parasuraman, R. (1983) 'Monotony and Boredom', in Hockey, G. R. J. (ed.), *Stress and Fatigue in Human Performance*. Chichester: Wiley, pp. 1–32.

Davies, H. (1926) 'Discussion on the Physical and Mental Effects of Fatigue in Modern Industry', *The British Medical Journal*, 2(3427), pp. 472–479. doi: 10.2307/25325687.

Davies, J., and Fortney, M. (2012) 'The Menton Theory of Engagement and Boredom', in Langley, P. (ed.) *First Annual Conference on Advances in Cognitive Systems*. Palo Alto, CA, pp. 131–143.

Delamont, S., and Atkinson, P. (2001) 'Doctoring Uncertainty: Mastering Craft Knowledge', *Social Studies of Science*, 31(1), pp. 87–107.

Dexonline: Dicționare ale limbii române. (n.d.) *Plictiseală*. Available at: https://dexonline.ro/definitie/plictiseală (Accessed: 29 January 2021).

Diccionario de la lengua Española. (2001) *Enojo*. Available at: https://www.rae.es/drae2001/enojo (Accessed: 29 January 2021).

Dienstag, J. F. (2006) *Pessimism: Philosophy, Ethic, Spirit*. Princeton, NJ and Oxford: Princeton University Press.

Digitales Wörterbuch der deutschen Sprache. (n.d.) *Langeweile*. Available at: https://www.dwds.de/wb/Langeweile (Accessed: 29 January 2021).

Donnelly, K. (2013) 'On the Boredom of Science: Positional Astronomy in the Nineteenth Century', *The British Journal for the History of Science*, 47(3), pp. 479–503. doi: 10.1017/S0007087413000915.

Dooley, D. & Prause, J. (2004) *The Social osts of Underemployment. Inadequate Employment as Disguised Unemployment*. Cambridge: Cambridge University Press.

Dorfman, E. (2016) 'Everyday Life between Boredom and Fatigue', in Gardiner, M., and Haladyn, J. J. (eds.), *Boredom Studies Reader*. New York, NY and London: Routledge, pp. 180–192.

Drory, A. (1982) 'Individual Differences in Boredom Proneness and Task Effectiveness at Work', *Personnel Psychology*, 35(1), pp. 141–152. doi: 10.1111/j.1744-6570.1982.tb02190.x.

Eastwood, J. *et al.* (2007) 'A Desire for Desires: Boredom and Its Relation to Alexithymia', *Personality and Individual Differences*, 42(6), pp. 1035–1045. doi: 10.1016/j.paid.2006.08.027.

Eastwood, J. *et al.* (2012) 'The Unengaged Mind: Defining Boredom in Terms of Attention', *Perspectives on Psychological Science*, 7(5), pp. 482–495. doi: 10.1177/1745691612456044.

Ecclesiastes. (n.d.) *New King's James Bible*. Available at: https://www.bible.com/bible/114/ECC.1.NKJV (Accessed: 29 January 2021).

Ejder, Ö (2005) *Spaces of Boredom: Imagination and the Ambivalence of Limits*. Bilkent University.

Ellis, C., Adams, T., and Bochner, A. (2011) 'Autoethnography: An Overview', *Forum Qualitative Sozialforschung/Forum: Qualitative Social Research*, 12(1), p. Art. 10. Available at: http://www.qualitative-research.net/index.php/fqs/article/view/1589/3095 (Accessed: 29 January 2021).

Elpidorou, A. (2014) 'The Bright Side of Boredom', *Frontiers in Psychology*, 5, pp. 3–6. doi: 10.3389/fpsyg.2014.01245.

Elpidorou, A. (2016) 'The Significance of Boredom: A Sartrean Reading', in Dahlstrom, D. O., Elpidorou, A., and Hopp, W. (eds.), *Philosophy of Mind and Phenomenology: Conceptual and Empirical Approaches*. New York, NY and London: Routledge, pp. 268–288.

Elpidorou, A. (2017a) 'The Bored Mind Is a Guiding Mind: Toward a Regulatory Theory of Boredom', *Phenomenology and the Cognitive Sciences*, 17(3), pp. 455–484. doi: 10.1007/s11097-017-9515-1.

Elpidorou, A. (2017b) 'The Moral Dimensions of Boredom: A Call for Research', *Review of General Psychology*, 21(1), pp. 30–48. doi: 10.1037/gpr0000098.

Epstein, J. (2011) 'Duh, Bor-Ing. What's so Interesting About Boredom?', *Commentary*, 131(6), pp. 43–48. Available at: https://www.commentarymagazine.com/articles/joseph-epstein/duh-boring/ (Accessed: 29 January 2021).

Esman, A. (1979) 'Some Reflections on Boredom', *Journal of the American Psychoanalytic Association*, 27(2), pp. 423–439.

Etzkowitz, H. (2008) *The Triple Helix: University-Industry-Government. Innovation in Action*. New York, NY and London: Routledge.

Evans, V. (2004) *The Structure of Time: Language, Meaning and Temporal Cognition*. Amsterdam, Philadelphia, PA: John Benjamins Publishing.

Fahlman, S. et al. (2009) 'Does a Lack of Life Meaning Cause Boredom? Results from Psychometric, Longitudinal, and Experimental Analyses', *Journal of Social and Clinical Psychology*, 28(3), pp. 307–340. doi: 10.1521/jscp.2009.28.3.307.

Fahlman, S. et al. (2013) 'Development and Validation of the Multidimensional State Boredom Scale', *Assessment*, 20(1), pp. 68–85. doi: 10.1177/1073191111421303.

Fehr, B., and Russell, J. (1984) 'The Concept of Love Viewed From a Prototype Perspective', *Journal of Experimental Psychology: General*, 113(3), pp. 464–486.

Fenichel, O. (1951) 'On the Psychology of Boredom', in *Organization and Pathology of Thought*. New York, NY and London: Columbia University Press, pp. 349–361.

Ferrell, J. (2004) 'Boredom, Crime and Criminology', *Theoretical Criminology*, 8(3), pp. 287–302. doi: 10.1177/1362480604044610.

Finkielsztein, M. (2013) *Nuda Na Zajęciach Uniwersyteckich. Percepcja Nudy Wśród Studentów Uniwersytetu Warszawskiego*. Uniwersytet Warszawski.

Finkielsztein, M. (2016) 'Nuda a wstręt. Przesyt, ennui i wstręt do życia', *Stan Rzeczy*, 11(2), pp. 61–73.

Finkielsztein, M. (2018) 'Nuda a Lenistwo, Gnuśność I Acedia [Boredom and Laziness, Sloth and Acedia]', *Maska*, 37, pp. 36–50.

Finkielsztein, M. (2020) 'Class-Related Academic Boredom Among University Students: A Qualitative Research on Boredom Coping Strategies', *Journal of Further and Higher Education*, 44(8), pp. 1098–1113. doi: 10.1080/0309877X.2019.1658729.

Firestein, S. (2015) *Failure: Why Science Is So Successful*. Oxford, New York, NY: Oxford University Press.

Fisher, C. (1987) *Boredom: Construct, Causes and Consequences*. Texas A&M University and Virginia Polytechnic Institute. Available at: https://www.researchgate.net/publication/235196139_Boredom_Construct_Causes_and_Consequences (Accessed: 29 January 2021).

Fisher, C. (1993) 'Boredom at Work: A Neglected Concept', *Human Relations*, 46(3), pp. 395–417. doi: 10.1177/001872679304600305.

Fisher, C. (1998) 'Effects of non-Task-Related Thoughts on Attributed Boredom, Job Satisfaction and Task Perceptions', *Journal of Organizational Behavior*, 19(5), pp. 503–522.

Fisher, M. (2009) *Capitalist Realism. Is There No Alternative?* London: Zero Books.

Fleck, L. (1979) *Genesis and Development of a Scientific Fact*. Chicago, IL and London: The University of Chicago Press.

Földényi, L. (2016) *Melancholy*. New Haven, CT and London: Yale University Press.

Forrest, P. (2016) 'The Identity of Indiscernibles', in Zalta, E. (ed.) *The Stanford Encyclopedia of Philosophy*. Available at: https://plato.stanford.edu/entries/identity-indiscernible/ (Accessed: 29 January 2021).
Frankl, V. (1988) *The Will to Meaning. Foundations and Applications of Logotherapy*. New York, NY: New American Library.
Frankl, V. (2000) *Man's Search for Meaning. An Introduction to Logotherapy* (4th ed.). Boston, MA: Beacon Press.
Frederiksen, M. (2013) *Young Men, Time, and Boredom in the Republic of Georgia*. Philadelphia, PA: Temple University Press.
Frederiksen, M. (2017) 'Joyful Pessimism: Marginality, Disengagement, and the Doing of Nothing', *Focaal*, 78, pp. 9–22. doi: 10.3167/fcl.2017.780102.
Freidson, E. (1990) 'Labors of Love in Theory and Practice', in Erikson, K., and Vallas, S. P. (eds.), *The Nature of Work, Sociological Perspectives*. New Haven, CT: Yale University Press, pp. 149–61.
Freud, S. (1953) 'Mourning and Melancholia", in *Collected Papers*, vol. IV. London: Hogarth Press and The Institute of Psychoanalysis, pp. 152–170.
Freud, S. (1961) *Beyond the Pleasure Principle*. New York, NY, London: W.W. Norton & Company.
Frijda, N. (1986) *The Emotions*. Cambridge: Cambridge University Press.
Fromm, E. (1986) 'Affluence and Ennui in Our Society', in *For the Love of Life*. New York, NY: The Free Press, pp. 1–38.
Fromm, E. (2002) *The Sane Society*. London and New York, NY: Routledge.
Fromm, E. (2011) *The Pathology of Normalcy*. Lantern Books.
Gabelman, D. (2010) 'Bubbles, Butterflies and Bores: Play and Boredom in *Don Juan*', *The Byron Journal*, 38(2), pp. 145–156. doi: 10.3828/bj.2010.23.
Gabriel, M. (1988) 'Boredom: Exploration of a Developmental Perspective', *Clinical Social Work Journal*, 16(2), pp. 156–164.
Gadacz, T. (2002) 'Nuda' [Boredom], in *O Umiejętności życia [On Art of Life]*. Kraków: Znak, pp. 176–187.
Gambetta, D., and Origgi, G. (2013) 'The LL Game: The Curious Preference for Low Quality and Its Norms', *Politics, Philosophy & Economics*, 12(1), pp. 1–21. doi: 10.1177/1470594X11433740.
Gamsby, P. (2012) *The Black Sun of Boredom: Henri Lefebvre and the Critique of Everyday Life*. Laurentian University, Sudbury, Ontario. Available at: https://zone.biblio.laurentian.ca/dspace/bitstream/10219/2018/1/Gamsby_Patrick_PhD_thesis.pdf (Accessed: 29 January 2021).
Gardiner, M. (2000) *Critiques of Everyday Life*. London and New York, NY: Routledge.
Gardiner, M. (2012) 'Henri Lefebvre and the "Sociology of Boredom"', *Theory, Culture & Society*, 29(2), pp. 37–62. doi: 10.1177/0263276411417460.
Gardiner, M. (2014) 'The Multitude Strikes Back? Boredom in an Age of Semiocapitalism', *New Formations: A Journal of Culture/Theory/Politics*, 82(82), pp. 29–46. doi: 10.3898/NEWF.82.02.2014.
Gardiner, M., and Haladyn, J. J. (eds.)2016) *Boredom Studies Reader: Frameworks and Perspectives*. New York, NY: Routledge.
Garland, C. (2008) 'The McDonaldization of Higher Education?: Notes on the UK Experience', *Fast Capitalism*, 4(1). doi: 10.1353/jhe.2004.0014.
Gemmill, G., and Oakley, J. (1992) 'The Meaning of Boredom in Organizational Life', *Group & Organization Management*, 17(4), pp. 358–369.

Gennep, A. (1960) *The Rites of Passage*. Chicago, IL: The Chicago University Press.
Gerritsen, C. et al. (2014) 'I can't Get No Satisfaction: Potential Causes of Boredom', *Consciousness and Cognition*, 27(1), pp. 27–41. doi: 10.1016/j.concog.2013.10.001.
Giakoumis, D. et al. (2011) 'Automatic Recognition of Boredom in Video Games Using Novel Biosignal Moment-Based Features', *IEEE Transactions on Affective Computing*, 2(3), pp. 119–133. doi: 10.1109/T-AFFC.2011.4.
Gibbon, J. (1977) 'Scalar Expectancy Theory and Weber's Law in Animal Timing', *Psychological Review*, 84(3), pp. 279–325.
Gibson, G., and Morales, F. (1995) *'Ethnic and Gender Differences in Boredom Proneness'*. Oak Ridge: Technical Information Center.
Gkorezis, P., and Kastritsi, A. (2017) 'Employee Expectations and Intrinsic Motivation. Work-Related Boredom as a Mediator', *Employee Relations*, 39(1), pp. 100–111. doi: https://doi.org/10.1108/ER-02-2016-0025.
Glaser, B. (1964) 'Comparative Failure in Science', *Science*, 143(3610), pp. 1012–1014. doi: 10.1126/science.143.3610.1012.
Glaser, B., and Strauss, A. (1967) *The Discovery of Grounded Theory: Strategies for Qualitative Research*. New Brunswick and London: Aldine Transaction.
Gleick, J. (1999) *Faster: The Acceleration of Just About Everything*. Pantheon.
Godlewicz-Adamiec, J., Łuczyńska-Hołdys, M., and Opalińska, M. (2019) *List w Sprawie Awansu Adiunktów z Habilitacją*. Available at: http://wh.uw.edu.pl/list-dr-hab-joanny-godlewicz-adamiec-dr-hab-malgorzaty-luczynskiej-hildys-i-dr-hab-moniki-opalinskiej-z-wydzialu-neofilologii-w-sprawie-awansu-adiunktow-z-habilitacja/ (Accessed: 16 May 2019).
Goetz, T. et al. (2014) 'Types of Boredom: An Experience Sampling Approach', *Motivation and Emotion*, 38(3), pp. 401–419. doi: 10.1007/s11031-013-9385-y.
Goffman, E. (1956) *The Presentation of Self in Everyday Life*. Edinburgh: University of Edinburgh, Social Sciences Research Centre. Available at: https://monoskop.org/images/1/19/Goffman_Erving_The_Presentation_of_Self_in_Everyday_Life.pdf (Accessed: 29 January 2021).
Goffman, E. (1982) *Interaction Ritual: Essays on Face-to-Face Behavior*. New York, NY: Pantheon Books.
Goldberg, Y. et al. (2011) 'Boredom: an Emotional Experience Distinct From Apathy, Anhedonia, or Depression', *Journal of Social and Clinical Psychology*, 30(6), pp. 647–666. doi: 10.1521/jscp.2011.30.6.647.
Goldberg, Y., and Danckert, J. (2013) 'Traumatic Brain Injury, Boredom and Depression', *Behavioral Sciences*, 3(3), pp. 434–444. doi: 10.3390/bs3030434.
Goodstein, E. (2005) *Experience Without Qualities. Boredom and Modernity*. Stanford, CA: Stanford University Press.
Graeber, D. (2015) *The Utopia of Rules. On Technology, Stupidity, and the Secret Joys of Bureaucracy*. Brooklyn, London: Melville House.
Gramota (n.d.) скука. Available at: http://gramota.ru/slovari/dic/?lop=x&bts=x-&ro=x&zar=x&ag=x&ab=x&sin=x&lv=x&az=x&pe=x&word=скука (Accessed: 29 January 2021).
Green, D. (2016) 'Conference Rage: 'How Did Awful Panel Discussions Become the Default Format?', *The Guardian*, (7 June). Available at: https://www.theguardian.com/global-development-professionals-network/2016/jun/02/conference-rage-how-did-awful-panel-discussions-become-the-default-format (Accessed: 29 January 2021).

Greenson, R. (1953) 'On Boredom', *Journal of the American Psychoanalytic Association*, 1, pp. 7–21.
Gurycka, A. (1977) *Przeciw Nudzie. O Aktywności*. Warszawa: Nasza Księgarnia.
GUS (2005) *Szkoły Wyższe i Ich Finanse w 2004 r. [Higher Education Institutions and Their Finances in 2004]*. Available at: https://stat.gov.pl/obszary-tematyczne/edukacja/edukacja/szkoly-wyzsze-i-ich-finanse-w-2017-roku,2,14.html (Accessed: 28 January 2021).
GUS (2011) *Szkoły Wyższe i Ich Finanse w 2010 r. [Higher Education Institutions and Their Finances in 2010]*. Available at: https://stat.gov.pl/obszary-tematyczne/edukacja/edukacja/szkoly-wyzsze-i-ich-finanse-w-2017-roku,2,14.html (Accessed: 28 January 2021).
GUS (2018) *Szkoły Wyższe i Ich Finanse w 2017 r. [Higher Education Institutions and Their Finances in 2017]*. Available at: https://stat.gov.pl/obszary-tematyczne/edukacja/edukacja/szkoly-wyzsze-i-ich-finanse-w-2017-roku,2,14.html (Accessed: 28 January 2021).
Halffman, W., and Radder, H. (2015) 'The Academic Manifesto: From an Occupied to a Public University', *Minerva*, 53, pp. 165–187. doi: 10.1007/s11024-015-9270-9.
Han, H. C. (2015) *The Burnout Society*. Stanford, CA: Stanford University Press.
Harju, L., Hakanen, J., and Schaufeli, W. (2014) 'Job Boredom and Its Correlates in 87 Finnish Organizations', *Journal of Occupational and Environmental Medicine*, 56(9), pp. 911–918. doi: 10.1097/JOM.0000000000000248.
Harris, J., and Segal, D. (1985) 'Observations from the Sinai: The Boredom Factor', *Armed Forces & Society*, 11(2), pp. 235–248.
Harris, M. (2000) 'Correlates and Characteristics of Boredom Proneness and Boredom', *Journal of Applied Social Psychology*, 30(3), pp. 576–598. doi: 10.1111/j.1559-1816.2000.tb02497.x.
Hayes, D., Wynyard, R., and Mandal, L. (2002) *The McDonaldization of Higher Education*. Westport, CT: Praeger.
Healy, S. D. (1984) *Boredom, Self, and Culture*. Rutherford, NJ: Fairleigh Dickenson University Press.
Heidegger, M. (1995) *The Fundamental Concepts of Metaphysics World, Finitude, Solitude*. Bloomington, IN: Indiana University Press.
Heidegger, M. (2013) *What is Metaphysics?* Available at: https://wagner.edu/psychology/files/2013/01/Heidegger-What-Is-Metaphysics-Translation-GROTH.pdf (Accessed: 29 January 2021).
van der Heijden, G., Schepers, J., and Nijssen, E. (2012) 'Understanding Workplace Boredom Among White Collar Employees: Temporary Reactions and Individual Differences', *European Journal of Work and Organizational Psychology*, 21(3), pp. 349–375. doi: 10.1080/1359432X.2011.578824.
Helmes-Hayes, R., and Santoro, M. (eds.)2016) *The Anthem Companion to Everett Hughes*. London and New York, NY: Anthem Press.
Helvétius, C. A. (1810) *De L'Esprit: or, Essays on the Mind and Its Several Faculties*. London: Albion Press. Available at: https://archive.org/details/delespritoressa-02helvgoog (Accessed: 29 January 2021).
Hermanowicz, J. (1998) *The Stars Are Not Enough. Scientists – Their Passions and Professions*. Chicago, IL and London: The University of Chicago Press.
Hill, A. B. (1975) 'Work Variety and Individual Differences in Occupational Boredom', *Journal of Applied Psychology*, 60(1), pp. 128–131. doi: 10.1037/h0076346.

Hill, A. B., and Perkins, R. E. (1985) 'Towards a Model of Boredom', *British Journal of Psychology*, pp. 235–240. doi: 10.1111/j.2044-8295.1985.tb01947.x.

van Hooff, M., and van Hooft, E. (2014) 'Boredom at Work: Proximal and Distal Consequences of Affective Work-Related Boredom', *Journal of Occupational Health Psychology*, 19(3), pp. 348–359. doi: 10.1037/a0036821.

Høyer, K., and Naess, P. (2001) 'Conference Tourism: A Problem for the Environment, as Well as for Research?', *Journal of Sustainable Tourism*, 9(6), pp. 451–470. doi: https://doi.org/10.1080/09669580108667414.

Hughes, E. (1958) *Men and Their Work*. London: The Free Press.

Hunter, A., and Eastwood, J. (2016) 'Does State Boredom Cause Failures of Attention? Examining the Relations between Trait Boredom, State Boredom, and Sustained Attention', *Experimental Brain Research*, 236(9), pp. 2483–2492. doi: 10.1007/s00221-016-4749-7.

Inge, W. (1940) 'Escape', in *The Fall of the Idols*. London: Putnam, pp. 386–399.

Irvine, I. (2001) *The Angel of Luxury and Sadness. Vol. 1: The Emergence of the Normative Ennui Cycle*. BookSurge Publishing.

Ivancheva, M. (2015) 'The Age of Precarity and the New Challenges to the Academic Profession', *Studia Europaea*, 60(1), pp. 39–47.

Izdebski, A. et al. (2015) *Raport: Ogólnouniwersytecka Ankieta Oceniająca Jakość Kształcenia (Piąta Edycja)*. Warszawa. Available at: http://pejk.uw.edu.pl/wp-content/uploads/sites/289/2017/12/OAOJK_5edycja.pdf (Accessed: 29 January 2021).

Jackson, S. (1985) 'Acedia the Sin and Its Relationship to Sorrow and melancholia', in Kleinman, A., and Good, B. (eds.), *Culture and Depression. Studies in the Anthropology and Cross-Cultural Psychiatry of Affect and Disorder*. Berkeley, LA, London: University of California Press, pp. 43–62.

Jacobs, J. (2004) 'The Faculty Time Divide', *Sociological Forum*, 19(1), pp. 3–27. doi: https://doi.org/10.1023/B:SOFO.0000019646.82538.cc.

Jacobs, J., and Gerson, K. (2004) *The Time Divide: Work, Family, and Gender Inequality*. Cambridge, MA, and London, England: Harvard University Press.

Jacobsen, M. H. (ed.) (2019) *Emotions, Everyday Life and Sociology*. London and New York, NY: Routledge.

Jacobson, D. (2016) *Causes and Effects of Teacher Burnout*. Walden University. Available at: https://scholarworks.waldenu.edu/cgi/viewcontent.cgi?article=3938&context=dissertations (Accessed: 29 January 2021).

Jaucourt, C. (1772) 'Ennui', in Diderot, D. (ed.) *Encyclopedie, Ou Dictionnaire-Raisonné Des Sciences, Des Arts Et Des Métiers*. Available at: https://fr.wikisource.org/wiki/L'Encyclopédie/1re_édition/ENNUI (Accessed: 29 January 2021).

Jeronimus, B., and Laceulle, O. (2017) 'Frustration', in Zeigler-Hill, V. and Shackelford, T. (eds) *Encyclopedia of Personality and Individual Differences*, pp. 1–5. doi: 10.1007/978-3-319-28099-8.

Jervis, L., Spicer, P., and Hanson, S. (2003) 'Boredom, "Trouble," and the Realities of Postcolonial Reservation Life', *Ethos*, 31(1), pp. 38–58. doi: https://doi.org/10.1525/eth.2003.31.1.38.

Kabzińska, K. (2015) *Nuda W Kulturze Nadmiaru [Boredom in the Culture of Excess]*. Uniwersytet im. Adama Mickiewicza w Poznaniu.

Kahn, W. (1990) 'Psychological Conditions of Personal Engagement and Disengagement at Work', *Academy of Management Journal*, 33, pp. 692–724.

Kass, S, Vodanovich, S., and Callender, A. (2001) 'State-trait Boredom: Relationship to Absenteeism, Tenure, and Job Satisfaction,' *Journal of Business and Psychology*, 16(2), pp. 317–327.

Kenny, L. (2009) *Boredom Escapes Us: a Cultural Collage in Eleven Storeys*. University of Toronto. Available at: https://tspace.library.utoronto.ca/bitstream/1807/30046/1/Kenny_Lesley_200906_PhD_thesis.pdf (Accessed: 29 January 2021).

Kerce, E. (1985) *Boredom at Work: Implications for the Design of Jobs With Variable Requirements*. San Diego, CA: Navy Personnel Research and Development Center. Available at: https://apps.dtic.mil/dtic/tr/fulltext/u2/a160337.pdf (Accessed: 29 January 2021).

Kierkegaard, S. (1843) *Either/Or*. Available at: http://sqapo.com/CompleteText-Kierkegaard-EitherOr.htm (Accessed: 29 January 2021).

Kierkegaard, S. (1971) *Either/or, Vol. 1*. Princeton, NJ: Princeton University Press.

Kierkegaard, S. (1980) *The Sickness Unto Death*. Princeton, NJ: Princeton University Press.

Kinman, G., and Wray, S. (2013) *Higher Stress. A Survey of Stress and Well-Being Among Staff in Higher Education*. Available at: http://www.ucu.org.uk/media/pdf/4/5/HE_stress_report_July_2013.pdf (Accessed: 29 January 2021).

Kirova, A. (2004) 'Lonely or Bored: Children's Lived Experiences Reveal the Difference', *Interchange*, 35(2), pp. 243–268. doi: https://doi.org/10.1007/BF02698852.

Klapp, O. (1986) *Overload and Boredom. Essays on the Quality of Life in the Information Society*. New York, NY, Westport, CT, London: Greenwood Press.

Klibansky, R., Panofsky, E., and Saxl, F. (1964) *Saturn and Melancholy*. New York, NY: Basic Books.

Knabb, K. (ed.) (2006) *Situationist International Anthology*. Berkeley, LA: Bureau of Public Secrets.

Knowles, R. (1986) *Human Development and Human Possibility*. Lanham, MD: University Press of America.

Kołakowski, L. (1999) 'On Boredom', in *Freedom, Fame, Lying and Betrayal: Essays on Everyday Life*. London: Penguin Books, pp. 85–94.

Kołakowski, L. (2017) 'Z Obywatelem Urzędnikiem – rozmowa' [With Citizen Official – Conversation], in *Wejście i wyjście oraz inne utwory ku przestrodze i dla zabawy*. Kraków: Znak, pp. 195–200.

Komunikat Ministra Nauki i Szkolnictwa Wyższego z Dn. 18 Stycznia 2019 r. w Sprawie Wykazu Wydawnictw Publikujących Recenzowane Monografie Naukowe (2019). Available at: http://www.bip.nauka.gov.pl/g2/oryginal/2019_01/1c2912c1f994b8d37a305fac21b8ab54.pdf (Accessed: 29 January 2021).

Konferencyjny Savoir-Vivre [Conference Savoir-Vivre] (n.d.) Studencka Konferencja Starożytnicza. Available at: https://studenckakonferencjastarozytnicza.wordpress.com/abstrakty/konferencyjny-savoir-vivre/ (Accessed: 28 January 2021).

Kowzan, P. et al. (2015) *Nie Zostaje Mi Czasu Na Pracę Naukową. Warunki Pracy Osób Ze Stopniem Doktora, Zatrudnionych Na Polskich Uczelniach [I don't Have Time Left for Scientific Work. Working Conditions of People With Doctoral Degrees, Employed at Polish Universit*. Gdańsk, Bydgoszcz, Warszawa: Nowe Otwarcie Uniwersytetu. Available at: https://noweotwarcie.files.wordpress.com/2016/04/nie-zostaje-mi-czasu-na-pracc499-naukowc485-raport-nou3.pdf (Accessed: 29 January 2021).

Kowzan, P., and Zielińska, M. (2016) 'Pochłaniacze czasu – doktorzy na uczelniach w Polsce wobec organizacji czasu ich pracy' [Time eaters - PhDs at universities in Poland and the organisation of their working time]', *Nauka i szkolnictwo wyższe*, 48(2), pp. 41–62. doi: 10.14746/nisw.2016.2.2.

Krajewski, M. (2017) *'Smart Boredom, Biweekly'*. Available at: www.biweekly.pl/article/4907-smart-boredom.html (Accessed: 28 January 2021).

Krasicki, I. (1994) *Pan Podstoli*. Olsztyn: Wyższa Szkoła Pedagogiczna.

Kroes, S. (2005) *Detection Boredom in Meetings*. Available at: http://citeseerx.ist.psu.edu/viewdoc/download?doi=10.1.1.406.8560&rep=rep1&type=pdf (Accessed: 29 January 2021).

Kubiak, J. (2019) *Walka o Punkty Zabija Naukę [Fighting for Points Kills Science], PAUza Akademicka*. Available at: http://pauza.krakow.pl/460_3_2019.pdf (Accessed: 29 January 2021).

Kuhn, R. (1976) *The Demon of Noontide. Ennui in Western Literature*. Princeton, NJ: Princeton University Press.

Kuhn, T. (1996) *The Structure of Scientific Revolutions, Chicago and London*. Chicago, IL and London: The University of Chicago Press.

Kulczycki, E. (2011) *Siedem grzechów polskich konferencji naukowych [Seven sins of Polish scientific conferences], Historia i media*. Available at: http://historiaimedia.org/2011/08/31/siedem-grzechow-polskich-konferencji-naukowych/index.html (Accessed: 29 January 2021).

Kulczycki, E. (2012) *Czytanie referatów na konferencji/de-komentarz #2 [Reading presentations on conference/de-comentary]*. Available at: http://ekulczycki.pl/design/czytanie-referatu-na-konferencji-de-%E2%80%8Bkomentarz-2/ (Accessed: 29 January 2021).

Kulczycki, E. (2016) *Ile czasu pożera naukowcom praca administracyjna? [How much time do scientists spend on administrative work], Warsztat badacza*. Available at: http://ekulczycki.pl/teoria_komunikacji/ile-czasu-pozera-naukowcom-praca-administracyjna/ (Accessed: 29 January 2021).

Kulczycki, E. (2017) 'Punktoza jako strategia w grze parametrycznej w Polsce' [Punktosis as a strategy in the parametric game in Poland]', *Nauka i Szkolnictwo Wyższe*, 49(1), pp. 63–78. doi: 10.14746/NISW.2017.1.4.

Kundera, M. (1999) *Identity*. New York, NY: HarperCollins.

Kustermans, J., and Ringmar, E. (2011) 'Modernity, Boredom, and War: A Suggestive Essay', *Review of International Studies*, 37(4), pp. 1775–1792. doi: 10.2307/23025575.

Kwiek, M. (2015) *Uniwersytet W Dobie Przemian. Instytucje i kadra akademicka w warunkach rosnącej konkurencji [University in a time of change. Institutions and academic staff in an increasingly competitive environment]*. Warszawa: PWN.

Kwiek, M. (2016) 'Kariera akademicka w Europie: niestabilność w warunkach systemowej konkurencji' [Academic careers in Europe: instability in systemic competition], *Nauka i Szkolnictwo Wyższe*, 47(1), pp. 203–245.

Kwiek, M. (2017) 'A Generational Divide in the Academic Profession : A Mixed Quantitative and Qualitative Approach to the Polish Case A Generational Divide in the Academic Profession : A Mixed Quantitative and Qualitative', *European Educational Research Journal*, (5), pp. 1–25. doi: 10.1177/1474904116689684.

de la Peña, A. (2006) 'Consequences of Increments in Cognitive Structure for Attentional Automatization, the Experience of Boredom, and Engagement in Egocentric, Hyperdynamic, Interest-Generating Behaviors: A Developmental

Psychophysiologic Approach', *Proceedings of the 50th Annual Meeting of the ISSS – 2006, Sonoma, CA*. Available at: https://journals.isss.org/index.php/proceedings50th/article/view/290/124 (Accessed: 29 January 2021).

Laird, J. (2007) *Feelings: The Perception of Self*. Oxford, New York, NY: Oxford University Press. doi: 10.1093/acprof:oso/9780195098891.001.0001.

Larousse (n.d.) *Ennui*. Available at: http://www.larousse.fr/dictionnaires/francais/ennui/29681?q=ennui#29569 (Accessed: 29 January 2021).

Larson, R., and Richards, M. (1991) 'Boredom in the Middle School Years: Blaming Schools Versus Blaming Students', *American Journal of Education*, 99(4), pp. 418–443. doi: 10.1086/443992.

Latin Dictionary (n.d.) *Nudo*. Available at: https://www.online-latin-dictionary.com/latin-english-dictionary.php?parola=nudo (Accessed: 29 January 2021).

Latour, B., and Woolgar, S. (1986) *Laboratory Life. The Construction of Scientific Facts*. Princeton, NJ: Princeton University Press.

Laugesen, A. (2012) *Boredom Is the Enemy. The Intellectual and Imaginative Lives of Australian Soldiers in the Great War and Beyond*. Farnham: Ashgate. doi: 10.7748/nop2014.03.26.3.5.s1.

Leary, M. et al. (1986) 'Boredom in Interpersonal Encounters: Antecedents and Social Implications', *Journal of Personality and Social Psychology*, 51(5), pp. 968–975. doi: 10.1037/0022-3514.51.5.968.

van Leeuwen, M. (2009) 'The Digital Void: E-NNUI and Experience', in Dalle Pezze, B., and Salzani, C. (eds.), *Essays on Boredom and Modernity*. Amsterdam, New York, NY: Rodopi, pp. 177–202.

Lehner, N. (2015) 'Is Boredom Inevitable?', *Antae*, 2(3), pp. 145–157.

Leopardi, G. (1882) 'Remarkable Sayings of Philip Ottonieri', in *Essays and Dialogues*. London: Trubner & Co., Ludgate Hill. Available at: https://www.gutenberg.org/files/52356/52356-h/52356-h.htm#Footnote_1_29 (Accessed: 29 January 2021).

Leopardi, G. (1893) *Essays, Dialogues, and Thoughts*. London: Walter Scott.

Leopardi, G. (2015) *Zibaldone*. Edited by M. Caesar and F. D'Intino. New York, NY: Palgrave Macmillan.

Levecque, K. et al. (2017) 'Work Organization and Mental Health Problems in PhD Students', *Research Policy*. Elsevier B.V., 46(4), pp. 868–879. doi: 10.1016/j.respol.2017.02.008.

Lévi-Strauss, C. (1961) *Tristes Tropique*. New York, NY: Criterion Books.

Liddell, H., and Scott, R. (1940) 'κένωσις', in *A Greek-English Lexicon*. Oxford: Clarendon Press. Available at: http://www.perseus.tufts.edu/hopper/text?doc=Perseus%3Atext%3A1999.04.0057%3Aentry%3Dke%2Fnwsis&highlight=empty (Accessed: 29 January 2021).

Linde, S. B. (1994) *Słownik Języka Polskiego, T. 3 M-O [Polish Language Dictionary]*. Warszawa: Gutenberg-Print.

Lipps, T. (1904) *Leitfaden Der Psychologie*. Leipzig: Verlag von Wilhelm Engelmann.

Lodahl, T., and Kejner, M. (1965) 'The Definition and Measurement of Job Involvement', *Journal of Applied Psychology*, 49(1), pp. 24–33.

London, H., and Monello, L. (1974) 'Cognitive Manipulation of Boredom' in London, H., and Nisbett, R. (eds.), *Thought and Feeling: Cognitive Alteration of Feeling States*. Oxford: Aldine, pp. 74–84.

Lorenz, C. (2012) 'If You're So Smart, Why Are You Under Surveillance? Universities, Neoliberalism, and New Public Management', *Critical Inquiry*, 38(3), pp. 599–629. doi: 10.1086/664553.

Loukidou, E. (2008) *Boredom in the Workplace: a Qualitative Study of Psychiatric Nurses in Greece*. Loughborough University. Available at: https://repository.lboro.ac.uk/articles/thesis/Boredom_in_the_workplace_a_qualitative_study_of_psychiatric_nurses_in_Greece/9495515 (Accessed: 29 January 2021).

Lunsford, T. (1968) 'Authority and Idealogy in the Administered University', *American Behavioral Scientist*, 11(5), pp. 5–14.

Van Maanen, J. (1974) *Working the Street: A Developmental View of Police Behavior*. Available at: http://dspace.mit.edu/bitstream/handle/1721.1/1873/SWP-0681-14451100.pdf?sequ. (Accessed: 29 January 2021).

MacDonald, D., and Holland, D. (2002) 'Spirituality and Boredom Proneness', *Personality and Individual Differences*, 32(6), pp. 1113–1119. doi: 10.1016/S0191-8869(01)00114-3.

Macklem, G. (2015) *Boredom in the Classroom. Addressing Student Motivation, Self-Regulation, and Engagement in Learning*. New York, NY: Springer. doi: 10.1007/978-3-319-13120-7.

Mael, F., and Jex, S. (2015) 'Workplace Boredom: An Integrative Model of Traditional and Contemporary Approaches', *Group & Organization Management*, 40(2), pp. 131–159. doi: 10.1177/1059601115575148.

Maeland, B., and Brunstad, P. O. (2009) *Enduring Military Boredom. From 1750 to the Present*. London: Palgrave Macmillan.

Malamud, R. (2016) 'One Big Yawn? The Academics Bewitched by Boredom', *Times Higher Education*, (14 July). Available at: https://www.timeshighereducation.com/features/one-big-yawn-the-academics-bewitched-by-boredom (Accessed: 28 January 2021).

Malinowski, B. (1989) *A Diary in the Strict Sense of the Term*. London: The Athlone Press.

Malkovsky, E. et al. (2012) 'Exploring the Relationship between Boredom and Sustained Attention', *Experimental Brain Research*, 221(1), pp. 59–67. doi: 10.1007/s00221-012-3147-z.

Malmor, I. (2009) *Słownik Etymologiczny Języka Polskiego [Etymological Dictionary of Polish Language]*. Warszawa – Bielsko-Biała: Park Edukacja, PWN.

Maltsberger, J. (2000) 'Case Consultation: Mansur Zaskar: A Man Almost Bored to Death', *Suicide and Life-Threatening Behavior*, 30(1), pp. 83–90.

Mann, S. (2016) *The Upside of Downtime. Why Boredom Is Good*. London: Robinson.

Mansikka, J. E. (2009) 'Can Boredom Educate Us? Tracing a Mood in Heidegger's Fundamental Ontology from an Educational Point of View', *Studies in Philosophy and Education*, 28(3), pp. 255–268. doi: 10.1007/s11217-008-9116-0.

Marciniak, Ł. (2008) 'Stawanie Się Nauczycielem Akademickim. Analiza Symboliczno-Interakcjonistyczna [Becoming Academic Tearcher. Symbolic-Interactionist Analysis]', *Przegląd Socjologii Jakościowej*, 4(2). Available at: http://przegladsocjologiijakosciowej.org/Volume7/PSJ_monografie_3.pdf (Accessed: 29 January 2021).

Markowski, M. P. (1999) 'L'Ennui. Ułamek historii', in *Nuda W Kulturze*. Poznań: Rebis, pp. 290–316.

Martin, M., Sadlo, G., and Stew, G. (2006) 'The Phenomenon of Boredom', *Qualitative Research in Psychology*, 3, pp. 193–211. doi: 10.1139/b87-051.

Martin, M., Sadlo, G., and Stew, G. (2012) 'Rethinking Occupational Deprivation and Boredom', *Journal of Occupational Science*, 19, pp. 54–61. doi: 10.1080/14427591.2011.640210.

Marx, K. (1992) *Early Writings*. London: Penguin Books.

Maslach, C., Schaufeli, W., and Leiter, M. (2001) 'Job Burnout', *Annual Review of Psychology*, 52, pp. 397–422. doi: 10.1146/annurev.psych.52.1.397.

Mauss, M. (2004) *Seasonal Variations of the Eskimo: A Study in Social Morphology*. London and New York, NY: Routledge.

Mayenowa, M. R. (ed.) (1988) *Słownik Polszczyzny XVI Wieku, T. XVIII [Dictionary of Polish Language of the 16th Century]*. Wrocław - Warszawa - Kraków - Gdańsk - Łódź: Zakład Narodowy im. Ossolińskich.

Maynard, D., and Feldman, D. (2011) 'Introduction', in *Underemployment: Psychological, Economic, and Social Challenges*. New York, NY: Springer, pp. 1–12.

McCall, G. (1984) 'Systematic Field Observation', *Annual Review of Sociology*, 10, pp. 263–282.

Merriam-Webster (2004) *Webster's Student Dictionary. International Encyclopedic Edition*. Bellavista.

Merriam-Webster (n.d.) *Boredom*. Available at: https://www.merriam-webster.com/dictionary/boredom (Accessed: 29 January 2021).

Meyer, C. (2012) *Emotions Versus Feelings*. Available at: http://emotionaldetective.typepad.com/EMOTIONAL-DETECTIVE/2012/04/EMOTIONS-VS-FEELINGS.HTML (Accessed: 29 January 2021).

Michaelis: Dicionário Brasileiro da Língua Portuguesa (n.d.) *Aborrecimento*. Available at: https://michaelis.uol.com.br/moderno-portugues/busca/portugues-brasileiro/aborrecimento/ (Accessed: 29 January 2021).

Mijuskovic, B. (1979) *Loneliness in Philosophy, Psychology, and Literature*. Assen, The Netherlands: Van Gorcum.

Mikulas, W., and Vodanovich, S. (1993) 'The Essence of Boredom', *Psychological Record*, 43(1), pp. 237–247. doi: 10.1007/s11606-012-2196-0.

Miller, M. (1974) *Plain Speaking: An Oral Biography of Harry S. Truman*. New York, NY: G.P. Putman's Sons.

Mills, W. (2000) *The Sociological Imagination*. Oxford, New York, NY: Oxford University Press.

Miłosz, C. (1982) *Visions from San Francisco Bay*. New York, NY: Farrar Straus Giroux.

Misztal, B. (2016) 'The Ambiguity of Everyday Experience: Between Normality and Boredom', *Qualitative Sociology Review*, 12(4), pp. 100–119. Available at: http://www.qualitativesociologyreview.org/ENG/Volume39/QSR_12_4_Misztal.pdf (Accessed: 29 January 2021).

Monbiot, G. (2009) *These Men Would've Stopped Darwin, The Guardian*. Available at: https://www.theguardian.com/commentisfree/2009/may/11/science-research-business (Accessed: 29 January 2021).

Montoya, A., and Perez, M. (2016) *Unravelling Academic Precarity*, *Allegra Laboratory*. Available at: http://allegralaboratory.net/unravelling-academic-precarity-universitycrisis/ (Accessed: 29 January 2021).

Moravia, A. (1965) *The Empty Canvas*. London: Penguin Books.

Mosurinjohn, S. (2015) *Boredom, Overload, and the Crisis of Meaning in Late Modern Temporality*. Queen's University, Kingston, Ontario, Canada. Available at: https://qspace.library.queensu.ca/bitstream/handle/1974/13387/Mosurinjohn_%20Sharday_C_201506_PhD.pdf?sequence=1&isAllowed=y (Accessed: 29 January 2021).

Mosurinjohn, S. (2016) 'Overload, Boredom and the Aesthetics of Texting', in Gardiner, M., and Haladyn, J. J. (eds.), *Boredom Studies Reader*. New York, NY and London: Routledge, pp. 143–156.

Mulligan, K., and Scherer, K. (2012) 'Toward a Working Definition of Emotion', *Emotion Review*, 4(4), pp. 345–357. doi: 10.1177/1754073912445818.

Musharbash, Y. (2007) 'Boredom, Time, and Modernity: An Example from Aboriginal Australia', *American Anthropologist*, 109(2), pp. 307–317. doi: 10.1525/AA.2007.109.2.307.308.

de Musset, A. (2006) *Confession of a Child of the Century*. Available at: http://www.gutenberg.org/files/3942/3942-h/3942-h.htm (Accessed: 29 January 2021).

Nagucka, E., and Zawadzki, M. (2015) 'Piekielna pustka. Patologie kształcenia w uniwersytecie neoliberalnym' [The Infernal Void. Pathologies of Education in the Neoliberal University]', in Ignatowski, G., Sułkowski, Ł, and Dobrowolski, Z. (eds.), *Oblicza patologii zawodowych i społecznych [Faces of professional and social pathologies]*. Warszawa: Difin, pp. 123–142.

Nett, U., Goetz, T., and Hall, N. (2011) 'Coping With Boredom in School: An Experience Sampling Perspective', *Contemporary Educational Psychology*, 36(1), pp. 49–59. doi: 10.1016/j.cedpsych.2010.10.003.

Neu, J. (1998) 'Boring from Within. Endogenous Versus Reactive Boredom', in Flack, W. F., and Laird, J. D. (eds.), *Emotions in Psychopathology: Theory and Research*. New York, NY: Oxford University Press, pp. 158–170.

Newcomb, S. (1903) *Reminiscences of an Astronomer*. Boston, MA: Houghton Mifflin.

Ng, A. et al. (2015) 'Culture and State Boredom: A Comparison between European Canadians and Chinese', *Personality and Individual Differences*, 75, pp. 13–18. doi: 10.1016/j.paid.2014.10.052.

Ngai, S. (2005) *Ugly Feelings*. Cambridge, MA, London, England: Harvard University Press.

Nietzsche, F. (1924) *Human All-Too-Human*. London: George Allen & Unwin.

Nietzsche, F. (1980) *On the Advantage and Disadvantage of History for Life*. Indianapolis, IN and Cambridge: Hackett Publishing Company.

Nietzsche, F. (2011) *Beyond Good and Evil*. Available at: https://www.saylor.org/site/wp-content/uploads/2011/09/PHIL101-5.3.3.pdf (Accessed: 29 January 2021).

Nisbet, R. (1983) 'Boredom', in *Prejudices: A Philosophical Dictionary*. Cambridge, MA: Harvard University Press.

O'Brien, W. (2014) 'Boredom', *Analysis*, 74(2), pp. 236–244. doi: 10.1093/analys/anu041.

O'Hanlon, J. (1981) 'Boredom: Practical Consequences and a Theory', *Acta Psychologica*, 49(1), pp. 53–82. doi: 10.1016/0001-6918(81)90033-0.

O'Neill, B. (2014) 'Cast Aside: Boredom, Downward Mobility, and Homelessness in Post-Communist Bucharest', *Cultural Anthropology*, 29(1), pp. 8–31. doi: 10.14506/ca29.1.03.

O'Neill, B. (2017) *The Space of Boredom. Homelessness in the Slowing Global Order*. Durham and London: Duke University Press.

Oatley, K., and Jenkins, J. (1996) *Understanding Emotions*. New York, NY: Wiley.
Online Etymology Dictionary (n.d.-a) *Bore*. Available at: https://www.etymonline.com/word/bore#etymonline_v_52968 (Accessed: 29 January 2021).
Online Etymology Dictionary (n.d.-b) *Dull*. Available at: https://www.etymonline.com/word/dull#etymonline_v_45750 (Accessed: 29 January 2021).
Organisation for Economic Co-operation and Development (OECD) (2007) *Revised Field of Science and Technology (FOS) Classification in the Frascati Manual*. Available at: http://www.oecd.org/sti/inno/38235147.pdf (Accessed: 29 January 2021).
Osbaldiston, N., Cannizzo, F., and Mauri, C. (2019) '"I Love My Work but I Hate My Job" – Early Career Academic Perspective on Academic Times in Australia', *Time & Society*, 28(2), pp. 743–762. doi: https://doi.org/10.1177/0961463X16682516.
Parker, M., and Jary, D. (1995) 'The McUniversity: Organization, Management and Academic Subjectivity', *Organization*, 2(2), pp. 319–338. doi: 10.1177/135050849522013.
Parkinson, A., and McBain, R. (2013) 'Putting the Emotion Back: Exploring the Role of Emotion in Disengagement', in Zerbe, W., Ashkanasy, N., and Härtel, C. (eds.), *Individual Sources, Dynamics, and Expressions of Emotion*. Bingley: Emerald, pp. 69–86.
Pascal, B. (1910) *Thoughts, Letters and Minor Works*. New York, NY: P.F. Collier & Son Corporation. Available at: https://archive.org/details/thoughtslettersm028185mbp/page/n7/mode/2up (Accessed: 29 January 2021).
Patton, M. (2001) *Qualitative Research & Evaluation Methods* (3rd ed.). London, Thousand Oaks, CA, New Delhi: SAGE.
Pauluk, D. (2016) *Ukryte programy uniwersyteckiej edukacji i ich rezultaty. Doświadczenia Studentów Pedagogiki [Hidden University Education Programs and Their Results. Experience of Students of Pedagogy]*. Kraków: Wydawnictwo Uniwersytetu Jagiellońskiego.
Pease, A. (2012) *Modernism, Feminism and the Culture of Boredom*. New York, NY: Cambridge University Press.
Pekrun, R. (2006) 'The Control-Value Theory of Achievement Emotions: Assumptions, Corollaries, and Implications for Educational Research and Practice', *Educational Psychology Review*, 18(4), pp. 315–341. doi: 10.1007/s10648-006-9029-9.
Pekrun, R. *et al.* (2007) 'The Control-Value Theory of Achievement Emotions: an Integrative Approach to Emotions in Education', in Schutz, P. and Pekrun, R. (eds) *Emotions in Education*. Amsterdam: Academic Press, pp. 13–36.
Pekrun, R. *et al.* (2010) 'Boredom in Achievement Settings: Exploring Control–Value Antecedents and Performance Outcomes of a Neglected Emotion', *Journal of Educational Psychology*, 102(3), pp. 531–549. doi: 10.1037/a0019243.
Perkins, R. E., and Hill, A. B. (1985) 'Cognitive and Affective Aspects of Boredom', *British Journal of Psychology*, pp. 221–234. doi: 10.1111/j.2044-8295.1985.tb01946.x.
Perlow, K. (1995) *The Image of Melancholy and the Evolution of Baroque Idiom*. Available at: https://www.edupsi.com/depresion/perlow.htm (Accessed: 29 January 2021).
Pessoa, F. (2002) *The Book of Disquiet*. London: Penguin Books.
Peters, E. (1975) 'Notes Toward an Archaeology of Boredom', *Social Research*, 42(3), pp. 493–511.

Petry-Mroczkowska, J. (2004) 'Acedia – lenistwo' [Acedie – Sloth], in *Siedem Grzechów Głównych Dzisiaj [Seven Cardinal Sins Today]*. Kraków: Znak, pp. 177–207.

Phillips, A. (1993) 'On Being Bored', in *On Kissing, Tickling, and Being Bored: Psychoanalytic Essays on the Unexamined Life*. Cambridge, MA: Harvard University Press, pp. 68–78. doi: 10.1037/034596.

Pieniądz, A. (2017) 'Model Kariery Akademickiej – Pokolenie Niepewności Między Nauką a dydaktyką' [The Academic Career Model – A Generation of Uncertainty between Research and Teaching], *Nauka i Szkolnictwo Wyższe*, 2(50), pp. 305–313.

Plutchik, R. (1991) *The Emotions (Revised Edition)*. New York, NY and London: University Press of America.

Preckel, F., Götz, T., and Frenzel, A. (2010) 'Ability Grouping of Gifted Students: Effects on Academic Self-Concept and Boredom', *British Journal of Educational Psychology*, 80, pp. 451–472. doi: 10.1348/000709909X480716.

Prinz, J. (2005) 'Are Emotions Feelings?', *Journal of Consciousness Studies*, 12(8–10), pp. 9–25.

Rabinow, P. (1977) *Reflections on Fieldwork in Morocco*. Berkeley, LA, London: University of California Press.

Raposa, M. (1999) *Boredom and the Religious Imagination*. University Press of Virginia: Charlottesville and London.

Reif, F., and Strauss, A. (1965) 'The Impact of Rapid Discovery upon the Scientist's Career', *Social Problems*, 12(3), pp. 297–311.

Rhodes, C. (2017) 'Academic Freedom in the Corporate University: Squandering Our Inheritance?', in Izak, M., Kostera, M., and Zawadzki, M. (eds.), *The Future of University Education*. London: Palgrave Macmillan, pp. 19–38.

Rhodes, E. (2015) 'The Exciting Side of Boredom', *Psychologist*, 28(4), pp. 278–281.

Riemann, G., and Schütze, F. (1991) '"Trajectory" as a Basic Theoretical Concept for Analyzing Suffering and Disorderly Social Processes', in Maines, D. (ed.), *Social Organization and Social Process: Essays in Honor of Anselm Strauss*. New York, NY: de Gruyter, pp. 333–358.

Ringmar, E. (2016) 'Attention and the Cause of Modern Boredom', in Gardiner, M., and Haladyn, J. J. (eds.), *Boredom Studies Reader*. New York, NY and London: Routledge, pp. 193–202.

Ritzer, G. (1983) 'The McDonaldization of Society', *Journal of American Culture*, 6(1), pp. 100–107.

Ritzer, G. (2011) *McDonaldization of Society (6th ed.)*. Los Angeles, CA, London, New Delhi, Singapore, Washington DC: Pine Forge Press.

Rodzik, P. (2016) 'Nadane Stopnie I Tytuły Naukowe – Czy Coś Się Zmieniło? [Awarded Degrees and Academic Titles – Has Something Changed?]', *Nauka i Szkolnictwo Wyższe*, 48(2), pp. 139–174.

Rogge, B. (2011) 'Boredom, the Life Course, and Late Modernity. Understanding Subjectivity and Sociality of "Dead Time" Experiences', *BIOS*, 24, pp. 284–299.

Rothlin, P., and Werder, P. (2008) *Boreout! Overcoming Workplace Demotivation*. London and Philadelphia, PA: Kogan Page.

Rozporządzenie Ministra Nauki i Szkolnictwa Wyższego z Dn. 12 Grudnia 2016 r. w Sprawie Przyznawania Kategorii Naukowej Jednostkom Naukowym i Uczelniom, w Których Zgodnie z Ich Statutami Nie Wyodrębniono Podstawowych

Jednostek Organizacyjnych (2016) *Dziennik Ustaw Rzeczypospolitej Polskiej (Dz. U.2016.2154)*. Available at: http://www.bip.nauka.gov.pl/g2/oryginal/2017_01/ eef3ce53f11d75c8345087358d8f65e4.pdf (Accessed: 28 January 2021).

Rozporządzenie Ministra Nauki i Szkolnictwa Wyższego z Dn. 2 Grudnia 2016 o w Sprawie Warunków Wynagradzania Za Pracę i Przyznawania Innych Świadczeń Związanych z Pracą Dla Pracowników Zatrudnionych w Uczelni Publicznej (2016) *Dziennik Ustaw Rzeczypospolitej Polskiej, poz. 2063*. Available at: http://www.bip.nauka.gov.pl/g2/oryginal/2017_01/03914228d37461557b613ffbdd75e3ac.pdf (Accessed: 28 January 2021).

Russell, B. (1932) 'Boredom and Excitement', in *The Conquest of Happiness*. London: George Allen & Unwin, pp. 57–67.

Safranski, R. (2017) *Czas. Co czyni z nami i co my czynimy z niego [Time. What It Does to Us and What We Make of It]*. Warszawa: Czytelnik.

Salkind, N. (2010) 'Triangulation', in *Encyclopedia of Research Design*. Los Angeles, CA, London, New Delhi, Singapore, Washington, DC: SAGE, pp. 1537–1540.

Sand-Jensen, K. (2007) 'How to Write Consistently Boring Scientific Literature', *Oikos*, 116(5), pp. 723–727. doi: 10.1111/j.2007.0030-1299.15674.x.

Sandywell, B. (2011) 'Boredom', in *Dictionary of Visual Discourse. A Dialectical Lexicon of Terms*. Farnham: Ashgate, pp. 177–178.

Sartre, J.-P. (1962) *Sketch for a Theory of the Emotions*. London: Methuen & Co.

Sartre, J.-P. (1989) 'Existentialism Is Humanism', in Kaufman, W. (ed.), *Existentialism from Dostoyevsky to Sartre*. Columbus, IN: Meridian Publishing Company. Available at: https://www.marxists.org/reference/archive/sartre/works/exist/sartre.htm (Accessed: 29 January 2021).

Sartre, J.-P. (2000) *Nausea*. London: Penguin Books.

Saunders, M. N. (1996) 'The Physiology of Boredom, Depression and Senile Dementia', *Medical Hypotheses*, 46(5), pp. 463–466. doi: 10.1016/S0306-9877(96)90026-2.

Schaufeli, W., and Salanova, M. (2014) 'Burnout, Boredom and Engagement in the Workplace', in Peeters, M., Jonge, J., and Taris, T. (eds.), *An Introduction to Contemporary Work Psychology*. New York, NY: Wiley, pp. 293–318.

Schielke, S. (2008) 'Boredom and Despair in Rural Egypt', *Contemporary Islam*, 2(3), pp. 251–270. doi: 10.1007/s11562-008-0065-8.

Schnabel, U. (2014) *Sztuka Leniuchowania. O Szczęściu Nicnierobienia [The Art of Laziness. On the Happiness of Doing Nothing]*. Warszawa: Muza.

Schneider, G. (2013) *Depicting Boredom: On Gestures and Facial Expressions*. Available at: http://comicsforum.org/2013/02/18/image-narrative-10-depicting-boredom-on-gestures-and-facial-expressions-by-greice-schneider/ (Accessed: 29 January 2021).

Schopenhauer, A. (1969) *The World as Will and Representation, Volume 1*. New York, NY: Dover Publications.

Schuster, J., and Finkelstein, M. (2008) *The American Faculty: The Restructuring of Academic Work and Careers*. Baltimore, MD: The Johns Hopkins University Press.

Seale, C. et al. (eds) (2006) *Qualitative Research Practice*. London, Thousand Oaks, CA, New Delhi: SAGE.

Seneca (1917) *Moral Letters to Lucilius*. Available at: https://en.wikisource.org/wiki/Moral_letters_to_Lucilius (Accessed: 29 January 2021).

Seo, H. (2003) *The Shock of Boredom: The Aesthetic of Absence, Futility, and Bliss in Moving Images*. Evanston: Northwestern University.

Shapin, S. (2008) *The Scientific Life: A Moral History of a Late Modern Vocation*. Chicago, IL: The University of Chicago Press.

Shore, C. (2010) 'Beyond the Multiversity: Neoliberalism and the Rise of the Schizophrenic University', *Social Anthropology*, 18(1), pp. 15–29. doi: 10.1111/j.1469-8676.2009.00094.x.

Shore, C., and Wright, S. (2000) 'Coercive Accountability: The Rise of Audit Culture in Higher Education', in Strahern, M. (ed.), *Audit Cultures: Anthropological Studies in Accountability, Ethics and the Academy*. London: Routledge, pp. 57–89.

Siegel, D. (2017) *How Anarchy Can Save the University, The Chronicle of Higher Education*. Available at: https://www.chronicle.com/article/how-anarchy-can-save-the-university/ (Accessed: 29 January 2021).

Sievers, B. (2008) 'The Psychotic University', *Ephemera: Theory & Politics in Organization*, 8(3), pp. 238–257.

Silver, D. (2012) *Boredom, The Point, 3*. Available at: https://thepointmag.com/examined-life/boredom/ (Accessed: 29 January 2021).

Silverman, D. (ed.) (2004) *Qualitative Research: Theory, Method and Practice (2nd Ed.)*. London, Thousand Oaks, CA, New Delhi: SAGE.

Simmel, G. (1950) *The Sociology of Georg Simmel*. Glencoe, IL: The Free Press.

Simpson, R. et al. (eds) (2012) *Dirty Work. Concepts and Identities*. Palgrave Macmillan.

Skorupka, S. (1967) *Słownik frazeologiczny języka polskiego* [phraseological dictionary of Polish language]. Warszawa, Poland: Wiedza Powszechna.

Slaby, J. (2010) 'The Other Side of Existence Heidegger on Boredom', in Flach, S. and Soffner, J. (eds) *Habitus in Habitat II. Other Sides of Cognition*. Bern: Peter Lang, pp. 101–120. doi: https://doi.org/10.3726/978-3-0351-0164-5.

Slaughter, S., and Rhoades, G. (2004) *Academic Capitalism and the New Economy. Markets, State, and Higher Education*. Baltimore, MD: The Johns Hopkins University Press.

Словник української Мови (1974) нудьга. Київ: АН УРСР, Ін-т мовознавства ім. О.О. Потебні.

Smith, R. (1981) 'Boredom : A Review', *Human Factors*, 23(3), pp. 329–340.

Sontag, S. (1967) *Against Interpretation*. New York, NY: Dell Publishing.

Spacks, P. (1995) *Boredom: The Literary History of a State of Mind*. Chicago, IL: The Chicago University Press.

Steele, R. et al. (2013) 'Boredom Among Psychiatric in-Patients: Does It Matter?', *Advances in Psychiatric Treatment*, 19(4), pp. 259–267. doi: 10.1192/apt.bp.112.010363.

Steiner, G. (1971) 'The Great Ennui', in *In Bluebeard's Castle: Some Notes Towards the Redefinition of Culture*. New Haven, CT: Yale University Press.

Stendhal (1892) *Lettres Intimes*. Paris: Calmann Levy.

Stets, J., and Turner, J. (2006) *Handbook of the Sociology of Emotions*. Springer.

Straus, E. (1980) 'Disorders of Personal Time', in *Phenomenological Psychology*. New York, NY and London: Garland.

Strauss, A., and Glaser, B. (1970) *Anguish: The Case Study of a Dying Trajectory*. Mill Valley, CA: Sociology Press.

Strelau, J., and Doliński, D. (eds.)2011) *Psychologia Akademicka. Podręcznik, Tom 1 [Academic Psychology: A Handbook]*. Gdańsk: Gdańskie Wydawnictwo Psychologiczne.
Sułkowski, Ł (2017) 'The Culture of Control in the Contemporary University', in Izak, M., Kostera, M., and Zawadzki, M. (eds.), *The Future of University Education*. London: Palgrave Macmillan, pp. 85–110.
Sundberg, N., and Staat, K. (1992) 'Boredom and Culture', *Paper Presented at the Emotion and Culture Conference, Eugene, OR*.
Sundberg, R. I., and Bisno, H. (1983) *Boredom at Life Transitions – Adolescence and Old Age*.
Svendsen, L. (2005) *A Philosophy of Boredom*. Translated by J. Irons. London: Reaktion Books.
Svendsen, L. (2016) 'Boredom and the Meaning of Life', in Gardiner, M., and Haladyn, J. J. (eds.), *Boredom Studies Reader*. New York, NY and London: Routledge, pp. 205–215.
Szmidt, K. (2013) 'Nuda Jako Problem Pedagogiczny' [Boredom as a Pedagogical Problem], *Teraźniejszość - Człowiek - Edukacja*, 63(3), pp. 55–69.
Szwabowski, O. (2014) *Uniwersytet – fabryka – maszyna. Uniwersytet w perspektywie radykalnej [Uniwrsytet – fabryka – maszyna. Uniwersytet w perspektywie radykalnej]*. Warszawa: Instytut Wydawniczy „Książka i Prasa".
Szwabowski, O. (2019) *Nekrofilna produkcja akademicka i pieśni partyzantów. Autoetnografia pracy akademickiej i dydaktycznej w czasach zombie-kapitalizmu [Necrophilous academic production and partisan songs. Auto-Etnography of Academic and Teaching Work in the Times of Zombie-*. Wrocław: Instytut Pedagogiki Uniwersytetu Wrocławskiego.
Szymczak, M. (ed.) (1995) *Słownik Języka Polskiego, T. 2 L-P [Dictionary of the Polish Language]*. Warszawa: PWN.
Tardieu, É. (1913) *L'Ennui. Étude Psychologique*. Paris: Librairie Félix Alcan. Available at: https://gallica.bnf.fr/ark:/12148/bpt6k5658929w.texteImage (Accessed: 29 January 2021).
Therrien, G. (1973) *Ratopolis*. YouTube. Available at: https://www.youtube.com/watch?v=L51vxQ8ruVQ (29 January 2021).
Thesaurus Linguae Graecae (n.d.) νόος. Available at: http://stephanus.tlg.uci.edu/cunliffe/#eid=6714&context=lsj&action=from-ref (Accessed: 29 January 2021).
Thiele, L. P. (1997) 'Postmodernity and the Routinization of Novelty: Heidegger on Boredom and Technology', *Polity*, 29(4), pp. 489–517.
Thoits, P. (1989) 'The Sociology of Emotions', *Annual Review of Sociology*, 15(1), pp. 317–342. doi: 10.1017/CBO9780511819612.
van Tilburg, W., and Igou, E. (2011) 'On Boredom and Social Identity: A Pragmatic Meaning-Regulation Approach', *Personality and Social Psychology Bulletin*, 37(12), pp. 1679–1691. doi: 10.1177/0146167211418530.
van Tilburg, W., and Igou, E. (2012) 'On Boredom: Lack of Challenge and Meaning as Distinct Boredom Experiences', *Motivation and Emotion*, 36(2), pp. 181–194. doi: 10.1007/s11031-011-9234-9.
van Tilburg, W., and Igou, E. (2017) 'Boredom Begs to Differ: Differentiation from Other Negative Emotions', *Emotion*, 17(2), pp. 309–322. doi: 10.1037/emo0000233.
Todman, M. (2003) 'Boredom and Psychotic Disorders: Cognitive and Motivational Issues', *Psychiatry*, 66(2), pp. 146–167. doi: 10.1521/psyc.66.2.146.20623.

Todman, M. et al. (2008) 'Boredom, Hallucination-Proneness and Hypohedonia in Schizophrenia and Schizoaffective Disorder', in Yip, K. (ed.) *Schizoaffective Disorder: International Perspectives on Understating, Intervention and Rehabilitation*. New York, NY: Nova Science Publications.

Todorovsky, D. (2014) 'Follow-up Study: on the Working Time Budget of a University Teacher. 45 Years Self-Observation', *Scientometrics*, 101(3), pp. 2063–2070. doi: 10.1007/s11192-014-1284-9.

Tokarczyk, R. (2009) *Antologia Anegdoty Akademickiej [The Anthology of Academic Anecdote]*. Warszawa: Oficyna a Wolters Kluwer business.

Tomczyk, M. (ed.) (2008) *Wielki Słownik Wyrazów Bliskoznacznych [The Big Dictionary of Synonyms]*. Kraków: Krakowskie Wydawnictwo Naukowe.

Toohey, P. (2011) *Boredom: A Lively History*. New Haven, CT and London: Yale University Press.

Traweek, S. (1992) *Beamtimes and Lifetimes. The World of High Energy Physicists*. Cambridge, MA, and London, England: Harvard University Press.

Treccani (n.d.) *Noia*. Available at: http://www.treccani.it/vocabolario/noia/ (Accessed: 29 January 2021).

Le Trésor de la Langue Française Informatisé (n.d.) *Ennui*. Available at: http://stella.atilf.fr/Dendien/scripts/tlfiv5/visusel.exe?13;s=2556936765;r=1;nat=;sol=2 (Accessed: 29 January 2021).

Turner, J. (2000) *On the Origins of Human Emotions*. Stanford, CA: Stanford University Press.

Tymkiw, A. (2017) 'Emotions Involved in Shopping at the Airport', *The Catalyst*, 4(1), pp. 5–17. doi: 10.18785/cat.0401.02.

Tze, V. et al. (2013) 'Canadian and Chinese University students' Approaches to Coping With Academic Boredom', *Learning and Individual Differences*, 23(1), pp. 32–43. doi: 10.1016/j.lindif.2012.10.015.

Ustawa z Dn. 18 Marca 2011 r. o Zmianie Ustawy - Prawo o Szkolnictwie Wyższym, Ustawy o Stopniach Naukowych i Tytule Naukowym Oraz o Stopniach i Tytule w Zakresie Sztuki Oraz o Zmianie Niektórych Innych Ustaw (2011) *Dziennik Ustaw Rzeczypospolitej Polskiej (Dz.U.2011.84.455)*. Available at: http://prawo.sejm.gov.pl/isap.nsf/download.xsp/WDU20110840455/U/D20110455Lj.pdf (Accessed: 28 January 2021).

Ustawa z Dn. 20 Lipca 2018 r. Prawo o Szkolnictwie Wyższym i Nauce' (2018) *Dziennik Ustaw Rzeczypospolitej Polskiej (Dz.U.2018.1668)*. Available at: https://www.uw.edu.pl/wp-content/uploads/2018/09/ustawa.pdf (Accessed: 28 January 2021).

Ustawa z Dn. 27 Lipca 2005 r. Prawo o Szkolnictwie Wyższym (2005) *Dziennik Ustaw Rzeczypospolitej Polskiej (Dz.U.2005.164.1365)*. Available at: http://prawo.sejm.gov.pl/isap.nsf/DocDetails.xsp?id=WDU20051641365 (Accessed: 28 January 2021).

Velasco, J. (2017) 'Boredom: A Comprehensive Study of the State of Affairs', *Themata. Revista de Filosofia*, 56(2), pp. 171–198.

Vodanovich, S. (2003) 'Psychometric Measures of Boredom: A Review of the Literature', *The Journal of Psychology*, 137(6), pp. 569–595. doi: 10.1080/00223980309600636.

Vodanovich, S. et al. (2011) 'Culture and Gender Differences in Boredom Proneness', *North American Journal of Psychology*, 13(2), pp. 221–230.

Vodanovich, S., and Watt, J. (1999) 'The Relationship between Time Structure and Boredom Proneness: An Investigation Within Two Cultures', *Journal of*

Social Psychology, 139(2), p. 143–10.1080/00224549909598368. doi: 10.1080/00224549909598368.
Vodanovich, S., and Watt, J. (2016) 'Self-Report Measures of Boredom: An Updated Review of the Literature', *The Journal of Psychology*, 150(2), pp. 196–228. doi: 10.1080/00223980.2015.1074531.
Voegelin, E. (1999) 'Nietzsche and Pascal', in *The Collected Works of Eric Voegelin, Vol. 25*. Columbia, Missouri: University of Missouri Press.
Vogel-Walcutt, J. et al. (2012) 'The Definition, Assessment, and Mitigation of State Boredom Within Educational Settings: A Comprehensive Review', *Educational Psychology Review*, 24(1), pp. 89–111. doi: 10.1007/s10648-011-9182-7.
Voltaire (2006) *Candide*. Oxford and New York, NY: Oxford University Press.
Wagner, I. (2011a) *Becoming Transnational Professional*. Warszawa: Scholar.
Wagner, I. (2011b) *Polish Reform of Higher Education: "Operation Was Successful and Patient Is Dead, Universities in Crisis. Blog of the International Sociological Association (ISA)*. Available at: http://isa-universities-in-crisis.isa-sociology.org/?p=858 (Accessed: 28 January 2021).
Wagner, I. (2012) 'Selektywna Analiza Problemu Pbulikacji Humanistów i Przedstawicieli Nauk Społecznych w Języku Angielskim [Selective Analysis of the Problem of Purging Humanists and Representatives of Social Sciences in English]', *Przegląd Socjologii Jakościowej*, 8(1), pp. 166–187.
Wagner, I. (2014a) 'Kariera Naukowa w Polsce. Czy Obecny Model Sprzyja Wyłanianiu i Awansowaniu "najlepszych" Naukowców [Scientific Career in Poland. Is the Current Model Conducive to the Selection and Promotion of the "Best" Scientists?]', *Przegląd Socjologiczny*, 63(3), pp. 39–65.
Wagner, I. (2014b) 'Work and Career Aspects of "ghetto Laboratories"', in Prpić, K., van der Weijden, I., and Asheulova, N. (eds) *(Re)Serching Scientific Careers*. St. Petersburg, pp. 145–170.
Wagner, I. (2015) *Producing Excellence: The Making of Virtuosos*. New Brunswick, NJ: Rutgers University Press.
Wagner, I. (2016) 'Sociology of Excellence(S) in the Knowledge Society', in Załęska, M., and Okulska-Łukawska, U. (eds.), *Rhetoric, Discourse and Knowledge*. Frankfurt am Main: Peter Lang, pp. 101–121.
Wagner, I. (2018) 'Academia Ut Ratopolis, Ars Salvandi', in *the Presentation at IEiAK UW, 21 February 2018, Warszawa*.
Wagner, I., and Finkielsztein, M. (2014) *Raport z Ewaluacji Polsko-Szwajcarskiego Programu Badawczego (PSPB) [Report on the Evaluation of the Polish-Swiss Research Programme (PSPB)][unpublished]*.
Wagner, I., Finkielsztein, M., and Czarnacka, A. (2017) 'Being Polish Scientists and Women – between Glorious Past and Difficult Present: The "reverse Dynamic of Equality Construction"', *European Educational Research Journal*, 16(2–3), pp. 141–165. doi: 10.1177/1474904116688023.
Wallace, D. F. (2011) *The Pale King: An Unfinished Novel*. New York, NY: Little, Brown.
Wallbott, H. (1998) 'Bodily Expression of Emotion', *European Journal of Psychology*, 28, pp. 879–896.
Wangh, M. (1975) 'Boredom in Psychoanalytic Perspective', *Social Research*, 42(3), pp. 538–550.

Watt, J. D. (2002) *Fighting More than Fires: Boredom Proneness, Workload Stress, and Underemployment Among Urban Firefighters*. Kansas State University.

Wechter-Ashkin, L. (2010) *The College Freshman's Lived Experience of Boredom: A Phenomenological Study*. [PhD dissertation] Capella University.

Wierzbicka, A. (1999) *Emotions Across Languages and Cultures: Diversity and Universals*. Cambridge: Cambridge University Press.

Wilcock, A. (2006) *An Occupational Perspective of Health* (2nd ed.). Thorofare, NJ: Slack.

Winokur, J. (2005) *Ennui to Go. The Art of Boredom*. Seattle, WA: Sasquatch Books.

Winter, R. (2002) *Still Bored in a Culture of Entertainment. Rediscovering Passion & Wonder*. Westmont, IL: InterVarsity Press.

Witkiewicz, S. (2005) *Pożegnanie Jesieni [Farewell to Autumn]*. Wrocław: Wydawnictwo Dolnośląskie.

Wycisk, A. et al. (2018) *Potrzeby I Oczekiwania Młodych Naukowców Związane Z Rozwojem Zawodowej Kariery Naukowej. Raport Z Badania Społecznego [The Needs and Expectations of Young Scientists Regarding the Development of a Professional Scientific Career. Report from a Social Study]*. Warszawa: Krajowy Punkt Kontaktowy Programów Badawczych Unii Europejskiej. Available at: http://www.kpk.gov.pl/wp-content/uploads/2018/07/Raport PL-ERADays.pdf (Accessed: 29 January 2021).

Yerkes, R., and Dodson, J. (1908) 'The Relation of Strength of Stimulus to Rapidity of Habit-Formation', *Journal of Comparative Neurology and Psychology*, 18, pp. 459–482. doi: 10.1002/cne.920180503.

Zając, T. et al. (2014) *Raport: Ogólnouniwersytecka Ankieta Doktorancka*. Warszawa. Available at: http://pejk.uw.edu.pl/wp-content/uploads/sites/289/2018/03/Badanie-Doktorantow-2014.pdf (Accessed: 29 January 2021).

Zakay, D. (2014) 'Psychological Time as Information: The Case of Boredom', *Frontiers in Psychology*, 5(August), pp. 1–5. doi: 10.3389/fpsyg.2014.00917.

Zawadzki, M. (2017) '"The Last in the Food Chain": Dignity of Polish Junior Academics and Doctoral Candidates in the Face of Performance Management', in Izak, M., Kostera, M., and Zawadzki, M. (eds) *The Future of University Education*. London: Palgrave Macmillan, pp. 63–84. doi: 10.1007/978-3-319-46894-5.

Zawisławska, M. (2017) *Święta Krowa Naukowa [Scientific Sacred Cow]*. Available at: https://zawislawska.wordpress.com/2017/02/17/swieta-krowa-naukowa/ (Accessed: 28 January 2021).

Zhu, B., and Zhou, Y. (2012) 'A Study on students' Affective Factors in Junior High School English Teaching', *English Language Teaching*, 5(7), pp. 33–41. doi: 10.5539/elt.v5n7p33.

Zijderveld, A. (1979) *On Clichés. The Supersedure of Meaning by Function in Modernity*. London, Boston, MA and Henley: Routledge & Kegan Paul.

Zimniak-Hałajko, M. (2012) 'Tylko pesymizm może nas uratować' [Only pesimism can save us], *Mała Kultura Współczesna*, 12. Available at: http://malakulturaws polczesna.org/2012/12/17/marta-zimniak-halajko-rozmowa-uniwersytet-krytyczny/ (Accessed: 29 January 2021).

Žižek, S. (2006) *The Parallax View*. Cambridge, MA and London, England: The MIT Press.

Znaniecki, F. (1940) *The Social Role of the Man of Knowledge*. New York, NY: Columbia University Press.

Zuckerman, H. (1967) 'Nobel Laureates in Science: Patterns of Productivity, Collaboration, and Authorship', *American Sociological Review*, 32(3), pp. 391–403. doi: 10.2307/2091086.

Zuckerman, M. (1979) *Sensation Seeking. Beyond the Optimal Level of Arousal.* London and New York, NY: Taylor & Francis Psychology Press.

Index

academic boredom: dirty work 101–103; lack of belonging 108–123; (post)modern academia and (post)modern boredom 85–92; as systemic issue 83–123; workload 103–108; *see also* (post)modern academia
academic boredom in practice 125–184; research-related work 170–184; scientific conferences 126–148; staff meetings 148–156; teaching 157–169
academic capitalism 89
academic texts, writing 180–181
administrative duties 102–103, 106, 123n1, 124n6, 190
agitated boredom 47
alexithymia 29
Alvesson, M. 182
Anglo-Saxon boredom 38–39
animals, and boredom 57
anomic boredom 118
apathetic boredom 47
apathetic melancholy 47
apathy 70–71
Appelrouth, S. 66
Apple Inc. 24
arousal, and boredom 47–48, *48*
arousal theories 49–50
Asimov, I. 1
attention deficit 50–51
attention withdrawal 74–75
Augé, M. 115
autoethnography 10
aversion 73

Baghdadchi, A. 132, 141, 181
Baratta, P. 72, 73
Bargdill, R. 56
Baudelaire, C. 2

Baudrillard, J. 29
Bellow, S. 77
belonging: boredom and career dynamics 121–123; comparative failure 120–121; hierarchy 116–118; identity disturbance 118–120; lack of 108–123; non-place 114–116; precarity 109–112; recruitment system 112–114
Benjamin, W. 2, 37
Berlin, I. 184
"book sociology" 90
boredom: anomic 118; and career dynamics 121–123; chronic 106–108, 111–112, 118, 121, 173, 187, 189–191; conceptualization of 30–44; denial of 22–25, **25**; divisions of 45–49; field 173–176; frequencies according to activities and degree **126**; frequencies according to activities and disciplines **126**; invisibility of 17–18; laboratory 176–179; methodological problems in dealing with 15–44; methodology 6–10; overview 1; phenomenological problems 15–19; reactions for 19–30; researcher as distraction for 19; as serious issue 1–2; shameful vice of 26–28; situational 118, 125, 171, 189–191; social prevalence of 2–3; underestimation of 19–22; *vs.* venereal disease 1
boredom by something 61
Boredom [The Empty Canvas] (Moravia) 31
boredom with something 61–62
Borelli, G. 20
boring didactic tasks 166–168
boringness of meetings 150–153
Boyns, D. 66

Brodsky, J. 160
bureaucracy, and academia 92–103
bureaucratic duties 92–94, 96, 100, 102, 118, 125
burn out 106–108, 111, 116, 157, 160, 165–166, 169, 191
busyness, principle of 25–26

Camus, A. 2
career dynamics and boredom 121–123
chronic boredom 79–80, 90, 106–108, 111–112, 118, 121, 173, 187, 189–191
Cioran, E. 57, 61
The Citizens of Science movement *(Obywatele Nauki)* 165
clerk academic 92–103
cognitive theories 50–52; attention deficit 50–51; perception and attributions 51–52
Collins, R. 65
'common' boredoms 45–46, **46**
communicating science 179–183
comparative failure 120–121
'complex' boredoms 45, **46**, 61
conceptualization of boredom 30–44; applicability of essential elements 78–80; dictionaries and literature definition of boredom 35–38; essential elements in defining boredom 72–77; general population definition of boredom 30–35; multidimensionality of boredom 42–44; non-essential elements in defining boredom 69–72; transcultural/translingual differences between boredoms 38–42
conference assembly line 136–138
conference culture 131
The Confession of a Child of the Century (Musset) 77
Conrad, P. 5, 119
content of presentation 128–136
Covid-19 pandemic 185n9
Csikszentmihalyi, M. 2, 66, 91, 104, 127

Damrad-Frye, R. 51
Dangling Man (Bellow) 77
Dasein 60
data collection 7–9, **8**
definition of boredom: dictionaries and literature 35–38; frequently used words in *43*; general population 30–35; *see also* boredom

'demonic pantheism' 60
denial of boredom 22–25, **25**
dirty work: academic boredom 101–103; Hughes on 101
disengagement 74–75
disturbances in integration 142–148
'doctoral schools' 114
Donnelly, K. 86–87, 170–171
dragging time 61, 72; *see also* time, and boredom
duties: administrative 102–103, 106, 123n1, 124n6, 190; of attending faculty meetings 149; bureaucratic 92–94, 96, 100, 102, 118, 125; organizational 106, 113, 123; teaching 123, 158, 160–166

ego 54
Ejder, Ö. 39
Elpidorou, A. 74, 193n1
elusiveness 17–18
emotional detachment 37
emotional energy 66
emotions 72–73; *see also* feelings
EU Working Time Directive 106
existential boredom 62
existentialism 57
existential psychology 54–56
experience of boredom 28–30

Facebook 185n8
faculty meetings 125, **126**, 149–156
fatigue 15–17
feelings 29, 72–73; *see also* emotions
Ferrell, J. 90
field boredom 173–176
Fisher, C. 84
Fisher, M. 94
flow 66
Földényi, L. 39
format of presentation 128–136
Frankl, V. 55–56, 76
Fromm, E. 2, 37
frustration 76

Gabriel, Y. 182
Gambetta, D. 140, 162
Gamsby, P. 127
Gardiner, M. 4
Garsten, C. 24
Glaser, B. 6, 120
Goetz, T. 47–48
Goffman, E. 64–65

Goodstein, E. 28–29
Graff, A. 91
The Great French Encyclopaedia 37
Green, D. 127
Greenson, R. 53, 71

habitual boredom 56
Haladyn, J. 4
Heidegger, M. 2, 57, 60, 61–62, 79, 131
Hermanowicz, J. 120, 123
hidden employment 100
hierarchy 116–118
Hughes, E. 101

identity disturbance 118–120
idleness 69–70
ignotum per ignotum 36
individual attitude, and boredom 47
integration: disturbances in 142–148; networking and 142–143
interactional ritual 65
interestingness of the world 25–26
interviews 9–10

Jacobs, J. 124n10
Jenkins, J. 27

Kahn, W. 83
Kierkegaard, S. 57, 60, 63
Kolakowski, L. 58
Kuhn, R. 3
Kulczycki, E. 184n4
Kundera, M. 49
Kwiek, M. 102

laboratory boredom 176–179
lack of belonging 108–123
lack of interest 71
La Divina Commedia (Dante) 1
Laird, J. 51
Latour, B. 87
laziness 37, 70
Leopardi, G. 57, 58–59
Lévi-Strauss, C. 173
liminality 76–77
listlessness 73–74
London, H. 52
low emotional energy 65–66

Maier-Leibnitz, H. 127
Malamud, R. 181
Malinowski, B. 173

Maltsberger, J. 55
manic (stultifying) boredom 49
manic melancholy 47
Mann, S. 24
Man's Search for Meaning (Frankl) 55
Marciniak, L. 162, 164
McDonaldization 87
meaninglessness 75–76
meditative (relaxing) boredom 49
meetings: boringness of 150–153; faculty 125, **126**, 149–156; social 142
Menton theory of boredom 67n2
methodology: autoethnography 10; boredom 6–10; interviews 9–10; methodological approach 6–7; participant observation 10; research questions 7; sampling and data collection 7–9, **8**
microsociological perspective: low emotional energy 65–66; role distance 64–65; theories of boredom 63–66
Mills, W. 181
Milosz, C. 28
Monello, L. 52
mood 58
Moravia, A. 31
Mosurinjohn, S. 49
motivation: and boredom 51–52; and perception 51–52
multidimensionality of boredom 42–44
Musset, A. D. 77

negativity 73
New Public Management 87, 123n1
Nietzsche, F. 57
nihilism 56
non-place 114–116
'nonverbal character,' and boredom 18
noogenic neurosis 55–56

Oatley, K. 27
O'Brien, W. 74
On the Advantage and Disadvantage of History for Life (Nietzsche) 57
opportunism 138–141
organizational duties 106, 113, 123
Origgi, G. 140, 162
over-exploitation 107
overload: of conference assembly line 136–138; quantitative 106–108

Parson, T. 181
participant observation 10
Pascal, B. 56–57
passion triangle *192*
Paulsen, R. 182
Pease, A. 42
perception 51–52; and lack of motivation 51–52; of time dragging 52
personal trait, and boredom 46–47
pessimism 57
Peters, E. 42
phenomenological problems: boredom 15–19; elusiveness and invisibility of boredom 17–18; fatigue 15–17; researcher as distraction 19; sleepiness 15–17
philosophical perspective, boredom 56–63
Pieniadz, A. 111, 165
Platonian cave 60
Poland 109, 121, 140; academic teacher in 162; massification of higher education in 157; teaching load in 185n13
Polish academia 116, 123n2
Polish Academy of Science (Polska Akademia Nauk, PAN) 162
Polish National Science Centre 21
(post)modern academia: and bureaucracy 92–103; and (post)modern boredom 85–92; rationalization 86–92; secularization 85–86; *see also* academic boredom
precarious employment schemes 111
precarity 109–112
prevention: and coping techniques 144–148, 153–156, 168–169; and research-related work 183–184
Prinz, J. 29
profound boredom 62
protracted duration 52
psychodynamic boredom 47
psychodynamic theories 53–54
psychological perspective: arousal theories 49–50; cognitive theories 50–52; existential psychology 54–56; psychodynamic theories 53–54; theories of boredom 49–63
psychology domination 4–5
punktoza 91
'pure' boredom 78

qualitative underload 104–105
quantitative overload 106–108
quantitative underload 105–106

'ragbag conferences' 134
rationalization, and modern academia 86–92
reading scientific publications 181–182
recruitment system 112–114
repetition/monotony 71
repressed desires 54
researcher, as distraction 19
researching and teaching 163–166
research questions 7
research-related work 170–184; communicating science 179–183; field boredom 173–176; laboratory boredom 176–179; prevention 183–184; satiety/overload 172–173; tediousness 170–172
rest 70
restlessness 73–74
'reverse pantheism' 60
revolutionary (transformative) boredom 49
role distance 64–65
Russell, B. 2

sampling 7–9, **8**
Sand-Jensen, K. 181
Sartre, J.-P. 57
satiety/overload 172–173
School of Athens (Raphael) 85
Schopenhauer, A. 2, 57, 59
scientific conferences 126–148; disturbances in integration 142–148; format and content of presentation 128–136; opportunism 138–141; overload of conference assembly line 136–138
'scientific excellence' 114, 162
'scientific menopause' 120
scientific publications 181–182
shameful stigma, of boredom 26–28
situational boredom 78–79, 118, 125, 171, 189–191
sleepiness 15–17
social capital 116
social meetings 142
The Sociological Imagination (Mills) 181
sociology negligence 4–5

staff meetings 148–156; boringness of the meetings 150–153; prevention and coping techniques 153–156
standardization, and modern academia 86–87
Strauss, A. 6
Svendsen, L. 62
systemic contributors to work-related boredom of academics **191**
Szwabowski, O. 89

Tardieu, É. 2
teaching 157–169; boring didactic tasks 166–168; disengagement 163–166; prevention and coping techniques 168–169; and researching 163–166; teaching overload 160–162; underestimation of 162–163
teaching duties 123, 158, 160–166
teaching overload 160–162
tediousness 170–172
texts: academic 180–181; reviewing 182–183
theories of boredom: divisions of boredom 45–49; microsociological perspective 63–66; overview 45; psychological perspective 49–63; *see also* boredom
theory of LL game 140
time, and boredom 61, 72
Todorovsky, D. 93
Toohey, P. 27
transcultural differences between boredoms 38–42
transitionality 76–77
translingual differences between boredoms 38–42
Tristes tropiques (Lévi-Strauss) 173
Truman, H. 26, 28
Twitter 185n8

'underemployment' 124n4
underestimation of teaching 162–163
underload: qualitative 104–105; quantitative 105–106
University of Warsaw 121, 123n2; Laboratory of Education Quality Evaluation 114
University Study-Oriented System 124n3
US National Study of Postsecondary Faculty (NSOPF) 124n10

Van Maanen, J. 174
Velasco, J. R. 3
Vogel-Walcutt, L. 73

Wallace, D. F. 2
WechterAshkin, L. 19
Woolgar, S. 87
workload: academic boredom 103–108; qualitative underload 104–105; quantitative overload 106–108; quantitative underload 105–106; typology **103**
writing academic texts 180–181

Žižek, S. 127

Printed in Dunstable, United Kingdom